Praise for *The Freelance Consultant*

'This book is SO needed! If only a book like this existed when I took the plunge 18 years ago to go freelance, a companion like this would have been invaluable. If you're just setting up your independent advisory or consultancy business, or even if you're established and want to know if you could be doing things better, I strongly recommend you read this book.'

**Rafe Offer, entrepreneur; speaker;
Founder of Sofar Sounds and this & that**

'This is an immensely practical and grounded guide to succeeding as a freelancer. From the comprehensive coverage to the in-depth guides, real-world case studies and incredibly helpful checklists, it will take you through every step you need to launch and prosper in a freelance business. Its realistic and practical approach is a refreshing antidote to the hype and pie-in-the-sky thinking we're all far too used to having pushed at us when it comes to succeeding with your own business. This book beats a different path, and it's one that will lead you to success.'

**Ian Brodie, consultant; creator of
Value-Based Marketing; author of *Email Persuasion***

'Richard Newton's The Freelance Consultant *is a detailed guide to launching your business as a freelancer and keeping your sales funnel full of high-quality leads.*'

**Kai Davis, Growth Marketing for Indie
Consultants and Freelancers**

'The Freelance Consultant *by Richard Newton provides comprehensive, fact-based insights into a freelance consulting career. In this book, the author provides not only the inspiration but also the practical guidance required for independent consultants to successfully navigate their challenging career path.*'

**Uzma Aitqad, founder and CEO of Magna
People Change Consulting**

'For those in the wild world of independent consulting, this book is chock-full of wisdom for you. Despite the fact that we consider our firm to be somewhat larger than the target audience, the advice (everything from finding your focus to running successful and paid engagements) seems to apply to us, and, dare I say it, to larger firms as well!'

**Doug Sheperdigian, Managing Director
of Atlantic Customer Solutions**

The Freelance Consultant

At Pearson, we have a simple mission: to help people make more of their lives through learning.

We combine innovative learning technology with trusted content and educational expertise to provide engaging and effective learning experiences that serve people wherever and whenever they are learning.

From classroom to boardroom, our curriculum materials, digital learning tools and testing programmes help to educate millions of people worldwide – more than any other private enterprise.

Every day our work helps learning flourish, and wherever learning flourishes, so do people.

To learn more, please visit us at **www.pearson.com/uk**

The Freelance Consultant

Your comprehensive guide to starting an independent business

Richard Newton

Harlow, England • London • New York • Boston • San Francisco • Toronto • Sydney • Dubai • Singapore • Hong Kong
Tokyo • Seoul • Taipei • New Delhi • Cape Town • São Paulo • Mexico City • Madrid • Amsterdam • Munich • Paris • Milan

PEARSON EDUCATION LIMITED
KAO Two
KAO Park
Harlow CM17 9NA
United Kingdom
Tel: +44 (0)1279 623623
Web: www.pearson.com/uk

First edition published 2021 (print and electronic)

© Pearson Education Limited 2021 (print and electronic)

The right of Richard Newton to be identified as author of this work has been asserted by him in accordance with the Copyright, Designs and Patents Act 1988.

The print publication is protected by copyright. Prior to any prohibited reproduction, storage in a retrieval system, distribution or transmission in any form or by any means, electronic, mechanical, recording or otherwise, permission should be obtained from the publisher or, where applicable, a licence permitting restricted copying in the United Kingdom should be obtained from the Copyright Licensing Agency Ltd, Barnard's Inn, 86 Fetter Lane, London EC4A 1EN.

The ePublication is protected by copyright and must not be copied, reproduced, transferred, distributed, leased, licensed or publicly performed or used in any way except as specifically permitted in writing by the publisher, as allowed under the terms and conditions under which it was purchased, or as strictly permitted by applicable copyright law. Any unauthorised distribution or use of this text may be a direct infringement of the author's and the publisher's rights and those responsible may be liable in law accordingly.

All trademarks used herein are the property of their respective owners. The use of any trademark in this text does not vest in the author or publisher any trademark ownership rights in such trademarks, nor does the use of such trademarks imply any affiliation with or endorsement of this book by such owners.

Pearson Education is not responsible for the content of third-party internet sites.

ISBN: 978-1-292-36083-6 (print)
      978-1-292-36084-3 (PDF)
      978-1-292-36085-0 (ePub)

British Library Cataloguing-in-Publication Data
A catalogue record for the print edition is available from the British Library

Library of Congress Cataloging-in-Publication Data
Names: Newton, Richard, 1964- author.
Title: The freelance consultant: your comprehensive guide to starting an independent business / Richard Newton.
Description: 1 Edition. | New York: Pearson, 2021. | Includes bibliographical references and index.
Identifiers: LCCN 2020057887 (print) | LCCN 2020057888 (ebook) | ISBN 9781292360836 (paperback) | ISBN 9781292360843 (pdf) | ISBN 9781292360850 (epub)
Subjects: LCSH: Business consultants. | Consultants. | Self-employed.
Classification: LCC HD69.C6 N494 2021 (print) | LCC HD69.C6 (ebook) | DDC 001—dc23
LC record available at https://lccn.loc.gov/2020057887
LC ebook record available at https://lccn.loc.gov/2020057888

10 9 8 7 6 5 4 3 2 1
25 24 23 22 21

Cover design by Kelly Miller

Print edition typeset in Stone Serif ITC Pro 9/13 by SPi Global

NOTE THAT ANY PAGE CROSS REFERENCES REFER TO THE PRINT EDITION

Contents

Acknowledgements / ix
Publisher's acknowledgements / xi
About the author / xiii
Introduction / xv

part 1 The essentials

1. Why be a freelancer? / 3
2. Different types of freelancers and what they offer / 15
3. Understanding why clients hire freelancers / 26

part 2 Design your freelance business

4. Defining your specialisation / 41
5. Profiling your clients / 55
6. Pricing your services / 66
7. Preparing yourself for freelancing / 84

part 3 Selling and winning your first engagement

8. Marketing and finding clients / 97
9. Selling and making sure you get paid / 115
10. Running your first engagement / 135

part 4 Developing your business and your expertise

11. Improving your engagements / 147
12. Building relationships to drive your freelance success / 158
13. Developing your credibility and influence with clients / 173
14. Thriving and leveraging freelancing for other interests / 186

Further reading and other resources / 199
Index / 204

Acknowledgements

Through my decades as a consultant, I have had the pleasure of learning from many experts in a wide variety of fields, and from my clients too. There are far too many of them to acknowledge here, but I would not be where I am without their help. If you are one of them, thank you!

I will name 13 extraordinary people who show what running a great independent business can achieve, and what fantastic client service looks like. You'll get to meet them as you read this book and see what brilliant insights they have.

My thanks go to them all: Lyndall Farley, Alison Zakers, Theresa Coligan, Scott Gould, Daljit R. Banger, Diana Wiredu, Leonie Scholten, Alastair McDermott, Mike Lander, Ciprian Rusen, Ian Williamson, Charles Cowan and Uzma Aitqad.

Publisher's acknowledgements

Text credits:
17-18 Lyndall Farley: Copyright © Lyndall Farley, Beyond a Break. Used by permission; **25-26 Alison Zakers:** Copyright © Alison Zakers, Pinfold Consulting. Used by permission; **34-35 Theresa Coligan:** Copyright © Theresa Coligan, The Coaching Project. Used by permission; **44-45 Scott Gould:** Copyright © Scott Gould, Author, Speaker and Consultant. Used by permission; **52-53 Daljit R. Banger:** Copyright © Daljit R Banger, Seat Consulting. Used by permission; **65-66 Diane Wiredu:** Copyright © Diane Wiredu, Lion Words – Localization Expert, Translator, Content & Copywriter. Used by permission; **73-74 Leonie Scholten:** Copyright © Leonie Scholten, Purposeful Growth Coach and Consultant. Used by permission; **87, 96 Pearson Education**: Newton, R.; The Management Consultant: Mastering the Art of Consultancy, 2nd Ed, 2020. Reprinted by permission of Pearson Education, Inc.; **87-88 Alastair McDermott:** Copyright © Alastair McDermott, Marketing for Consultants. Used by permission; **103-104 Mike Lander:** Copyright © Mike Lander, Piscari Limited. Used by permission; **110-111 Ciprian Adrian Rusen:** Copyright © Ciprian Rusen, Digital Citizen. Used by permission; **119-120 Ian Williamson:** Copyright © Ian Williamson, Transformation Consultant. Used by permission; **119-120 Charles Cowan:** Copyright © Charles Cowan, ICC Wealth Management Limited. Used by permission; **139 Uzma Aitqad:**Copyright © Uzma Aitqad, Magna People Change. Used by permission.

Image credit:
1 Christopher Cornwell: Copyright © Christopher Cornwell. Used by permission.

About the author

Richard Newton is an independent business adviser. He worked for a number of international consultancies before going independent in 2004 with his own successful company, Enixus. He continues to be engaged as a freelance consultant for clients worldwide. Through his career, Richard has worked with hundreds of freelance consultants, contractors, coaches and other independent experts. He acts as a mentor to a steady stream of freelancers and employees looking to step out on their own. Outside of his consulting business, Richard is also a prolific author. His passion is fiction, but he is most well-known for his non-fiction books including *The Management Consultant: Mastering the Art of Consultancy* and the award winning *The Management Book*.

Introduction

This is your comprehensive and practical guide to starting and growing your freelance business. The book has four main aims. It will:

1. Help you to understand what the business of being a freelance expert is all about.
2. Guide you in shaping your services and setting up your own freelance business.
3. Explain the essentials of making money as a freelancer: getting clients to buy and pay for your services, and maximising your fees.
4. Explore the core skills of sharing expertise, building relationships with clients and running engagements.

When you have mastered these four areas you will be well on your way to being a successful freelancer.

Who is it aimed at?

This book is designed for people whose work has two characteristics: their work is provided on a freelance basis and it is based on providing expertise. It is both for people starting out as a freelancer who want the comprehensive guide to getting it right, and it is also for experienced freelancers looking for ways to progress their careers.

Freelancers provide services to any client from individuals, small businesses, governments, charities or the largest of global corporations. But whoever they provide their services to, they are their own boss. Their success is solely up to them.

Many freelancers make their living based on their expertise – the know-how that is in their heads. What they are selling is essentially themselves and their ability to help their clients: solve problems, get things done, become happier and more fulfilled, reduce risks and improve their ways of working.

A note on terminology

Freelancers with these two characteristics go under lots of titles, for example: consultant, coach, specialist, adviser, mentor, trainer, contractor and interim manager. We'll explore these titles and what they each mean a little later in the book, I just want to give you a flavour for now. When I need to refer to all of these different job titles together, I often use the word 'expert' as a catch-all title.

'Expert' is not a perfect word. Some of the people I am talking to in this book, such as coaches, sometimes don't like to be lumped into what could be a misleading word. Unfortunately, there does not seem to be a perfect collective noun that encapsulates everyone in this group of people. Go with me on this – in the end it's just a word!

A growing sector

Over the past few decades there has been an explosion of people working as freelance experts. In fact, generally, there has been an explosion of advice-giving. Flick through Twitter, Facebook, Instagram, LinkedIn or your platform of choice and in between the banter and jokes, it's full of people trying to advise you what to do. Let's not focus on the ones who just do this because they've got an opinion they want everyone to hear, but let's focus only on those who want to give advice for a living: professional experts, freelance experts.

The services experts offer are broad and include things no-one had heard of decades ago, such as health coach or social media adviser. In another 10 years there will certainly be new categories of experts we don't yet have. More and more of these experts are choosing not to work in big professional service firms but to work independently or in small companies. The services are offered not only to corporates with deep pockets, but to everyone. Whatever advice is needed and whoever needs it, there is probably someone out there offering it!

What this book covers

In 14 chapters, this book covers the core aspects of being a successful freelancer. I'm going to explore the work of freelancers, introduce you to your clients and all their needs, and then we'll look at how you can go about making a living by fulfilling those customer needs.

Let me start with a caveat. There are limits to what you can cover in one book, and there are two specific things I do not include. Firstly, as a freelancer there are lots of things you need to know related to your specialist area. So, for instance if you are a freelance coach, you need to know all about the tools and techniques of coaching. This book is not about the details of your specialisation, although it will help you choose, brand and sell that specialisation. Secondly, there are lots of general things you need to know, that anyone working needs to understand. For example, everyone at work needs to understand how to work in a team. That sort of advice is also not covered here.

What does that leave? It leaves those very important activities that are not often explained to anyone going into freelancing. Those specific tasks that are central to being a freelancer. At its core there are eight main areas that all freelancers have to be able to do. These are summarised in the following list with a reference to the chapters in this book that cover each topic:

1. *Identify a specialised area of advising:* what is the essence of the service you will be providing to your clients? How do you select the best service and describe it in a compelling way to clients? (Chapters 2, 4, 5 and 14)
2. *Work out a price for this service:* what are you going to charge for this service, and how do you charge more? (Chapters 6 and 14)
3. *Find clients who want this advice:* who is going to buy your service and how do you find enough clients for you to earn the livelihood you want? (Chapters 4, 5 and 8)
4. *Get those clients to buy this service and pay for it:* how do you sell to those clients in a way which means you get enough of the right clients, and won't spend your whole life worrying about selling? (Chapters 8 and 9)
5. *Understand how to deliver the service:* how do you set up and run engagements, so you get everything you need done from starting work to billing your client? (Chapters 2, 7, 11, 12 and 13)

6. *Please clients:* how do you satisfy your clients, so they keep coming back to buy more, and don't blink when you charge higher fees? (Chapters 1, 10, 11, 12 and 13)

7. *Run a business and protect your interests:* as a freelancer, you need to run your business. What do you need to know as a freelancer? How can you navigate your way around all those risks associated with working for yourself? (Chapters 9, 10 and 11)

8. *Thriving and leveraging freelancing:* how do you learn from your client feedback and from observing the trends going on in the market? How do you make sure the service you provide stays popular as the world changes? (Chapter 14)

This is a sketch that we are going to explore and flesh out as we go through the book, building up your understanding and ideas about making a living as a freelancer. There is one other thing which you do not have to do, but you may choose to do. Freelancing can be a great platform to do other activities and start another business. I'll look at this too at the end of the book in Chapter 14.

I have structured this book to cover every aspect of this lifecycle, in roughly the order shown. But some of the topics need revisiting as we go through the book. I think the best way to read this book is to start at the beginning and read through to the end, but I know not everyone does that. So, for those of you who like to jump around and pick and choose the parts to look at, Figure 1 should help you find the chapters you are most interested in.

An independent voice

This book contains one other part, in every chapter, which I hope you will find extremely useful. I have invited someone from my network who works as a freelance expert to share their story. I want to give a flavour of the diversity of experts there are, and to build your confidence by hearing from people you can personally relate to. These are all real people sharing their real experiences.

These stories are not meant to be self-promoting shout-outs of the form 'how I made a billion dollars'. Instead they are the stories of successful advisers who work as freelancers and lead the life they want.

My selected colleagues have a wide variety of services and include everyone from someone setting out at the very start of their career through to people who have being doing it for years and years. I have chosen individuals who have good advice that otherwise you might not think of.

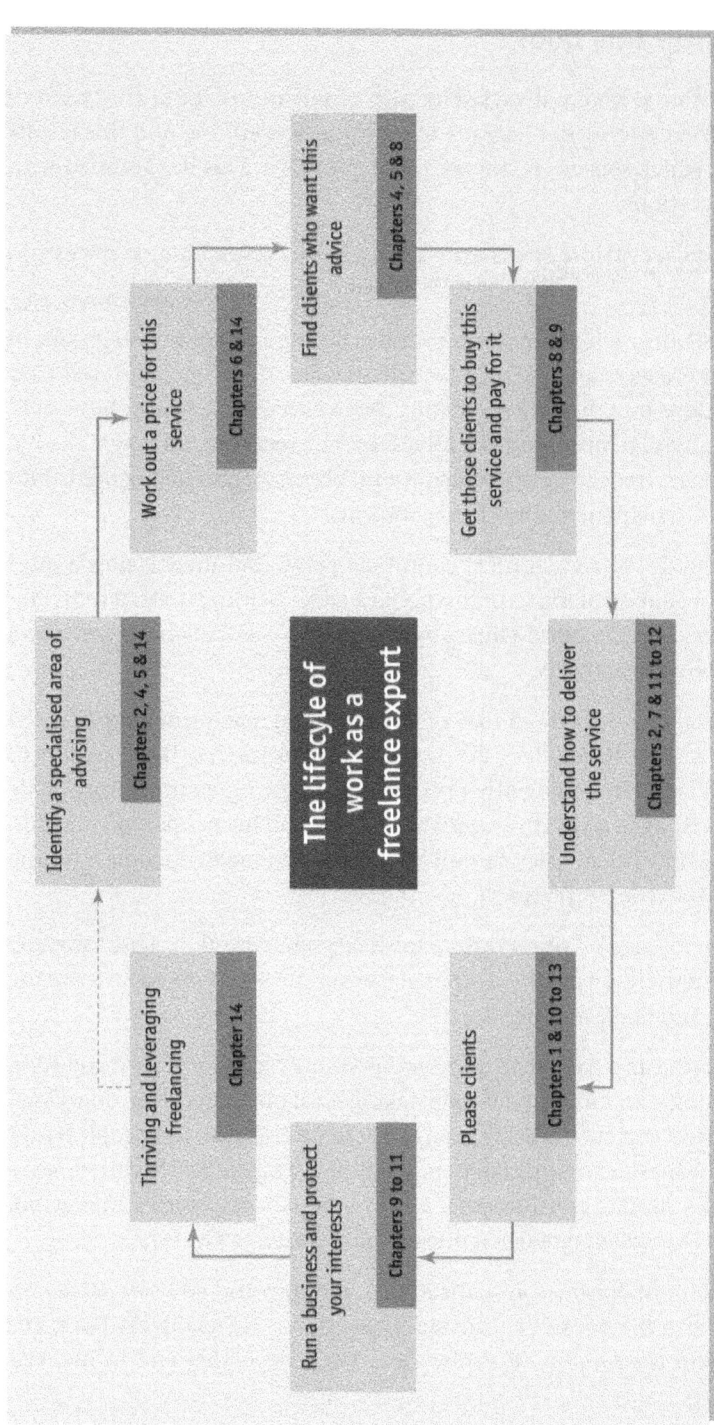

Figure 1 The 'lifecyle of work' mapped against the chapters of this book

Why did I write this book?

My professional books always start with observations about the world of work – observations that lead me to question something, and this results in a book which sets out to answer those questions. This book started with four observations.

My **first observation** is that the business of professional services has changed.

There was a time when advisory work was largely limited to two groups of people. There were a few senior executives who after a long and well-paid career decided that they did not want to be an executive anymore but would prefer to advise or coach other executives. The second group were the big consultancies, hoovering up graduates with big brains and selling them onto businesses to help them solve their problems.

Both the groups I just identified continue to exist, but there is now a third group who I am speaking to in this book: a large, swirling mass of individuals who are trying to make a living by giving advice as freelance experts and independent consultants.

These freelancers provide all sorts of services, often making deft use of social media to market themselves. For instance, as I write this, there are lots of people on LinkedIn telling other people how to use LinkedIn. If my update feed is anything to go by, this seems to be about half the people on LinkedIn. So many LinkedIn advisers cannot all make a reasonable income advising others how to use the platform.

That led to my **second observation**: too many advisers often chase too small a pie, when there are plenty of other pies around. So how do you choose the right area and make money?

Search around and you'll will find people willing to advise you on anything from starting your business or career, taking breaks in your career, doing well in your career and even retiring from it. There are also a fair few people trying to build businesses advising advisers. Some of these people will thrive, some won't. They need to consider what makes a domain of expertise interesting or attractive, and what makes it one no one is going to pay for.

I talk to a lot of contractors, consultants, coaches and advisers. Based on my work and the books I've written in the past – especially my book *The Management Consultant: Mastering the Art of Consultancy* and influenced by my social media posts, a few reach-out to chat to me every week. They often want advice and help. I'm happy to share advice with them, the sort of advice I include in this book.

Not surprisingly, the **third observation** comes from these chats. There are many people doing well as independent advisers, grasping and playing the game skilfully and making a nice living for themselves doing what they love. But there are also a huge number who are just getting by or even struggling. This book explains what it takes to be a successful adviser or freelance expert.

There is another audience. The audience of professionals who desire independence from the corporate life, while still making corporate-level money by advising. Hence my **fourth observation** is that often these people assume that skills in business convert directly into skills as a freelance expert. They don't, not always. It's a different game with different rules. It's best not to jump until you understand what's on the other side!

With those four observations I started to collate my thoughts into a book specifically about being a freelance expert – this book.

Some ideas about having a career as a freelance expert come from the big professional services firms – such as management consultancies, IT services providers, law firms and so on. One thing these big firms have shown themselves to be good at is playing the advisory game, surviving its ups and downs, and making a lot of money on the way.

Whether you are a fan or critic of the big firms, there is something they are doing right. There is plenty to learn, which I will share from my many years as a management consultant. But I also want to impart my and other people's lessons about getting along very comfortably as *freelance experts*. Working independently has some tricks of its own.

Making a living as a freelance expert is not rocket science, but there are important things to understand. These can be lumped into two sets of lessons. The first are some business basics; basics that many would-be experts seem to forget and benefit from being reminded of.

The second set are some things about the advice-giving game itself. Straightforward ideas that anyone can use to develop confidence in yourself as an adviser, to develop trusted relationships with clients of your own, to persuade someone in a way that's helpful and, of course, to convert this into an income.

Why listen to me?

There are two reasons you should consider buying a professional book from a specific author. The first is that they can write in an appealing and accessible way that you will find helpful, and the second is that they know what they are talking about.

I have been writing for almost 20 years, and I focus specifically on practical books that help people overcome practical challenges – like becoming a successful freelance expert. I've worked hard to develop a style that is engaging and is based on solid knowledge. The feedback from my readers is that they like the hands-on practical nature of my books. I've set out to write this book in the same way.

But what about my knowledge of freelancing? Although I have done 'real' jobs, most of my long professional career has now been spent as a freelance consultant. As such, I've worked with dozens and dozens of different clients, in lots of countries, in various industries, helping them to overcome all sorts of problems.

As I've done this, I've learnt and become successful at it. I have a solid reputation and often someone will call or text and ask me for help. I've got to that nice point where I don't really have to work that hard to find clients. They often come to me because I have done the things explained in this book to make me well enough known among my target clients.

I've created a pleasant lifestyle for myself living in two countries, if not in absolute affluence, at least with a high degree of comfort. I certainly don't work 12 months a year. I haven't for years. Eight or nine months is typical. On top of work, I have plenty of time for the other things I enjoy in life: walking in the mountains, writing, studying philosophy and socialising with friends – real, physical friends. Somehow, and often it surprises me, I have acquired a lifestyle that others want.

I appear lucky: I largely do what I want when I want to. But like many other apparently lucky people, it has taken time and plenty of effort to get here. However, it is not magic – and you can achieve it too if you follow the advice in this book.

A large part of my success has come down to two things. Firstly, experimenting and learning as I go along. Not everything I have done has been successful, but the great thing about being willing to make a few mistakes is that you learn a lot, quickly! Those lessons are in this book.

Secondly, I have learnt from other freelance experts. I read a lot and will share the key references that have taught me how to be a successful freelancer. I am by no means the most successful freelancer I know. I've built up a network of other people who have done better than me and have really cracked the freelancing game. I'm going to take advantage of the generosity of these people and weave in their advice, stories and experiences directly into the book.

How does this relate to you? Everyone has different aspirations from work, but beyond the need to earn money, there are the common modern desires for flexibility, independence, remote working from wonderful locations, setting one's own targets and choosing clients who you like working with. My example shows that in being a freelance expert you can achieve these things – and in this book I am going to tell you how.

But I want to balance this positive with some realities. Before we get carried away and assume that by becoming a freelancer that you will enter some work–life balanced nirvana there is a reality as well, and while I and many others I know have thrived in the freelance business, it isn't for everyone. I will give you an honest picture so you can make up your own mind if it is, or is not, for you. We'll start doing this in the next chapter.

part
one

The essentials

chapter

Why be a freelancer?

I want to start this book by helping you to understand what your experience of being a freelancer will be like. This will answer two questions for you: what will I get from freelancing, and is it really for me?

There is often a lot of naivety about freelancing, and an assumption that it's an easy way to make a living. It can be wonderful, but it can also be challenging and throw up risks that an employee does not face. On the other hand, some people would love freelancing, but they don't take the leap away from the safety blanket of paid employment, because they worry too much about problems that are easily resolvable.

I want you to be able to assess freelancing calmly – understanding the benefits as well as the risks.

Let's look at the opportunities as well as the possible pitfalls. The good news is that on balance most people can thrive as freelancers, taking advantage of the opportunities and avoiding the pitfalls. We'll look at this in summary in this chapter and there will be more detailed advice throughout this book on how to do this.

Why should you consider freelancing?

A good question to start with is why freelance when there are lots of fantastic and interesting jobs around? Some of those jobs are well paid with incredible benefits. On top of this, there are very few services offered by freelancers that someone in an employed job does not also do. For instance, there are many employed consultants, coaches, mentors – and much of what contractors do is also done by someone who is an employee. So why go the freelance route?

There are three main reasons why you might consider becoming a freelancer:

1. You might make more money as a freelancer compared to an employee.
2. You want the independence that comes with being a freelancer.
3. You feel you have no choice. You cannot find a job in your field or you have been made redundant, and you think that if no one is going to offer you a job you might as well try freelancing.

I want to explore each of these, and what they require of you in return.

Money

Whatever your attitude to money and whatever your income aspirations, we all need some of it. This desire for money ties in closely with the other aspiration of freelancers – for independence. If your chosen route is to be a freelancer, there is one critical area in which you are not and will never be fully independent: you need clients from whom you can earn a living – you are not about to disappear off the grid!

Clients have expectations and may only hire you if you meet these expectations. At times you will find more clients than you can service, but at others you may struggle to find any at all. If you choose to work independently, the old phrase that *no one owes you a living* needs to be firmly in your sights.

I know some freelance experts who have made themselves seriously affluent, much richer than people doing similar roles in industry. A very comfortable lifestyle is achievable if you approach freelancing sensibly. If you follow the advice in the future chapters, you will have a firm foundation for achieving this. But it is important to understand the risks associated with earning a living as a freelancer.

You can earn very good money as a freelancer – if you get your services right and you find the sort of clients those services are valuable to. A lot of this book comprises explaining how to do this. But there are a couple of risks in the way: firstly, at any time, your revenues can dry up, and secondly, you may find yourself facing unexpected bills you have not got the finances to pay.

As a freelancer there is always a risk that your revenue can stop at very short notice. This comes from those global black swan events, such as the banking crisis of 2007 or the coronavirus pandemic of 2020. But they also come from individual issues, such as family problems and illness. Outside of crises, it's also true that an important client, for a million and one reasons, can just decide to stop hiring you.

Every so often I meet a freelancer in desperate straits. After years of earning a great income, and living a comfortable lifestyle, there is an interruption in their work. Bad luck, illness or the global economy creates a surprise and they cannot find work or cannot work. The bank account soon empties, and difficult times ensue. With a little planning and a little restraint on spending every dollar you earn, as you earn it, this is avoidable. This should be obvious, but it's surprising how often I find self-employed people who do not adhere to this principle.

Additionally, unlike employees whose tax is taken away before they get their pay, freelancers pay their taxes afterwards. It can be easy to lose track of how much those taxes are, and to overspend only to get into difficulty when that tax bill arrives.

A lot of people worry about these risks, but they are not so difficult to reduce. There are four ways to reduce these risks:

1. *Stay on top of the money.* What you have, what you are owed and what you owe. If you aren't naturally great at doing this, there is an easy answer. Hire a good accountant. There are lots of accountants who are skilled at helping freelancers. To me this is essential.
2. *Build up cash reserves.* I always recommend a minimum amount of money to be able to get by without a contract for 6 months. In the boom times, when the cash is rolling in, this may seem unduly pessimistic. In a freelance career across multiple decades, I have found that at times even the most highly demanded freelancer finds themselves without work from time to time. Being able to save up this reserve is helped by maximising your income when you can earn, which we will look at in Chapters 6 and 14.
3. *Don't depend on one client.* I've known freelancers earn great money for years from one client, only unexpectedly for that client to stop buying. The best answer to this is to have a set of clients. Most freelancers don't need hundreds, but you should try to have at least a handful. We'll explore how to do this in Chapters 5, 8 and 9.
4. *Optionally, have another income.* You don't need to do this, but lots of freelancers do. Some side hustle that keeps them interested, but also acts as a buffer if the main freelance income stalls for a while. For instance, I write. I know other freelance experts who own holiday properties, are professional musicians, offer training, run a farm or are

a director of other small companies. There is nothing stopping you doing anything else, save how you prioritise your time.

But while you can reduce these risks to your income in practice, there is also a psychological challenge. Some people just cannot stand the pressure of worry that comes from having to constantly think about the next sale.

Honestly, I think this concern is overblown, for the simple truth is that even most permanent jobs are not as safe as you may imagine. I've been involved in too many downsizing, relocation and radical cost-cutting programmes not to know this. But, if you are fundamentally someone who needs the perceived certainty of regular monthly pay into your bank account, freelancing probably isn't for you.

Independence

A higher degree of independence is a realistic expectation if you choose the freelance life. I know many people who, after years of feeling unfulfilled, have released themselves from the corporate world and made themselves independent.

I want to explore what this means and show you how you can achieve it while avoiding the pitfalls. Some of this I'm going to do in this chapter. It is also a repeated theme in the stories throughout this book, especially in the ones at the end of each chapter.

Years ago, most of the freelancers I used to meet primarily moved into freelancing for the money, but increasingly more and more of the freelancers I meet are doing it for quite a different reason – they want independence. And in practice this usually means the ability to choose when you work, where you work from and who you work with.

Most freelancers want something that money does not compensate for – independence. By this I mean the ability to be free of a lot of the issues and challenges that come with working for someone else; the chance to avoid some of the hassle, the politics and frankly, nonsense, that goes with working in a large organisation.

Freelancing enables this, but for most of us there are limits to quite how independent we can be.

There are a few people with a rare and in-demand specialisation who can decide exactly which hours of the week and which weeks of the year they choose to work. Most freelancers, though, are like me. I have a lot of flexibility over the times and days I work, but it's not always completely in my control. I typically take a few months off every year to do other things, such as writing. But sometimes I want some time off, but I can't take it because there is a bit of work that is too interesting or too valuable not to do.

You can, of course, always say no to any piece of work because you may not want to work at that point in time. That's what being independent means. I have rejected work that has come at the wrong time. But say no too often and the customer will stop asking and find someone else to do the work. Once they find someone else, next time they may not go back to you but stick with their new adviser.

The opposite is also true. Sometimes I want to be working and earning some money, but the customers aren't buying, or I need to spend time marketing and networking. After all, as a freelancer you have a business to run, and this takes time of its own. You cannot be billing every single hour.

The first point about independence then is to set yourself realistic expectations. You will be more independent, but not 100% free to do what you want when you want. Think of it as a more balanced life, rather than a completely independent one. I have taken a conscious choice that I will earn a bit less, but in return I get a bit more independence. What's great is that whatever the balance is, is up to you.

I also have flexibility as to where I work. Decades ago, when I started out as an independent consultant, clients expected me to show up at their premises five days a week. Fortunately, those days are long over. Home working is increasingly the norm. As I write this book I am in lockdown at home, like a lot of the world, due to coronavirus. I am still doing billable time for some of my clients. They are fine with this. Remote working is possible and increasingly normal. I expect this is a trend that will continue.

If you want to work remotely, it tends to be easier if your client perceives that they are buying a service from you with an agreed output, and are not just paying you a rate for working for them for an amount of time (see Chapters 4 and 6). When you hire yourself by the hour, clients tend to like to know you are really working for them. As a freelancer you may not enjoy the same trust as employees do. Before feeling an affront at this, ask yourself: why should you be trusted? Trust is earned, not given freely. The more value you show, the more a client will trust you. (See Chapter 12 for more on this topic.)

But even if you can work from home, it is not the same as being able to live anywhere in the world and successfully work with your clients. There are some clients who are happy to never physically meet, especially if you have a very solid reputation or already have a strong relationship with them. But most clients like to see you now and again. Once a week, or perhaps just a couple of times a month.

If your client is in the UK and you are living in Portugal this is manageable. If your client is in Northern Canada, and you are living in Bali, this probably won't work. Again, if you have sensible expectations, you will enjoy the freedom freelancing provides.

While there are trends, including the increasing acceptance of 100% remote working and dealing with suppliers based in other geographic regions, each client's attitudes are unique. You can pick and choose your clients to be the ones who want to work with you in the way you want. I have often rejected clients whose need for me to be in certain locations just was not for me. Lots of freelancers do this. But it's a competitive world and there are lots of freelancers. If you are too choosy you may find yourself with a thin order book.

To decide which clients are for you, and which are not, the starting point is to be clear about what is your essential level of independence. Reject the clients whose needs conflict significantly with your needs for independence, but try to be a little flexible. It's all about give and take!

Redundancy and the lack of an alternative

The other reason why people choose to become a freelancer is in some ways the simplest – they have no choice. There is no other job around and with bills to pay, some work needs to be found to keep the wolf from the door.

If this is you, the good news is that while many people have effectively been forced into freelancing and at first only did this as a necessary evil, they have gone on to find they love working this way. If you have found yourself without a job, then freelancing should be a serious option for you. I've known many people who made forced entry into freelancing but have gone on to wish they had done it years before.

If you really are a corporate beast, who loves the sense of working in a bigger business, then freelancing may not be for you as a permanent option. That does not mean you cannot do it as a short-term expedient. There is nothing stopping you freelancing for a while and then going back to permanent employment. It used to be that employers were sceptical of employing ex-freelancers. Those days are long gone, and many people happily flip between being employed and freelancing several times.

Later in this book we will look at transitioning to freelancing from another career which will give you a flavour of what to expect. The most important point to understand though is that freelancing is not just doing your old employed role but being self-employed. Freelancing is different – both in terms of the things you need to do, and the way it feels.

Let's look a little more at this.

The life of a juggler

OK – so far you can see there are real benefits, with some risks, but risks you can manage if you are sensible and have reasonable expectations. So, what's the catch? I don't think there is one, but it is different from being an employee. The best way to think of this is that as an independent, running your own business, you will need to learn to juggle. There are lots of different things you need to find time to fit in.

Let me make an analogy with my other job as an author. Most people imagine me sitting at my desk writing my books. In reality, writing is only one part of the life of an author – probably 50% of my working time as an author at most. There is the work coming up with ideas, researching, dealing with publishers and agents, working through editor's comments, promoting books and lots of chasing around on various topics like royalties and the like. When I write I'm not just thinking about this book, I'm still promoting the previous ones and usually thinking about the next one.

It is not so different for the freelancer. You may want to spend all your time working with and helping customers. But there are a lot of other things you need to do.

I've already introduced eight steps of freelancing in the introduction, but for a quick reminder here they are again:

1. Identify a specialised area of advising.
2. Work out a price for this service.
3. Find clients who want this advice.
4. Get those clients to buy this service and pay for it.
5. Understand how to deliver the advice.
6. Please customers.
7. Run a business and protect your interests.
8. Thriving and leveraging freelancing.

Each of these takes time. Only one of them, number 5, is concerned with doing the daily work of a freelance expert. You must find time or ways to do the other seven.

Some of these are infrequent tasks, while others need regular time. How much time depends on your business model. I'll explain this in detail in later chapters, but let me give you an example.

If your work is sold in hour-long chunks, you need to sell a lot of them to make an income. You are going to spend a lot of time doing steps 3 and 4 from the above list. However, if you sell your work in 6-month chunks you only need two sales a year at most, and so will spend a lot less time on steps 3 and 4.

There is no right or wrong here – it depends on your services and clients, and you will find yourself doing a unique balance of these eight steps. What balance you choose is largely in your control, based on the choices you make as explained in this book.

If this seems complex, it really isn't, it's just a way of working you need to get used to. And before you get too worried about all the things you need to do as a freelance expert, remember there are also lots of people to help you. Even as a freelancer you do not need to be on your own. You can work with other freelancers, some who complement your strengths and weaknesses, or do more of the things you don't like doing. Instead of being the freelancer, you can be the client for once!

For instance, you will easily find freelancers who will help you with marketing, social media presence, training or with running your business. You can also find other freelance experts who focus on selling work, and then partner with other freelancers to deliver the work.

Never think you need to do everything yourself even if you are only a one-person business. One of the joys of independence is thinking about where you want to spend your time and then building a network of reliable partners to do the other things that you need to get done.

Can you do this and get what you want from it?

Can you do this and get what you want from it? That is the central question that everyone wants to answer. Everyone is unique, but most people if they put their mind to it can find a niche as a freelance expert and make a good living. It certainly is not for everyone, but it can work for a lot of people. If you are starting out and wondering what to do, or if you are sitting in a corporate job that is driving you crazy, then freelancing could well be the answer.

It requires a little thought and planning, a willingness to be flexible with how you exactly spend your time – juggling between tasks. As we will see in the later chapters, you need to have some service or product you can sell, but most people have more skills than they realise. It helps to have a clear understanding of your strengths – and finding others to help you in the areas in which you are not so strong.

If your expectations are reasonable, you work at it and build a business; being a freelance expert gives the opportunity for great flexibility, significant independence and earning a good income. It can be hugely satisfying work. I know several independent coaches and consultants for whom their work really is their calling.

Professor Barry Schwartz, the psychologist who has often written and spoken about work, makes many good comments about satisfaction from work. In his book *Why We Work*, he says: 'Satisfied workers are engaged by their work. They lose themselves in it', and later in the same book: 'It is people who see their work as a "calling" who find it most satisfying. For them, work is one of the most important parts of life'. Being an independent expert might be your calling.

The life of a freelancer

Some people reading this book will be working as a coach, consultant, or other form of freelance expert, already used to the lifestyle and wanting to move to the next level. On the other hand, some of you will be new, making your first tentative steps into this world. This book will give you guidance on your journey, whether it is starting out or stepping up to the next level. But before you make that journey, you may be thinking what it's going to be like to work as a freelancer.

There is no universal answer as each of us is ploughing our own furrow. But I believe I can give you a flavour of it with a few examples of my own working life, and from the lives of other experts I know well.

To keep my business going I must do several different important activities on a regular basis. I spend time promoting myself, talking to prospective clients and convincing them to hire me, and keeping in touch with old clients so they don't forget me and use me again when they have a problem of the type I'm good at solving. I write proposals and, of course, I do the work of helping clients. I bill my clients and check those bills are paid. And I must do all the things that have to be done to run any small business. I am constantly planning and prioritising where I spend my time.

I used to travel a lot. I do that less, but still do it a bit. Clients can be based anywhere in the world and my expertise is not specific to any country or culture. One must be very aware of cultural differences to be able to advise successfully in different countries. Some work is easy to do remotely, other work is best done face-to-face. I have worked in 14 countries in Europe, Asia, Australasia and North America. I know some consultants who have worked in dozens more, but I also know some who have only ever worked in their home country and even just their hometown. This will be, to a large extent, up to you.

I have a lot of flexibility over the times and days I work, but it's not always completely in my control. I typically take a few months off every year to do other things, such as writing. But I try to be flexible with my clients.

Good consultants, coaches and contractors make very comfortable livings, but most do not live the life of professional sport stars or billionaire entrepreneurs. It can be a fulfilling and well-paid role, but it is not a get quick rich scheme. It is a long-term commitment if you want to make the best of it.

My work is interesting and varied. I have been involved with dozens of clients helping them sort out a wide range of problems. I actively choose variety, and I enjoy it. I know some colleagues who have very specific niche skills, and every engagement is rather similar. But they like that and are well paid as well-recognised subject matter experts.

It's nothing like being an employee. There are no regular hours, teams, offices or fixed ways of working. There is a huge amount of freedom, but it can sometimes come with a lack of a sense of belonging. On the other hand, while you may not have a fixed team, most independents build a strong network of freelancers who share experiences, ideas and clients.

There is no fixed career path or professional development structure. That is up to you to define for yourself, and fulfilment does not come from job titles and seniority, but from satisfied clients, recommendations and quickly paid bills.

I am mostly not a stressed person with my work, but I am always conscious that there is an element of risk to it. The work can dry up. Consultancy and similar services are usually in the nice-to-have category and not the essential-to-business one. During the 2020 coronavirus outbreak many freelancers found their incomes dropping to zero without much notice. When times are hard, clients usually reduce their spend on these non-essential services. As mentioned before, any sensible freelancer builds up a safety buffer of money in the bank for the lean times. This can be hard at the start of a career, but it is essential for the longer run.

Although over time there are patterns and commonalities between engagements, the work is varied, and no engagement is ever quite the same as another. For me, some are long full-time gigs for a few months, whereas others are part-time relationships. I've known some clients for years, and regularly do a day or two's work for them but have never done anything large. There are other clients who hired me for one large piece of work and who I have never worked with again. I also know other freelancers whose work is sold by the hour, and some clients may only buy a few hours' help.

The clients are mostly enjoyable people to work with, but occasionally they are a nightmare. In the end, they are all human beings and have all the variations that any other group of people have. On balance, even though there have been stressful times, I find it great fun. I feel fulfilled by my work.

An independent voice

Lyndall Farley, Beyond a Break

I help people and companies use the power of time off to stay recharged and thriving.

Through coaching, workshops and programs, I help people make the most of extended breaks from work so they can pause, recharge, reflect and return to work stronger than before. My clients have usually reached a certain level of success in their career but have plateaued and are ready to get off the 'hamster wheel' life they created for themselves. They want a real break to disconnect and figure out what's next, but they need some support to get there – that's where I deliver the most value. I help them navigate the experience and get the most value out of their time off.

I also help companies implement leave programs that deliver real wellbeing benefits to employees. This helps businesses attract and retain the best talent, stay innovative and avoid the disruptive effects of burnout. I learnt early on, not to work with companies who haven't yet figured out that it's important to look after their people.

I look for companies who have already started taking steps towards improving employee wellbeing; for example, resilience courses, meditation programs or flexible work policies. Once a company has a wellbeing focus, I help them design great leave or sabbatical policies, then complement this with a complete implementation program that communicates the benefits of taking breaks and institutionalises the concept of taking time off to stay happy, healthy and productive.

My tips for anyone considering a freelance career

There is just one thing I tell people to think about when they're starting out. Design your life, not just your business. I did this when I was on my nineth sabbatical in Bali. I looked at my ideal life and what I valued, then created my business around that. I came up with my business 'Guiding Principles' and still use these today. For me, that was critical in making sure I didn't create a business that became a cage, but one that facilitated my life.

My three Guiding Principles are:

1 **Location independent.** Having a business I can operate from anywhere in the world. The life I designed was to have nine months in one home base, then three months in different locations. So, I designed for remote flexibility from the outset.

2 **Independent.** Having the freedom to choose how to run the business and not be constrained by the rules of partnerships, memberships, franchise networks or costly IP licencing deals. I want to be able to control my business.

3 **Scalable.** Escaping the 'time for money' trap. My aim has always been to create productised services that are bought for the value they provide, not the hourly cost of delivering the service. Selling IP and value, not time so I can scale back my involvement over time.

I'm still working towards some of these, but the Guiding Principles are like North Stars for how I make decisions in my business. If you start there, you'll always be able to navigate your way to a business and life you love.

If you want to get in touch with me, connect with me on LinkedIn or at www.beyondabreak.com

chapter 2

Different types of freelancers and what they offer

There are three things I want to cover in this chapter. They are all essentials that will help you think more systematically about your freelance career. If you are planning to become a freelancer, they are essentials that you can spend a little time getting right before you take the plunge.

Firstly, I am going to explore the various broad categories of freelance experts. These categories are reflected in the names freelancers give themselves. Of course, as you are now independent you can give yourself any job title you like. I know people who call themselves all sorts of things. However, I find it is best to stick with one of the tried and tested names such as consultant, coach, mentor and so on. When clients hear one of these names they gain a rough understanding of what they will be getting when they hire you. By choosing one of these names you make it easier for them to understand you, and why would you want to make it difficult for them?

Secondly, I want to spend a little more time exploring the various things that freelance experts generally need to do. I want to go deeper into the list of eight key activities mentioned in the introduction. Think of this section as describing *what* you need to do.

Thirdly, I am going to look at some of the skills, competencies, attitudes and behaviours that freelancers need. Whereas the previous section describes what you need to do, this section focuses on *how* you should go about doing it.

Let's start then by exploring why it matters what title you give yourself.

Why does it matter what I call myself?

No two experts do exactly the same thing in precisely the same way. We are all wonderfully different and unique. Many of us shy away from simplistic labels and job titles. We want to be recognised as special and individual. But there are broad categories we usually fit into. It is often useful, and occasionally essential, to label ourselves with one or two known terms like 'consultant', 'coach', 'adviser', 'expert' and so on.

With these labels our customers, and the other people we need to interact with, get a rough idea of what we do. Through the label someone gives themselves, we conclude what sort of role they perform. This works to some extent, but it's rough and ready as no one uses these labels in quite the same way – although some people get very hot and bothered if you don't use them in exactly the way they do! Even though the labels can be ambiguous, it's generally helpful to understand these labels and what the implications of them are.

It's important at any one time to signal to clients which type of expert you are acting as. There are lots of freelancers and, if you use the wrong label to name your service, clients will often ignore you without giving you a chance to explain how wonderful your service is. So, for instance, with the title 'contractor' or 'coach' a client is much less likely to think about using you as an interim manager. That's fine if you don't want to win work as an interim manager – but if you do, it is a problem.

Hence, we want to avoid using the wrong label so clients give us a chance to sell to them. But we also use the label so clients buy the right thing. For instance, just because you call yourself a coach, doesn't make you one. This is one of the most common mistakes I see. I know some wonderful coaches. I also know some people who call themselves coaches, but what they do is not coaching. It's not helpful to use the wrong label as it sets the wrong expectation with clients about what they are buying. You may end up with some irritated and disappointed clients if you sell to them with the wrong sort of role title.

Some people worry that such labels trap them into a certain type of work. It does not need to, as there is no reason you cannot use more than one label or use different labels for different clients. For instance, to some clients I am a consultant, with others I am a mentor. But I am doing different things when I use the different labels.

The roles signified by the different labels overlap. For instance, I know some excellent career coaches, and career coaching is the only thing they do, but some coaches provide other advice as well, such as health and lifestyle advice. I know some consultants who, while they focus on advising their clients in a fact-based way, often drift into using some coaching techniques. They may sometimes work as interim managers and from time to time may position themselves as subject matter experts. I know some people who call themselves mentors, but who are also practitioners and fully trained and accredited as coaches. I know many contractors who are adept at advising like a consultant.

For these reasons it's good to be cautious and avoid thinking in terms of absolute boundaries between these roles. For an expert, it's very helpful at times to be able to flow into different roles as different situations and different clients require. Skilled advisers do this all the time. Nevertheless, you will often need to quickly describe your service to clients, and starting with common labels that they understand is best.

What are the labels?

The way I think about these labels, is that each label represents a different type of role performed by experts. To categorise the roles, I start by thinking about what it is that I have as an expert. To advise there must be something I know, believe or can share to advise anyone else. What is the type of knowledge I have which I base my advice on? Then I think about how I want to use this knowledge. Another way of putting this is: what is my core proposition to my clients? Knowing these two things, I can come up with a label that reflects what I am.

I've done this in Table 2.1.

Each of these roles has specific skills, knowledge and techniques. Given your expertise, you should be able to position what you do with the right sort of label.

Clients seek out people with these labels for different reasons and look for different types of experience and expertise. For instance, someone hiring an interim manager will want someone with significant experience of doing a specific management role before. Some of these roles, for instance a coach, are associated with formal qualifications such as a coaching certificate.

Table 2.1 The types of freelance expert

	What type of expert I am – this is the label naming my role	What I have	What my proposition to my clients is/what my clients will expect me to do
1	**Guru** or **Influencer**	I know a lot about something, and have strong and interesting opinions about it	I will **influence** you with blogs, talks, podcasts, books and posts
2	**SME** (Subject Matter Expert)	I know the valuable answers to some tricky questions	I will tell you the **answers** to your problems
3	**Consultant**	I know how to do something people struggle to do themselves	I will **advise** you on how it's done, and **guide** you in doing it
4	**Coach**	I know that you can do more than you think you can, and I can show you this and help you to grow	I will help you to **understand** and help yourself
5	**Mentor**	I understand your situation and have wisdom that will be useful to you	I'll stand by you as you make your journey providing advice, tips and acting as a wise sounding board
6	**Contractor** (e.g. IT contactor) or **Freelance Expert** (e.g. freelance translator or freelance writer)	I am an expert who knows how to do something people struggle to do themselves	I will **do** it for you
7	**Interim Manager** or just **Interim**	I have performed a job as a manager successfully lots of times before	I take on and work as one of your managers for you for a limited time (This might be because it's a temporary role, or the client needs the time to find the right person to permanently do it, or because the person who normally does it is not available for a period of time, such as being on maternity leave)
8	**Jack of all trades**	I am a useful person who can turn their hands to many things	I'll do **whatever** you want done

Occasionally, I come across freelancers using the last label, number 8 – the jack of all trades. This is the sort of freelancer who makes it clear they can put their hand to many different things. I strongly advise you against doing this. We will explore why in detail later, but put simply it is because the people who succeed as freelancers are specialists, not generalists. We all know the follow-on words to the phrase 'jack of all trades' is 'master of none'. When clients hire a freelancer for their expertise, they want a master! It is true clients will also hire generalists sometimes, but when they hire a generalist, normally they don't expect to pay very much.

Choosing your label

How do you go about choosing the right label for yourself? There are no hard rules, and you must decide yourself, but I can guide you.

1. *You can call yourself what you like:* there are no rules (as long as you avoid prescribed titles, e.g. Doctor of Medicine, unless you are qualified to use them). The list I gave above is incomplete as I could have written a book just of freelancer's titles. But it does contain the most common ones.
2. *What you call yourself affects how your clients perceive you:* clients are unique, what will be good for one client will not work for another. But generally, stick to a tried a tested label, at least until you are established. The better you understand your clients, the easier it is to choose the right label. If you are a world-famous expert, you can safely call yourself anything you like including more off-the-wall names like 'wizard'! Until you are though, you risk sounding like a joker or a fool if you call yourself something like this. Avoid anything that makes clients think 'jack of all trades'.
3. *You can use more than one label:* it's increasingly common for people to have multiple labels. My view is that there is a risk of confusing clients, and it is clearer to have just one – at least one for any one situation.
4. *You can change your label when you want:* if you get it wrong and decide to change your label, just do it. However, there is a 'memory' of your previous labels – both literally in clients' memories, but also on things like social media and web sites. So, avoid changing it too often as it creates work, and may confuse some clients.
5. *What's important is not how you feel about it, but how your clients react to it:* the label is there to help you sell and do your work. Put your ego to one side and choose what works with your clients. If you do not know, look at what similar freelancers use, and select this to begin with. As you win business and learn about your clients, update it if you find a better one.

A couple of other bits of terminology

While we are talking terminology, I want to quickly cover a couple of other things. Just as there are different types of advisers, there are different types of clients. I don't want to get too bogged down in this as I don't think it makes much difference.

Some advisers call the people who they work for, and who pay them, 'customers'. Others call them 'clients'. For me there is not much between these words, save personal choice. In the corporate world 'client' tends to be favoured over 'customer'.

I'm going to call all of these people *clients*. Don't read anything into this other than it is the word I've chosen.

When an expert does some work for the client it might be a project, a task, a meeting or a service. I'm going to use the word from the world of consulting and call that an *engagement*. Client engagements take many shapes and forms and may be as short as an hour, or as long as several years.

The main elements of a freelancer's work

There are two sets of common areas of work that all freelancers have to understand. The first set is what I call the *lifecycle of work*. I've already introduced this, but I want to explain it some more. This lifecycle covers all the things you have to do – in other words **what** you do. The second set describes characteristics in the work of an expert which relate to **how** you do it. For now let's think about what you do.

The following list gives an overview of each of the steps in this lifecycle:

1. *Identify a specialised area of advising:* are you a specialist in technology implementation, keeping healthy or managing finances? Are you primarily a coach or a consultant? Do you work with clients on lots of small pieces of work or occasional large ones? Understanding this often starts with two questions: what do you know that other people might find useful, and how do you want to work with your clients to apply this knowledge?

2. *Work out a price for this service:* pricing is often opaque and there is not a standard price that everyone charges. It can be quite a challenge getting your prices right. Some charge low fees that everyone can afford, others charge huge amounts that only the largest of corporates can find the budget for. It's obviously going to make a huge difference to your lifestyle which you do.

3 *Find clients who want this advice:* this is often the thing that newcomers to the advisory business find hardest of all. How do I find enough clients for me to earn the livelihood I want? If you are starting out, this question may be terrifying you. Calm down: you are not alone and there is an answer.

4 *Get those clients to buy this service and pay for it:* that ongoing battle to sell and sell again. It's nice giving advice. It's better to be paid well for it. If you don't, you won't be doing it for very long, unless you are one of those happy rare people who does not need or want any money.

5 *Understand how to deliver the service:* how do you set up and run engagements? How do you interact with your clients when it comes to sharing the help?

6 *Please clients:* you want your clients to be happy with the service you give. That's because doing a good job is much more fun than doing a bad one! But it's also because then they will buy again and tell their colleagues and friends to do the same, and they will pay to use your services as well. This is also central to earning higher fees.

7 *Run a business and protect your interests:* whether you want to be a sole freelancer, or work as part of a firm, you need to run a business. Some of this is administrative, and other parts are about avoiding the risks that come with running a business. Unfortunately, some of this is terribly dull, but it is essential, and you need to get used to it. The good news is that if you are sensible, it can be a small part of your workload.

8 *Thriving and leveraging freelancing:* you may know a lot about something that everyone wants you to tell them today, but is anyone going to be interested in 5, 10 or 20 years' time? How do you keep people coming back to you for a career of freelancing?

The skills and behaviours to perform these activities

In the previous section of this chapter I outlined the eight main tasks that freelancers need to do. But you will know that to be great at something it's not just *what* you do, it is *how* you do it. Underlying these eight tasks are some skills and competencies, along with some behaviours and attitudes that ensure that freelancers who do these tasks do them well.

In terms of this book, think of these as themes that will flavour the way you should do the eight tasks that are mentioned above. I am outlining them here both to set your expectations about what it feels like to work as a freelancer, but also to get you thinking about how you might develop these skills and adopt these behaviours and attitudes.

Whatever you are doing at any time, these themes will weave their way into your daily life as a freelancer, and you will need to be comfortable with them if you are going to enjoy your life of advising.

They are:

1. *Knowledge:* your clients hire you for what's in your brain: your ideas, insights, observations and ways of helping and explaining. You may tell them things, question them in a helpful way, share experiences or help them through conversation. Whichever way you interact requires knowledge, whether that knowledge comes from experience, training or research, and whether that knowledge is given as direct advice or by helping a client think something through for themselves. Knowledge needs to be useful, reasonably up-to-date and in short supply. If it's not in short supply, no one wants to pay much for it.

2. *Being helpful:* at its heart, being an adviser is all about helping people and organisations, whether you are advising, influencing, guiding, or temporarily at least even directly doing things for your clients. A successful adviser learns how to be helpful. This isn't difficult, but it is not always as obvious as you might think it is. And don't fall into the trap of thinking that there is only one way to give advice. There isn't. To bring some focus on this, always remember the mantra that I was taught a long time ago as a junior consultant: *you are not paid to be right, you are paid to be helpful.* (Chapters 3 and 12)

3. *Credibility:* for a client to consider paying you for advice, you have to have a level of credibility as a source of that advice. There are different sources of credibility, which are more or less important for different sorts of experts. For instance, credibility may come from qualifications, experience, track record, recommendations, or a recognised brand. Credibility is not some fixed aspect of you, you can deliberately work to improve your credibility. (Chapter 13)

4. *Trust:* whatever type of expert you are, your clients need to trust you. If they don't, they will soon stop listening or buying your service. The way you develop trust varies depending on the type of adviser you are, but all advisers need to understand trust. There are different sources of trust and different advisers need to tap into these different sources. But whatever it derives from, trust is essential. (Chapter 12)

5. *Being persuasive and influential:* this goes hand in hand with trust. If you want to advise, and you want people to value that advice, you must develop the ability to persuade them that your advice is the right advice. There are lots of sources of advice, and most people are

overloaded with suggestions and recommendations. In the modern world I am bombarded with advice all the time: so, why should I listen to you? (Chapter 13)

6 *Temporary involvement, long-term influence:* you may have a long-term relationship with a client, but for any one piece of advice your work is normally temporary. The client asks for help in one form or another – you give it, and then the client gets on with their own work for a while without you. But although you only work with the client for a short period of time, the effect should be long lasting. And that's one of the clever bits about good advice giving, changing someone or some organisation's future with just a short involvement with them. The better you are at this, the higher fees you can charge. (Chapters 12 and 13)

7 *Working as an outsider:* as a freelance expert you are always an outsider. You don't do the work your clients do. Most of the time, you aren't sitting with them while they do it, and even if you are, usually you only need to worry about one part of their work. You might be their best friend, a trusted partner or it may be a cool professional relationship. But whichever it is, you are always living outside of your client's world. Advising or helping is not the same as being a manager, employee or a business partner. This is one reason why just because you are great at a job, does not mean you will necessarily be a great adviser or helper. Doing and helping are different.

You don't need to remember this second list, as we are going to go into all these topics in more detail as we go through the book.

An independent voice

Alison Zakers, Pinfold Consulting

My career hasn't been one where I set out with a clear ambition, but I've followed my passions and interests, and I've ended up in a good place. Initially, I worked in operational roles and then in my 30s took a step back to think about the next steps in my life and career. I took a year out to do an MBA, after which I moved into management consulting.

Working with some of the top consulting firms was an amazing experience. I was privileged to work with some brilliant people on some extraordinary transformation programmes. This is where I learnt the ropes of consulting and client engagement management.

▶

I set up Pinfold Consulting in 2005. I had been living out of a suitcase for years, travelling around the world working long hours on very challenging programmes. It was tiring, but I loved my job and the variety it brought. However, there were things I wanted to change. I wanted more time with my young family. I was sometimes mis-assigned. I sometimes found myself in organisations where there was a mismatch with my values.

While I was thinking about my next career move, my father was diagnosed with untreatable prostate cancer. This was the catalyst that started my thinking about an independent consulting career. I wanted to continue to do interesting, challenging, projects, but to have the ability to manage my diary and free up time to spend with dad.

Pinfold Consulting has now been running for 15 years, focused on helping clients realise their strategic ambitions. I guide them in shaping their future organisation, defining how that will impact ways of working and navigating the change.

My tips for anyone considering a freelance career

Making the leap to an independent pathway has given me more choices about what I work on and how much I want to work, but it's not always in my gift to engineer it perfectly.

1. Before you set out **think about what you want to get out of an independence status**. For me I wanted to balance interesting work with the opportunity to have extended time off when I needed it. I didn't set out to make lots of money.

2. **There's a lot of work that goes on behind the scenes** of the on-the-job role, from business development, to collateral development to the administration of running a small business. This is all non-chargeable to the client, but is essential to run your business.

3. There are usually **a range of trade-offs with any opportunity**. Getting the perfect role that suits your skills, calendar and geography preferences is rare, so think about what's really important for you.

4. **Be flexible as far as you can … and a bit more … to provide your services for your client.** You'll have your own reasons for pursuing independence but you'll need to make sure those reasons don't impact on client service. For example, I invest time up front to understand their expectations and schedule my personal appointments and holidays around their plans.

5. **Be realistic about the ups and downs of independence and plan for them.** Sometimes I have had very busy years with good income. Other years have been lean. I always try to keep a reasonably healthy business bank

balance so that I can pay myself a small salary in leaner times. I also have a range of other business or personal activities that I can get on with when not on full time assignments. I offer training services which can be turned on or off at short notice and I volunteer. I write up case studies and prepare points of view for future opportunities. And I enjoy time to spend with my family and turning my focus to hobbies.

My experience as an independent advisor has been rich and varied. It can be both rewarding and scary; intensively 24/7 and then suddenly fallow for a while. If you pursue this route think about what being independent might mean for you and any time spent exploring both the pros and cons will be time well spent.

chapter

3

Understanding why clients hire freelancers

To make a living from freelancing, you must choose a service to offer your clients, price it and sell it to them. The obvious place to start thinking about the type of freelance service you will offer, is by asking questions like 'what do I know, or can I do, that other people would find useful and be willing to pay for?'.

You might look at how other freelancers make money and think that you could do something similar. But as anyone who has started a thriving business before will tell you, the best place to start thinking is not with yourself, but with your clients.

The best strategy to build any successful enterprise starts by understanding what clients want and are willing to pay for. In this regard, freelancing is like any other business. Before you think about anything else, if you want to make a living as a freelancer, it's important to have an appreciation of why people hire freelancers. If you don't understand this, then you will never thrive and meet your full potential.

In this chapter, I'm going to explore what motivates people to seek advice or help. I want to give you a sense of the reasons there are. The material in this chapter will help you get ready for the advice in the next section of this book. It sets out some groundwork, which supports three things:

1 It will help you decide what sort of expert you want to be. Clients have different reasons for hiring different sorts of experts. By thinking

about why clients seek help, you can consider which kind of help giving you are stronger at or prefer, and from that decide what sort of expert you will position yourself as. We will go further on this in Chapter 4.

2 It will help you in working out more precisely who your client is. The most successful businesses are designed to sell to a clearly defined client. We will explore your specific clients in Chapter 5.

3 It will help you to price and sell your service, which we will work through in Chapters 6, 8 and 9.

Why do clients hire freelancers?

Clients hire freelancers for a variety of reasons. There are lots of things individuals and organisations need doing, but for one reason or another, they cannot or do not want to do these themselves. When this happens, there is an opportunity for a freelancer to earn a living.

We can think of the reasons a client might want to hire you in terms of something they lack. There are five main things clients lack: motivation, capacity, capability, confidence and remit. Let's briefly look at each of these:

- *Motivation:* we all have tasks we can do, but don't like doing. For instance, I hate cold calling customers. I can do it, but I really don't enjoy it. Fortunately, I don't need to do it much, but some businesses do need to cold call potential clients often, and when they do, they prefer to hire an external person to do it.

- *Capacity:* sometimes clients just don't have the time to do everything they need to do. Clients' days fill up with all sorts of activities involved in running their businesses. There are no hours left in the day to do anything else. These clients often have additional tasks they want done quickly and that means they must find someone to do them.

- *Capability:* in every business there are tasks clients need doing, but they cannot do. The task requires knowledge or skills the clients do not have. The client seeks a specialised expert and hires them to do it.

- *Confidence:* there are many problems which clients can work out the answer to, but they are not quite sure if their answer is right. When the consequences of making a decision based on that answer are significant, the client may falter. This is when an expert is approached to check the answer. The client is not necessarily expecting a different answer, but they want that sense of security that comes with a credible expert agreeing with them.

- **Remit:** there are some tasks where it does not matter whether the client can or cannot do them, they are not allowed to. For instance, if you run a business you legally must hire an independent and qualified accountant to do some of your accountancy tasks. If you want to buy certain financial products you must talk to an accredited financial adviser.

The better we understand these reasons, the better we can design our services. Also depending on the nature of these reasons, a client will be willing to pay more or less for a freelancer to help them.

To give a simple example, there are many things I have limited motivation to do, but I'm only going to pay so much for someone to do something for me that I could do. Make the price too high and I'll think 'oh well, I'll just do it myself'. On the other hand, I am more likely to pay well for a task that I really need doing, but which I do not have the faintest idea how to do. I may have no choice.

To bring this to life, I have created a table (Table 3.1) which simplifies the sort of dialogue you might have with a client, and from this how you might sell a related service to them.

Thinking a little bit further, it is not just how we sell the service to the client, but also how much they are willing to pay. Depending on the client's beliefs about a task they will be willing to pay more or less. You can influence this, by the way you encourage certain client beliefs by what you say or demonstrate about your service. This is summarised in Table 3.2.

From these two tables you can see that if you understand what the clients lack you can talk to them in a way that encourages them to buy your service, and to pay most highly for it. You can also think which services are most attractive to offer. For instance, offering to do an easy task, which requires few skills, is unlikely to be an attractive freelance business for you. But if you find a critical service that busy clients hate doing themselves, which relies on rare skills, they will be willing to pay you well to take it off their hands.

Table 3.1 Client reason checklist

The client lacks:	The client says:	The freelancer says:	In selling this service the freelancer stresses:
Motivation	I don't like doing this	I can painlessly take this unpleasant task away from you	How unpleasant the task is, and how easily I will take this task away from you. You do not need to do anything, and I will get it done.
Capacity	I don't have the time to do this	I can efficiently process this work for you	How much client time will be wasted doing this task, and how slickly and quickly I can do it for you, freeing up your time to do more important things.
Capability	I don't know how to do this	I have the skills and knowledge to do this work to a high standard	How difficult this task is for someone who does not understand it, and how much knowledge and experience I have to do it.
Confidence	I am uncertain or unsure about my choices	Let me help you and make sure you are doing it right	I am an experienced and helpful person who will put my arm around you and guide you, making sure you make the right choices.
Remit	I am not allowed to do this	I have the necessary accreditations / approvals / qualifications to do this task	You must have the right accreditations to do this, and I do. You can trust me to do it well for you.

Table 3.2 Implications for pricing your service

The client lacks:	The client will tend to pay more for this service if they believe:	The client will tend to pay less if they believe:	You can improve your fees by:
Motivation	They really hate doing the task	They prefer not to do it, but they will if they cannot find an easy alternative	Showing the client how unpleasant the task is, and how much easier their life would be if you did it.
Capacity	It is an essential task they must get done quickly, and they are very busy with other essential activities	It's an optional task, they would like to do, but is not essential – or they are not busy at present	Showing the client how much time they will free up if you do the task for them, and how much better you will do the task than them.

Table 3.2 (continued)

The client lacks:	The client will tend to pay more for this service if they believe:	The client will tend to pay less if they believe:	You can improve your fees by:
Capability	The skills needed to do the task are recognised as being rare and difficult to acquire	The skills needed to do the task are very widespread, or easily acquired with a little research	Showing the client how high your skills are, how difficult they were to acquire, and why they are safe in your hands.
Confidence	The implications of getting the decision wrong are very high	It's a small decision	Developing client trust in you and your knowledge, and client enjoyment in working with you.
Remit	The activity requires a rare accreditation and a high level of trust	There are lots of people accredited to do this activity	Developing client trust in you, and client belief in your expertise.

Other motivations for clients to hire freelancers

I have explained the five key reasons clients hire freelancers – lack of motivation, capacity, capability, confidence, or remit. But in truth your clients, like most other human beings, will be complex and full of hidden feelings and thoughts. What this means is that on top of the reasons I have sketched out, a client may have other motivations for hiring you.

The nature of these client motivations is that they are sometimes hidden. Unless you have a very strong relationship with a client, they may not tell you what they are. One of the signs of great salespeople is their ability to encourage a client to share their personal motivations, and then to weave responses to these into their sales messages.

It takes time and experience to get a sense of these other motivations. In this subsection, I want to give you some sense of the sort of hidden reasons clients sometimes have. The most important point from this subsection is to understand that clients' real needs may not always be explicit and therefore it's important to learn how to get beyond the obvious and expose their real needs. In doing this you will find their needs are often more complex than you originally thought. This may only become apparent over time. I have not included these for you to remember verbatim, but just to give you an impression of the complexity of the client's mind.

I need support for my idea

Sometimes a client has a great idea, but they cannot get the support from other people they need. This often happens in business. For example, one manager wants to invest in a project but cannot get approval to spend the money because none of the other managers is convinced it's such a great idea.

In a situation like this, clients often hire an expert to help them argue their case – perhaps building a stronger business case or maybe simply explaining why the idea is so good in a better way. Being able to communicate persuasively is an important skill for most freelance experts.

This can be interesting work to do, but caution is needed. There is always the risk that when you look at the client's idea you too, as an expert in the field, will think it's not very good. Instead of supporting the client, you may end up with a conundrum – pretending to support their idea which is ethically dubious or telling them that the idea is a bad idea, which will normally irritate them and may threaten your relationship and fees!

This challenge can be reduced significantly by the way you agree with a customer up front about your levels of independence when starting work. If your client knows at the start of your work that you may end up disagreeing with them, they have less cause for annoyance if you do.

I want someone to listen to me

Rarely does anyone say this out loud, but sometimes a client really wants a friendly ear to listen to them. They may want some advice that goes with this, but they may also just want someone who can nod and smile and show interest in their words.

Some jobs can be very demanding and stressful, and it can be difficult to discuss this with colleagues at work. This is when a client, often senior in an organisation, may seek someone who can listen to them. We all know there is something about talking things through that can clear our minds.

I have worked with customers who have been very happy with the engagements I have done, but when I think back to it, I have often done little more than listened to them. Never underestimate the value of listening to someone – and how much they may pay for this!

Although coaches do a lot more than this, parts of the relationship a coach builds with their clients are based on being good listeners.

I've been told I must work with you

Clients sometimes hire experts because they have been told to by someone else. A classic example in business is the manager who is well valued in an organisation but is struggling with some problem which is holding them back. A more senior leader decides they need some help and brings on a freelancer to give that help.

One thing to note is that you regularly won't immediately know this when you start working with the client. Often, even if your client has been told to get help, they won't tell you this. It usually doesn't feel great admitting we have been told to get help. However, it is useful for the expert to know, as you can be more appropriately sensitive to the client.

Some clients are happy when their boss tells them to get some help, but occasionally you may find that your client seems oddly prickly or difficult. You may find yourself thinking 'well why did you hire me if you are going to make it so hard to work with you?' There may be a simple reason for this – they never wanted to hire you in the first place.

This may sound like an impossible situation. It's not, but it does require a careful tread to make sure your client develops trust in you, rather than just resents your presence.

I want someone to take the blame

Occasionally, a client hires an expert because they think there is a big risk of making a mistake. That would be fine if what they were looking for was someone to help them find the right answer. But hidden in some client's requests for help is the desire to have someone else to take the blame if it all goes wrong. This is the finger-pointing motive.

If you think this is what a client is trying to do, take care. It is possible to gain very profitable engagements from clients for this sort of work. But of course, if you keep getting blamed for mistakes, you won't gain a great reputation as a useful expert to know. Additionally, there is always the risk of being sued if the decision has important consequences. This is one reason why many of us have professional indemnity insurance.

Fortunately, this client motivation is not something the freelancer has to worry about too often. Unless you are an internationally recognised expert in a specialised area, this is rarely a motivation for hiring an independent expert. For a client, being able to say that a single freelancer agreed with their decision is normally not a big enough target to point the finger at if it all goes wrong. The client needs a big target – usually a large professional services firm with a well-known brand, deep pockets and a widely recognised name. Often one of the reasons people hire the well-known and expensive, big professional services firms is to have someone to blame if it goes wrong.

Years ago, it used to be said that 'no one got fired for hiring IBM', in the days when IBM dominated the IT business. If clients wanted a risk-free option, which you would never be blamed for, they hired IBM.

As an aside, don't worry about the big firms. They understand very well that their clients do this, and they make a lot of money because of this. They are adept at avoiding the finger being pointed at them, caveating all their advice with all sorts of phrases and get-out clauses, which makes holding them accountable rather tricky.

Guide me

There are many situations in which a client is not looking so much for *an* answer to *a* problem from an expert, but for a long-term relationship that will help guide them through the ups and downs of their career. They want someone they can reach out to on a regular basis to talk things through. This might be perceived as a shoulder to lean on, someone to give wise counsel and someone who can help them solve their own problems.

This is the domain of truly trusted advisers, mentors and coaches. Whether it is for a few months or a whole career, such advisers develop deep relationships with their clients – and their focus is usually their client as a person, rather than any one specific work situation. These long-term relationships can both be very fulfilling for freelancers and offer a long-term revenue stream.

What does this mean for the freelance expert?

To become a successful expert, you need to be able to work out the reasons clients have hired you. Success depends on fulfilling client needs, and it's difficult to do this if you don't know what they are. Now this would be easy if the motives causing clients to hire us were just written down and given to us at the start of an engagement. Life is not always so simple. Sometimes the motivations behind people hiring a freelance expert are hidden and unexpressed.

One important aspect of your ability to expose a client's true reasons for wanting help is trust. When clients trust you, they will tell you more, even their hidden motivations. Being able to develop trust is a key capability of freelance experts. In Chapter 12, we will explicitly look at building trust further.

Understanding the reasons clients hire us will help you to sell and maximise your prices. Also, it will help you avoid mismatches in expectations. This is when you think you have been hired for one reason, but you find out as you go through your work that there is a different reason. You cannot avoid this happening in every situation, but you can protect yourself, by clearly specifying to the client exactly what you will do for them and why. In this way, if the reasons change, you have a basis to discuss what the change means for your service, and the fees you will charge.

In the end, all of these client motivations are generalisations. Each client you meet will be unique. No matter how good you are, there will be somebody somewhere that you cannot work with and who will not ever buy services from you. You are not the right freelance expert for that person. Don't worry. You don't want to be the right expert for everyone. There are lots of people, and there will also be somebody somewhere who wants what you have. You should not be seeking to serve every client, only enough clients, who will pay the fees you want. One of your jobs will be to find the right ones which, if you follow the advice in this book, you will be able to do.

Sometimes this is about tailoring your services and the way you interact with your clients, but it is also about choosing clients who want the services you have and like your style of working. We too easily forget that not only do clients have a choice whether to hire us or not – we also have a choice as to which clients we work for.

Your attitude towards helping your clients

I want to conclude by thinking about your attitude to your clients. As I have explained, there are a variety of reasons for why they will work with you. Sometimes you will know these, occasionally there will be other hidden motivations. We can say that, always, the overall reason you will be hired is because a client needs some help. Your first response to this statement might be *surely everyone hires an expert because they need help*. Yes, you'd be right with that response, but it is important to think about your attitude to being helpful. If you develop the right attitude you will succeed!

Your primary job when you provide expertise is not to be right, it is to be helpful. Fortunately, most of the time being helpful entails being right. But there is a critical attitude of mind to develop to be a successful freelancer. If your first thought in responding to any customer is that you must at all costs be right, then you are in the wrong frame of mind. The first thought should be: what is the most helpful thing to say or do?

Imagine someone asks you a question which you, as an expert, know the answer to. Do you tell them the right answer? Often that is the best thing to do. But sometimes being helpful requires asking a question in return rather than saying the answer. Sometimes being helpful means reducing the complex precise truth into a simplified, not totally accurate but good enough, answer. Sometimes being helpful means telling someone they are asking the wrong question in the first place. And so on . . . because what is helpful depends on the situation and what help that client needs at that point in time. Successful experts judge what is needed in which situation.

I always think of it this way. When I was a teenager and learning to drive, I wanted to get everything right and always to be in the right as I drove. It is great to want to do things right. It is not always helpful to insist though on being in the right. My father always cautioned me: the graveyards are full of drivers who thought they were in the right and so didn't press the breakpedal. It's a lesson I have not forgotten. Sometimes being right isn't the right thing to try to be!

Following on from this, there is no point advising clients in a way that is of no use to them, even if the advice is factually correct. A good adviser puts the advice in a form that is useful to the client. By this I mean a couple of things.

The first is that they must understand it. As an expert it's easy to forget you are the expert and your client isn't. You need to talk in their language, not yours. Secondly, the advice must be useable. There is no point advising clients about all sorts of wonderful things they don't have the resources or capability to make use of. Of course, sometimes this really is not possible and the only answer to a problem is that the client cannot solve it. Then the best help is to try and get them to focus on other things they do have the resources and capability to resolve. Your advice might entail explaining why they can't resolve the problem and pointing out some other things they can resolve that are in their power to sort out.

No adviser, who keeps telling their customers things that are right but not helpful or usable by them, is going to build a successful business. It's extremely irritating to clients to be continually told by some smart Alec something that is correct but unhelpful.

Always remember, your job is not to be right, it is to be helpful – and help comes in many forms.

Clients may already know the answer!

I want to end this chapter with a quote which I often reflect on. When anyone asks for help, we usually assume they do not already know the answers to their problem. Jean-Paul Sartre would disagree. In his 1946 book *Existentialism is a Humanism* he wrote:

> But if you seek counsel – from a priest, for example – you have selected that priest; and at bottom you already knew, more or less, what he would advise. In other words, to choose an adviser is nevertheless to commit oneself by that choice.

An independent voice

Theresa Coligan, The Coaching Project

After 18 years in the advertising industry and at the grand old age of 40, I was ready for a change. Three years earlier I had done what everyone told me not to do and crossed the 'great divide'. I was headhunted to become Sales Director at a big publishing company responsible for 180 people. Little did I know that those 180 people were on the floor in terms of their motivation. I was really shocked by what I had walked into. Three years later, however, we won Campaign Media Sales Team of the Year (a big industry award) and I knew my job was done. I was also exhausted! Not just by the scale of the challenge, but also by the hideous politics and daily battles with one of the key companies we served.

On discussing my future with my own coach and mentor at the time, he asked if I had ever considered becoming a coach saying he thought I would be excellent at it. I was a little taken aback. I really rated this guy and the idea hadn't even crossed my mind. I had only got as far as planning to take a year out to do a foundation course in acting – something I had wanted to do since I was knee-high to a grasshopper!

Well, much as the course was a great experience, it turned out that I didn't want to tread the boards in a local theatre for £300 a week or be one of the 97% of actors who are unemployed. I had become accustomed to quite a nice lifestyle. So, my thoughts turned to coaching and after re-training as a coach and NLP Master Practitioner in the mid-2000s I have never looked back.

I realised I had been putting on an excellent front for 18 years, utilising those innate acting skills, which is also exhausting. In complete contrast to that, coaching has felt like a vocation since day one and, while it might sound clichéd, I can genuinely say that it doesn't feel like work. More importantly, as I always say, it has brought me back to me.

My tips for anyone considering a freelance career

A lot of people contact me to ask about getting into coaching and I am happy to discuss it with anyone. However, much as I love it, I am always sure to point out three things:

1. If you are the main breadwinner or a key financial contributor to the household, be aware that there are a lot of coaches in the market (including internal ones) and **it is hard to make a good living**. A relatively small percentage make a six-figure sum and for those that do it has probably taken many years of hard graft.

2. You don't just need to be an excellent coach, **you need to be a confident salesperson too**. There is no-one building your pipeline or securing business for you; it's all down to you. Many coaches find this the hardest part of running their own business and it is probably the main reason many fail or seek to supplement it in some way.

3. You can call yourself a coach after attending a weekend course, but please don't. Find a reputable company and **accredited training course** that requires many hours of practice and observation. These are peoples' lives, careers and businesses you will be working with and they deserve to be treated with the utmost care, professionalism and respect. Moreover, it is the new entrants looking for this low cost, quick fix who often disappear most quickly from view.

part

two

Design your freelance business

chapter 4

Defining your specialisation

What kind of expert are you going to be?

Many people have read my book *The Management Consultant*. Some of those readers will contact me with comments, feedback and sometimes questions. One of the topics of discussion will often arise from their surprise at learning that there is no such thing as a general management consultant. Some people assume that all management consultants essentially do the same thing. They don't.

Consultants must specialise. Of course, there are some general skills that all consultants must have, but they alone will not make anyone a successful consultant. When clients spend money on consultants, they want to know the consultants they are hiring are experts in the specific area they are advising on.

Whether it is corporate strategy, organisational design, IT systems delivery, how to set up a pension fund or the thousands of other things that people seek consultants for, there are experts in each area. If you look inside any of the large consultancies, they break their businesses down by all sorts of dimensions – usually including geographies, client sectors and specialist service. So, a client might hire a consultant who knows the best IT systems for the US retail market. This isn't true just for consultants. This also applies for all freelancers.

As a freelance expert you may want to offer services that are different from those of a large consultancy. Nevertheless, you also need to specialise. You need to have your own niche. You will not succeed as a jack of all trades.

The need for a niche

I want to get one point out of the way quickly, although often I find I can't without a debate. This is the fundamental need for a niche. If you get this and don't need any further convincing, you can skip this section. If you don't, read on, as I really do want to convince you to specialise.

In Chapter 2, I introduced a list of names or titles for different types of freelancers. This is an element in finding your niche or a starting point, but it is not enough on its own. For instance, there are millions of IT contractors. But there are no generic IT contractors. Every IT contractor has an area they help in. This is what we are now going to focus on.

None of us likes being simplified into a single area that tries to encapsulate us. We are complex and there are lots of different parts to our personalities. We all reflect Walt Whitman's famous phrase 'I am large – I contain multitudes'.

But when it comes to selling yourself as a freelance expert, you are not selling every aspect of yourself, your personality or your experience – you are selling a particular service. The truth is that people tend not to buy the jack of all trades who claims to be able to put their hand to everything. Perhaps you really are an expert at lots of things. Even if you are, your clients won't believe that or be interested. Too broad expertise is not credible, and credibility is essential to a successful career as a freelance expert. As an expert your product is always you . . . it's just which you is it?

When it comes to thinking about your service lines, park your ego for a moment. Don't focus on the breadth of your wonderfully colourful and varied career. Think about what you can be great at, not all the things you might be able to do. People always need help, and if you can help there is a business to be made.

Specialists make it, generalists don't. As a generalist you may think there is lots and lots of work you can do. But there're also lots and lots of other people who could do the work as well. As a generalist it is virtually impossible to stand out and differentiate your service.

Buying the services of a freelance expert is usually a discretionary spend. On the occasions that clients want to buy, they typically want to be sure you can do what they need. They don't want to hire a nice person who is putting their hand to a task for the first time; they want you to have done it many times before.

People don't always like it when I point this out. I remember quite a heated argument with someone who had reached out to me to help them increase their leads and sales, while positioning themselves as a business generalist. I challenged her, and suggested she needed to refine her niche. She claimed it was her strength to be a business generalist. I resisted the urge to point out the irony of her confidence, given that she had contacted me to increase her sales!

Now there are three exceptions to what I have said. Firstly, anyone can get lucky. Maybe you will be lucky once or twice as a generalist and meet a client who hires you at a good rate. That's great, but luck is not really a sustainable way to build a business. Secondly, you can sell yourself as a jack of all trades if you are happy to work for the lowest possible rate. But, if you want to earn a decent living, you need a specialisation.

The third situation in which being a generalist can work is when you have a particularly deep and long-standing relationship with a client, who over time has come to appreciate the range of your skills. Then you may well be asked to do things without the constraints of your niche, but this takes time to achieve. Once a client has a high degree of trust in you, they may well ask you to do things outside of your specific niche. Instead of being a niche specialist, you become a specific customer specialist. Because you have trust and work regularly with this client, you will learn what is important to them and understand their real desires and interests. Based on this, they will be more likely to engage you in a wider set of work than that purely related to your subject matter expertise. (See Chapter 12 for more on long-term relationships.)

This point of specialisation is eloquently argued for by McMakin and Fletcher in their book *How Clients Buy*. They use a phrase that consultants should constantly be 'shrinking the pond'. They argue that you should be making your target market smaller and smaller until you can say for that market you are the best in the world.

Is it the same for a freelance expert? Well, perhaps confusingly, I'd answer that in two ways: 'yes' and 'not exactly'!

The reason I say the answer is yes is that some of the readers of this book will be truly ambitious, seeking to completely dominate some area of expertise. If you are this, perhaps you are looking to become a global influencer. The sort of person who is invited to give TED talks, key note speeches at major conferences, and has hundreds of thousands of followers who follow you to learn. If this is what you want to be then you absolutely need to have a very clear, and ideally unique, niche. When you have this niche, you have the potential to become that person.

So, why did I also say the answer is 'not exactly'? That's because for many of the people reading this book, wanting to become a freelance expert, you are not aiming for global domination. Usually, all you want is a steady stream of good clients. Let me assure you there are lots of customers to go around, but I can equally assure you that there are also lots of alternative sources of advice and expertise.

You need to be good enough, and you need to be differentiated enough for the client to want to hire you as opposed to anyone else. In this case you do not need to be the most specialised in the world, but you do want to be the best choice available to your clients at the time they need help. Perhaps that is just the best in your local area, or for a specific sector of the market. This still requires a reasonable degree of specialisation, but you can worry less about being unique.

The client, the client, the client ... it's all about the client

In the next chapter we will talk about who your client might be. At this stage we are talking about your service, but you cannot think of your service completely independently of clients. Every service needs a customer, without one it's a hobby not a business. Before we get into the details of targeting clients, it's useful to think about the fundamental characteristics that your clients must have to be the sort of clients you want.

There are four factors to think about.

- There needs to be enough people who would find your service useful. Now don't get me wrong, that does not need to be millions of clients. Most of us can only deal with one client at a time. Depending on your service, you may need dozens of customers a year or perhaps only one. You just need enough, no more.
- Secondly, those people must either have money directly, or an ability to access the money required to pay for your service. There is no point targeting a group who have no finances unless you are offering your work as a public service. I do some pro-bono work and it's very satisfying, but I can only do this because I have plenty of paying clients too.
- A slight twist on the point about money is that your target clients must have the propensity to spend money on the sort of service you are planning to offer. Now sometimes we won't know this until we try, but please bear this point in mind when thinking about your services. Just because someone has money, doesn't automatically mean they are going to spend it on you!

- Finally, you need to have access to those clients. For instance, there's no point coming up with a service line that targets the CEOs of major corporations if you don't personally know any of them, don't know anyone else who knows them, or have no idea how to access them. Inaccessible clients are as useless as no clients at all, except they are probably even more frustrating!

This boils down to a single important question: are there enough people interested in your service with money they are willing to spend, who you have some level of access to? If your answer to this is 'no', then you will need to think again about your service lines.

Of course, there are people who have invented new services which initially had no clients. It can be done and can be hugely successful. But if you go down this route, understand that you are going to be spending a lot of time explaining your service and creating that new market.

I have summarised these points in the short checklist presented in Table 4.1.

Often the answer to these questions for the new freelancer is, 'I don't know'. The truth is, you won't know with absolutely certainty until you start, but there are ways you can reduce the risk and avoid looking at the world with rose-tinted glasses. There are five ways to find out more.

1. **Reflect:** what do you know about, what are you interested in, how do you like working? Honestly and critically reflect on yourself and your abilities. Avoid being overly hard on yourself and being overly optimistic. The rest of this chapter describes the key things for you to reflect on.

2. **Research:** there are quite a lot of ideas and information available beyond this book. But much of it is unstructured and you must take the time to search, filter and find the gems. As I write this, one of the best places to look is LinkedIn, but a general web search can also help. Look at some websites freelancers have. What services are being offered, and do they seem to be successful? This won't give you a reliable answer, but it will help you to identify some niches you may not have thought about.

Table 4.1 Are there clients for your niche?

	Your target clients . . .	Yes?
1	Are there enough people who would find your service useful?	☐
2	Do these people have access to resources to pay for your services?	☐
3	Do these people tend to spend money on the sort of service you are offering?	☐
4	Do you have access, or a way of gaining access, to these people?	☐

3 *Ask:* use your network, and if you don't have one, build a network by reaching out to people who do the sorts of things you want to do. Read their social media posts and ask for advice. Look at who other people follow and follow them yourself. Some people will not be helpful, but many people will happily give you a few minutes of their time. It's amazing how much you can learn by asking experienced freelancers a few questions.

4 *Pay:* there are increasing numbers of people advising, mentoring or coaching freelancers about their business. They promote themselves on social media, particularly LinkedIn. The phrase *caveat emptor* holds, as these are paid-for services. There are some excellent and genuine freelance mentors around; there are also a lot of charlatans. Choose carefully. Look at their track record and seek references and recommendations. Generally, I'd say avoid those who have never actually worked as a freelancer themselves.

5 *Experiment:* try a niche and refine it over time. Frankly, this is the best approach, i.e. to learn by doing. Set yourself up, and then find out what works and what does not. If you are not getting enough business – refine your niche! All freelancers do this to some extent.

It starts with what you know

If you want to be a freelance expert, the starting question for you is 'what do you know that might be useful to someone else?'. A slight variation of this, is 'what can you learn that might be useful to someone else?'. You can always go out and learn some new expertise to sell.

As a freelance expert your clients hire you for what's in your brain: your ideas, insights, observations and ways of explaining. Every possible service requires knowledge, whether that knowledge comes from brilliant insights, experience, training or research.

You don't need to know everything. Sometimes you don't need to know very much, but you need to know something. You need to know *enough* to be helpful.

But it's not just *any* knowledge. If you want to make a living from your knowledge, it obviously needs to be useful. It also needs to be reasonably up to date. No one is going to hire you to advise them how the Victorians ran factories. But it does not need to be cutting-edge knowledge. In fact, many customers are slightly suspicious of novel ideas. Many clients are victims of the crowd mentality of trusting most easily what everyone else already trusts. Only some clients have the foresight to buy novel services.

Finally, that knowledge needs to be in short supply. If it's not in short supply, no one wants to pay much for it. But short supply is relative to demand. If you know something that thousands of other people know, but that can help millions of people who don't know it, then this knowledge is still short enough supply to make money.

It's wonderful to be a world-class expert and, based on such expertise, some of the most successful experts have built hugely successful careers. But you don't need to be a world-class expert to build a good business advising other people. Clients rarely need a truly unique perspective or total originality. Anyway, not all clients want or can afford the world-class expert.

You might worry about your levels of experience. Do you need decades of experience to be credible? It certainly can be helpful, and many of the most successful freelance experts have this. But the importance of experience built up over many years depends on the service you plan to offer.

You don't always need huge experience. If you want to help people with brand new technology, by its very definition there won't be much experience around. Your few months of knowledge may make you a leading-edge practitioner and may allow you to help clients tremendously.

I have come across one enterprising young and seemingly inexperienced consultant, whose service is to help businesses target his age group. His marketing explains that, as one of them, he understands this age group better than no end of highly experienced marketing professionals do. Brilliant!

Know-what versus know-how

Although more and more people want to make a living giving advice, there is one domain of knowledge that is becoming less and less valuable. This is 'know-what'. By know-what I mean straight facts, figures, information and so on. Decades ago, there were experts who could make a living just because they knew a lot of information. That's largely a dead business. If I can look it up with a short search on the internet, then I don't need advice or help from someone else. Even if I was lazy enough not to want to do a search, I'm not going to pay much for it.

There are a couple of exceptions to this. The first is new knowledge. This might be knowledge to do with brand new technology, social trends or novel ideas. For a short period of time – perhaps only a few months and rarely more than several years – there can be a business with new knowledge. Knowledge should disseminate quickly and seamlessly. In reality, it doesn't. Although you may not make your career telling others about the latest ideas, you may make some money for a while.

The other sort of know-what that has value is when someone brings knowledge from one domain, or better still several domains, to another one. Look at ideas like Lean and Six Sigma – they have been around for many decades. As I write this book, the word 'Agile' is shouted out like an innovative solution to every problem. Yet the Agile manifesto was created in 2001, and some of the ideas in Agile go back long before then. In many sectors Lean and Agile are established business practices which have been used for years and are engrained into everyone who works in the sector. However, decades on from their original development, these approaches still seem to be news in some sectors. There is still money to be made as an expert in these areas in some sectors.

Even with these two exceptions, know-what is a difficult business to grow and it is a challenge to make a sustained independent business from know-what. If customers don't buy much know-what – what is it that they buy? What they buy is *know-how*.

Now it may sound as if I am just playing with words. I am not. There is an important difference between know-what and know-how. When a client reaches out for help, it is rarely because they just want the answer to a question. What they usually want is practical solutions to real-world problems they have. The difference between know-what and know-how is one of application and direct relevance to that specific client.

For instance, a client rarely pays much to simply know what a new piece of government regulation is. They want to know what it means to their and their competitor's businesses, and what they need to do to become compliant with it. This does not just require information; it requires that 'seen-it, done-it' kind of experience that is able to take information and apply it in a specific situation.

How you share your knowledge with your clients

The other aspect to your niche, is how you utilise the knowledge you have. It is quite easy to think of two freelance experts with similar experience, qualifications and knowledge – but who work in different ways and appeal to different clients. They apply knowledge in different ways.

The most obvious example of this is the difference between a subject matter expert (SME) and a coach. An SME tends to provide knowledge directly – to support customers answering their questions and resolving problems. In simple terms, the SME tends to tell and to inform the client's thinking. A coach on the other hand tends to help a client think something through for themselves. In other words, coaches tends to facilitate the client's own thinking.

There are many different dimensions to consider in how you might apply your knowledge, but I think of them primarily in four categories. There are no right or wrong answers as to which is the best way to operate with these categories, and to some extent it comes down to personal preferences and personal styles. The answers you give are, however, important as they can be central aspects of defining your niche. The four dimensions can be phrased as questions:

- Are you a *doer* or an *adviser*?
- Do you *instruct* your clients or *encourage* them?
- Do you sell services *transactionally* or based on long-term *relationships*?
- When you sell, are you selling your *time* or a *product*?

There are significant differences between these approaches, some of which we will explore in future chapters. They are summarised in Table 4.2.

Table 4.2 Your approach to helping clients

Advise	You guide your client to solve their problems with ideas, techniques and approaches. You are paid to share your ideas and knowledge.	You take problems off your clients' hands and do the work required to resolve them. You are paid to get something done.	Do
Encourage	When you engage with your clients your style is to help them to help themselves. You facilitate their thinking with questions and help them reach their own answers.	When you engage your clients, you tell them the answers and provide direction and instructions based on good practice and experience.	Instruct
Transaction	When you engage with your clients it is a transaction based on your specific specialist service which is tried, tested and proven. It is the same for every client.	When you engage with your clients it is based on a deep understanding of each client and a strong relationship with them. Your service is tailored to fit their needs.	Relationship
Time	You client hires you, and pays for you, for an amount of time. For example, by the hour, the day or the month, irrespective of what you do or what you deliver.	Your client hires you to provide a specific product or service. Your prices are based on a price for the product, not how long you work.	Product

Advise |——————↑——————| Do
Encourage |——↑——————————| Instruct
Transaction |——————————↑——| Relationship
Time |↑————————————| Product

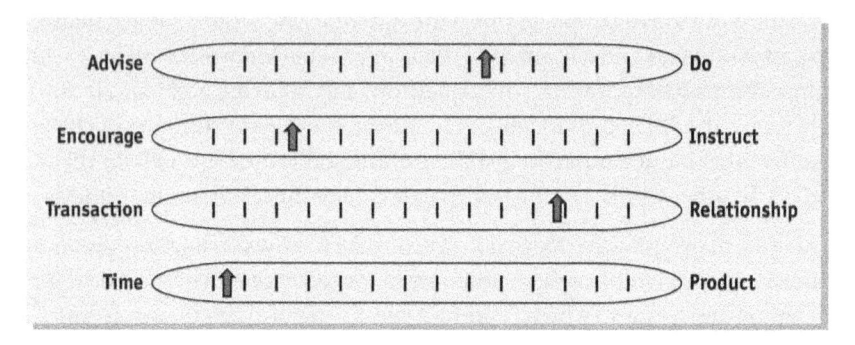

Figure 4.1 How do you provide your service?

One way to think of these are as extremes of a slider, like the volume control on some old-fashioned hi-fi systems (see Figure 4.1). You have a choice as to where you place these sliders, and what the balance of your approach is based on these sliders.

How you position yourself relative to these four dimensions does not have to be a static choice, it may change over time or even within a single engagement with a single customer. Great experts are adept at changing their style. In fact, excellent freelancers often discuss this explicitly with their clients for a specific piece of work.

Nevertheless, it's useful to understand the main style you will be using when you sell to clients, as this should be part of your sales message and, over time, will become ingrained into the reputation you have with clients.

Where to start?

If you have a great idea for a service that you can uniquely sell, then you may well be starting out on a fabulous freelance career.

If you don't, there is a simpler answer. Look around and see what is in demand and imitate what the successful ones are doing. Don't confuse the need for a niche with the need for originality.

There is a great case for this in social media. There are a few influencers really saying original things, but in my experience some of the most popular names with the largest groups of followers do little else than repeat popular wisdoms. They come up with little or nothing that is original, but they have hundreds of thousands of followers.

Now, we do have to be a little careful as being a successful expert and being a big social media name are not the same thing. But I mention this to make clear the point that while originality may be wonderful, it is not always or even often valued. People usually like to hear things they are comfortable with, and similarly people often like to buy advice and other expert services that they are familiar with.

This may sound too simple, but look around the market of freelance experts. Across the world there are lots of experts offering essentially the same service: IT contractors, life coaches, financial advisers and marketing consultants who are offering pretty much identical things. They all have a clear niche, but it's a niche they are far from being uniquely situated in. As James Altucher says in his book *Choose Yourself:* 'Pick a boring business. Everyone is always on the lookout for "the next big thing". The next big thing is finding rare earth minerals on Mars. That's HARD WORK.'

Going into an established niche can be low risk. As long as the demand for that service remains greater than the supply, there will be work for you to do. This will limit your income to what the market will bear for that service. You will never become one of those globally recognised experts, but it can provide enjoyable, fulfilling work and a good income. I know many freelance experts who have generated a very comfortable living without doing anything unique.

Of course, you must watch that the supply stays lower than the demand, else your rates will start to decline. Perhaps, this is a way for you to start. Begin with something specific that you know there is a business for. Once you have become established and understand the business more, you can experiment and improve your service, and make it a little more uniquely yours.

I am not trying to put you off coming up with a truly original service. Now and again someone does this and builds a hugely successful career for themselves. After all, when I started work the only coaches anyone knew were sports coaches, and yet now decades later the world is full of all sorts of coaches, some of whom are making very comfortable livings. This would not have happened without innovation.

If you can, and you believe there is a market for the service you want to offer, you should go for it. But if you don't see yourself as the source of innovative wisdom, yet still have plenty of useful non-unique knowledge, there is still going to be an opportunity for you.

What you like doing

One of the joys of being a freelancer is the independence you get, and how you take advantage of that freedom and flexibility. Now there's not much point seeking this independence if you don't take advantage of it. You might as well save yourself the bother of running your own business, and stay safe and secure in that corporate role, working for someone else.

So before homing in on your service line, it is worth reflecting for a moment on whether you are really going to enjoy offering this service and if it is going to give you the benefits of independence you first sought.

The ever-changing world

I hope you are now convinced that it's important to have a niche. When you have found the right one, it will become one of the critical foundations of your success. But I don't want you to think that having come up with your niche it's a once-in-a-lifetime exercise.

The world will continue to evolve, from time to time the unexpected will happen, you will learn and grow, new opportunities will arise, and some services will become outdated. Whatever your service is and no matter how successful it is to begin with, there will be a time at which demand starts to fall. Your service is a starting point. It is unlikely to be the basis of a life-long career.

But there is also the opportunity to continually refine your niche, to go back to McMakin and Fletcher's phrase of 'shrinking the pond', you can do this. Perhaps you may start in a busy niche, but as you get confident, learn the business and start to develop a deeper understanding of your clients' need, you can specialise further. This is the way to create a truly great freelance business.

I have changed my focus as an expert several times in my career in response to shifts in the market and opportunities to specialise. I don't see this as a pain, but as a wonderful aspect of the world of freelancing. The great thing about independent working is that you always have the opportunity to shift your services and invent yourself again under a new guise. (See Chapter 14 for more on this.)

An independent voice

Scott Gould, Author, Speaker and Consultant

As far as freelance expert stories go, I've got a bit of a peculiar one – mainly because I didn't choose to become an expert, I was forced to!

I used to be a church minister, and as you might imagine, being a church minister is something you devote everything to – your career progression is pretty much focused exclusively on developing those skills and working in that context.

So, when it came time for me to make the decision to move out of being a church minister, the transition was extremely difficult. I had run lots of different initiatives within church, in addition to some business ventures on the side, which meant that while I had a fair amount of experience with people, I didn't have one clear skill that I could hang my hat on and get a job with.

Out of 100 job applications I only got two interviews – and zero job offers – because I simply didn't have the career progression that they were looking for, and it just wasn't clear what I did. I was forced into offering my services as a freelancer in order to find some way to earn an income.

After two years of doing a range of freelancer jobs, from event planning to running a crowdfund to copy writing to leadership coaching, I had the superb fortune of reading Richard's book, *The Management Consultant*. This book switched the lights on for me, because I saw that consulting was what I always actually *had* done as a minister – using my knowledge to help people find solutions to their problems, especially in the realm of how they engaged with people.

Some years on, and now I'm an author, speaker and leadership consultant in people engagement.

My tips for anyone considering a freelance career

The advice that I give to people is the story of my journey: you *do* have expertise, but uncovering what that expertise is will likely be the hard part, even though it's probably staring you right in the face!

The reason why it is hard is because you can't read the label from the inside of the bottle. Your expertise is such a part of you that you don't actually recognise it as expertise, you just think it's normal.

Even if you have a very distinct industry and skillset, you will have a unique expert view – and this is the very thing that makes you in demand as a freelance expert, and also helps you command the expert fee that should go with it.

But it will take time to see your expertise for what it is, especially if you're just starting out. The best approach, I think is to start with what tangible skill you have, but seek regular feedback that will help uncover the nuances that are your unique perspective, and your true expertise. In fact, I encourage people to be willing to work outside of their niche or historic skillset if they need the income, as applying your approach in new environments is often what shines the light on your expertise all the more.

Don't be too eager to rush this: it is trial and error, and getting it wrong is just as important as getting it right, because learning where your weaknesses are is part of your learning your strengths.

You can contact me via email, scott@scottgould.me, and on Twitter, @scottgould

chapter

5

Profiling your clients

In Chapter 4 we explored how experts need to specialise to build a successful business. We asked a crucial question: 'what work will you do?'. There is another important question you must ask yourself: 'who is going to buy your services?'. Specialisation requires you to answer both questions.

You want to know who your client is to be able to refine your services to suit that client. You also need to know this so you can work out who you are going to approach to sell your services to. If part of your niche is the service you offer, another part of it is the clients you offer it to.

Let me make an analogy. When I write a book, I think very carefully who the book is aimed at. I imagine my ideal reader. Sometimes I even write some features of this person down, so I can carefully analyse who they are. Then as I am writing I hold this person in mind. As I write I am then able to ask myself questions like: *What would this person find useful to know? What would they already know? What would they benefit from understanding? What style of language will be best?* As I write, I imagine I am having a conversation with this person. As a freelance expert, I have also built up a similar view of my typical client, and this is important for my business.

In Chapters 8 and 9 we will talk about how you can find these clients and persuade them to buy your services. In this chapter we are going to explore who your client might be in a more generic sense. Marketing professionals call this your *client persona*. Marketeers spend a lot of time exploring personas – analysing the style, habits, wants, needs and propensities of their potential clients. They do this, because they have learnt that this is a great way to build a product or service that people want.

One successful small business adviser told me that the biggest problem he sees with small start-up businesses is the lack of clarity over who is the customer. This is a lesson worth remembering as a freelance expert.

But I don't want to miss out on sales . . .

One concern that is often raised when I talk about identifying your specific clients, is that there might be other clients who also want to buy your service. If you target your client too precisely, might you miss out on sales? Yes, you might, but you want to build a business in which this is not a problem. It should even be a good thing.

If you have a strong enough business, the fact that you have clients who you don't serve won't cause any problems. You will have enough clients to be able to generate the income you want without working for those who don't fit your chosen profile. Your attitude to clients who don't quite fit your ideal profile will depend on how successful you are. The more successful you are, the choosier you can be about your clients.

There are lots of advantages to being able to be choosey, not least of which is that you will be able to charge higher fees. Remember you do not need millions of clients. You are not setting up a global corporation who needs to sell to everyone. You simply need enough clients, and for a freelance expert usually that is not that many. After all, most of us can only serve one customer at a time.

There is another point: if your service is going to be properly designed, it needs to be designed for someone. I use the term 'clients', and other businesses may talk about 'customers'. Whichever word we use, there is a risk that we start thinking of our clients or customers as some generic or abstract category. The person who buys your service is never anyone or everyone, it is always *someone*. A specific person with specific wants and needs. That is why your client persona needs to be realistic.

Remember, when thinking about your ideal client – that client is not you. One of the mistakes many freelancers make when setting out, and which frankly is a common mistake across small businesses, is for people to design their service with themselves in mind. But think about it for a moment, isn't that a little crazy? After all, you are one person who certainly is never going to buy a service from yourself!

Having said this, there is no reason to expect that all your clients must be exactly like your target client persona. The persona is just a tool you can use to check your service is right, and a tool to help you in sales and marketing. Everyone is unique, and you may have to tweak your sales messages and your services to individual clients. But if you can focus on a specific set of clients with similar wants and needs, this will all be much, much easier. Thinking through your client persona is simply intended to make it easier and more effective when thinking about your services and your sales messages.

I said in the introduction to this chapter that I am always clear about who my reader for my books is. Interestingly, I have found the more I write for one specific reader, the better I write – and the better I write, the more the book sells to other readers. I can't really explain this, but I do recommend you don't worry too much about excluding people by targeting your clients too precisely.

(To explore client persona's further in a structured way, you can use the empathy map from Alexander Osterwalder and Yves Pigneur's book *Business Model Generation,* or see www.strategyzer.com)

The first question – will you be selling to individuals or businesses?

In thinking about your clients, the first point to be clear about is whether you intend to sell to individuals or to businesses.

If I use myself as an example, most of my work is sold to large businesses. I have occasionally worked for clients with a few hundred employees, but most of my clients employ thousands or even tens of thousands of people.

I work mainly for large businesses because the sort of service I sell, and the sorts of problems I solve, exist solely in large businesses. The only exception to this is where someone has approached me as a writer to advise them on writing, or because of the books I have written, to give them some advice based on the content of those books. But this is not, currently, my core business. I do not actively seek this work, it just happens. Sometimes, I don't have the time to help and have to say no. Perhaps at some point I'll switch to focusing on mentoring those clients, but as I write this – not yet!

Most of the freelance experts I work with have businesses as their target clients. Usually this is for a very simple, practical reason. Businesses have more money to spend on expert support – whether that is contractors, interim managers, or consultants. However, there are many experts who have built very successful businesses that sell to individual customers. For instance, you have probably met and been offered services by financial advisers and health coaches. Whether you want to work with businesses or individuals you have a choice, which depends on your service line and your personal preferences.

I know some freelance experts who manage to sell both to individuals and businesses. For example, I know some coaches who have individual clients, and have managed to sell their services to businesses as well. The businesses ask these coaches to coach some of their staff. But for most freelance experts, you are selling either to individuals or businesses. It is hard to do both, because they are very different sorts of sales, often they need different services and usually they require different relationships.

If you do decide that your clients are always businesses, then you also need to think about the sort of business you want to approach. Are you thinking about large corporations? They often have deep pockets and buy a lot of services. But they also can be very difficult to find your way into and have complicated procurement processes and rules. Or is your service, more for small- and medium-sized enterprises, the sorts of businesses that are perhaps local to where you live? Small businesses can be tough, individually, to sell to because they often have very limited discretionary budget, but there are an awful lot of them and between them they spend a lot on expert support.

For most people, the decision on whether to sell to individuals or businesses is determined as soon as you know what your service will be. Some services are only bought by businesses and some by individuals. But if you cannot decide, remember the characteristics of customers I described in Chapter 4 (and in Table 4.1).

- There needs to be enough people who would find your service useful. That does not mean that you need millions of clients. Depending on your service, you may need dozens of clients a year or perhaps only one. You just need enough, no more.
- Secondly, those people must either have money directly, or an ability to access the money required to pay for your service. For individuals that means they need to be wealthy enough to afford your services. By wealthy, I mean they have money left over once they have paid all their normal monthly bills. For businesses that means that they must have an available budget to pay for your service. For both individuals and businesses, there are occasionally third parties who provide money to pay for expert support – for instance grants. I know a handful of experts whose income comes from grants. But it is a limited market.

- Your target clients must have the propensity to spend money on the sort of service you are planning to offer. Some people have a tendency and a track record in paying for expert services, some don't. I recommend you choose clients who are in the former group. It is possible to get people who have never paid for any advice to pay for it, but it is usually a challenge.
- Finally, you need to have access to those clients. We will explore this more in Chapter 8, but I recommend a balance of realism and optimism. If you become successful you will be able to sell to people you never expected to, but it would be very ambitious to start a business aimed at clients that you have absolutely no idea how you might get in contact with.

Where are you most likely to find enough people interested in your service with money they are willing to spend, who you have some level of access to? Is it going to be with individuals or by targeting businesses? Which sorts of individuals or which sort of businesses?

Your client is always a person

I have been a bit imprecise in the last section talking about businesses as opposed to individuals. While I might talk of my clients as being businesses, the truth is that even when dealing with the largest organisations in the world, my client is always a person.

Speaking of clients as businesses is a common way of talking. Anyone can speak about a company having difficulties or a company needing help, and we all understand what they mean. But it is shorthand for a more complex message. The reality is that companies don't have problems or need help, and they don't have wants or needs. Companies are not the sorts of things that can have a need or that can want help. A company is a collection of people, and it is those people who have problems and need help.

This may sound like an obvious point, but it is an important one. If you think back to the foundation stones I mentioned in Chapter 1, they are all concerned with relationships and interactions with people. As we go through this book you will find that I stress that your interpersonal skills, your ability to develop trusting relationships and your ability to persuade others that your advice is right are critical to your success.

Similarly, if you remember the reasons I listed in Chapter 3 for why people hire an expert to help them, these are all very human-centric needs. Practical and emotional needs that only human beings have.

I stress this because interpersonal skills are more important, in the longer run, than your expertise. It is not the person with the greatest expertise who makes the best freelance expert. You need enough expertise, that is all. The most successful freelance experts are those who build the best relationships, have the greatest credibility and trust, and can communicate persuasively with their clients. In his book, *The Trusted Advisor*, Maister, Green and Galford put this neatly when he says '. . . a trusted advisor benefits from having trusting relationships because they lead to repeat business from the same client. These relationships also lead to new business through referrals from existing clients.'

In my career I have often met people who have fantastic subject matter knowledge. Knowledge that is in short supply and high demand. Yet some of these people were complete failures as freelance experts because they lost sight of the fact that their job depended on them being able to help people, not just know more than anyone else. In contrast, I know people who have some useful expertise – but it is not unique and they are not especially deep experts. Yet their help and support are valued far more highly by their clients because they have strong relationships based on trust and are found to be helpful at a human level. A freelance expert provides a service, and the human dimension of service provision is critical, even more critical than the expertise.

You can learn from the large professional services firms. If you peer inside the biggest management consultancies, the people who lead the firms and earn the most money are rarely the people with most in-depth expertise. Yes, they have expertise, but usually they have people working for them with lots more expertise. What they are truly skilled in is in managing relationships with clients, exploring their needs and then selling them a service to fulfil their needs. They understand who their clients are, and by understanding them have developed well-tailored marketing messages, sales approaches and services.

It is sometimes more than one person

Identifying a client can get more complex when it's not only one person I have to deal with. Normally, multiple people are involved in every piece of work I do. Multiple people with different needs, wants and opinions. This presents a challenge, and I am not unique in facing this problem.

In a business, the question 'who is the client?' can be rather complicated to answer. I wrote about this extensively in my book *The Management Consultant: Mastering the Art of Consultancy*. This can get quite complex, but for most freelancers it is good enough to think in terms of three types of people who may be clients:

- The one with the money, or who authorises the money to be spent
- The one who wants the service and benefits from it
- Others who may influence your success.

Sometimes these are three or more different people. I am not going to get into the complexity of dealing with this now, but it is important to understand this. For now, as we are thinking about client personas, I am going to focus on the person who directly wants the service – but we do need to remain aware of the others, especially anyone who has to be convinced to spend money on our work.

Even if you are selling to an individual, in reality you often have to consider the interests and needs of other people rather than just that individual. For example, if your service is advising teenagers on their career choices, then fundamentally the teenager is your client. But it is usually a parent who must be persuaded to pay for the service, and so when you sell you need to think about what will make the parent pay as well. Similarly, if you are providing personal advice to one person in a long-term relationship, you will often find that you also must convince their partner that the advice is helpful and worthwhile.

Dimensions of client persona

There are hundreds of ways you can think about your client persona. I suspect that some businesses have been very successful simply because they identified a way of looking at clients that no one else had thought of before.

But typically, there are some standard factors to consider, which we can consider as various dimensions of client personas. Here are some examples of important dimensions to get your own thinking going:

- *Job role:* are your clients CEOs, managers or job starters? If your services are for individuals are they writers, bakers, artists or parents?
- *Industrial sector:* do you want clients in the finance sector, public sector, manufacturing or telecoms?
- *Geographic location:* are you selling to local or global businesses, or businesses sharing a common regulatory or statutory regime?

- *Functional domain:* do your clients work in IT departments, HR or finance?
- *Demographics:* are your clients a particular age range or have a certain income level?
- *Shared interests:* do your clients like restaurants, theatre or foreign travel?
- *Common challenges:* are your clients starting a new business, returning to work, or dealing with stress?

You do not need to have an answer for every dimension. It may be that only one or two of these dimensions are relevant. For instance, as a coach you may not be concerned with sector or functional domain, but perhaps you want local clients with common personal challenges. In contrast, my services are independent on sector and geography, but my ideal clients have quite specific job roles and work in certain business functions.

Identifying your ideal client

Another way of thinking about client persona is to think in terms of who would be your ideal client. Who is going to benefit most from your services? Who will you be able to convince to buy them? What sort of people are you going to enjoy working with, and be able to learn from to develop your service and reputation further?

Try to be clear about who this person is, what they are like, what their needs are and what excites or interests them.

When I worked in large consultancies we talked about 'hot buttons'. A hot button is a topic or area of interest that, if raised, will generate interest from your clients and make it easier to engage them in conversation and sell to. You can only identify hot buttons when you have an idea of who your client is.

Not all expert services require a very precise definition of customers. But the tighter your definition is, the more focused your expertise can be tailored to those clients, and the more credible you can come across as an expert who understands their specific needs.

When I am advising freelancers, I go through the three steps outlined in Figure 5.1.

In the first step, I ask the freelancer to describe who their client is. I ask them to write it down, as this encourages clarity. Usually, the result of this first step is too broad a definition. Then I ask them to refine it, to make it clearer and

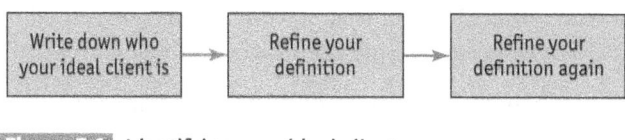

Write down who your ideal client is → Refine your definition → Refine your definition again

Figure 5.1 Identifying your ideal client

more specific. To help them, I will ask questions such as: Where are those clients? Who are they precisely? What sort of problems and challenges do they face? Where do they work? Why do they want help? What are their interests? What excites them or annoys them? (There are examples below.)

Then I do this again. At the end of this third iteration, we are usually getting to quite a clear and specific definition of the client. Sometimes I ask the freelancer to do it once more. The answer is not set in stone, and it is not always right first time, but it does start the process of getting clarity over the client.

Some examples

Let me end this chapter by sharing a few examples of ideal clients from six freelance experts I know. It may be interesting to you that the last two ideal clients are freelancers themselves.

- Change Management Offices Leaders for FTSE 100 companies.
- FDs/CFOs of organisations with greater than 1000 employees who want to do a software-system-enabled transformation of the finance function.
- 'C' level leader in the housing sector, wanting to pursue an IT enabled transformation.
- Parents returning to work after a prolonged period out of the job market raising children.
- Successful independent management consultants concerned with funding their retirement.
- IT contractors working in the public sector.

As far as I know, in none of these cases do the freelancers, for whom one of these profiles is the ideal client, have a rule that they will only work for that profile of client. Most freelance experts I know are opportunistic and will take other clients if they are approached by them. But these independent experts do not actively seek clients outside of these profiles – and they only take work from other clients if they have spare capacity. In all cases, the majority of their work comes from clients who fit these profiles.

Because these freelancers have an established reputation and have developed relevant expertise with clients with these profiles, they have a higher degree of recognition, they have high demand and they can charge higher fees. When you are in that position there is little point seeking other customers.

We will reflect again on client personas in Chapter 8, when we will discuss finding clients.

An independent voice

Daljit R. Banger, Seat Consulting

I am a British IT consultant with 37 years of experience, the last 21 years of which have been as an independent consultant. I obtained a master's degree in 1994 and have been a Fellow of the British Computer Society for 10 years.

As an independent consultant I have been fortunate enough to undertake engagements in several global locations, including Sweden, Finland, Brazil, Hong Kong and the USA. I started as an independent consultant on a short-term programming contract for the Swiss Bank UBS in Zürich. This was extended, and eventually lasted 2 years. This pattern has continued throughout my career, resulting in engagements with a typical length of around 1.5–2 years.

An observation I made early in my career was that a premium was paid for skills relating to the current flavour of technology, i.e. the latest products, but over time that technology becomes obsolete and the rates for skills relating to it drop. For example, AS400 RPG coders 20 years ago could demand in excess of $1k a day. Today they will earn, on average, 1/3 of this.

Having observed this trend early, I invested time in developing my core business and systems architectural skills – and in keeping those skills current. For instance, I participated in the TOGAF committee and then co-chaired the British Computer Society (BCS) Enterprise Architecture group 2015–2020(Q1).

During my two decades as an independent consultant I have developed reusable content, software tools and published several articles / blogs to keep myself relevant. Most recently I published a book entitled *Enterprise Systems Architecture*.

Information on my blogs, book, papers etc. can be found via my website www.s-ea-t.com

My tips for anyone considering a freelance career

- **Notice period:** You are only as good as your contractual notice period. As a contingent worker you are employed to perform tasks that deliver specific outcomes to the client. If the outcome is achieved prior to the end date of the contract, or the client's situation changes, then the client has every right to terminate the contract prior to the contractual end date. I have not experienced this personally. I have been fortunate to have my contracts extended, but I have witnessed other contractors having their contracts terminated on several occasions.

- **Mobility:** Not all assignments will be on your doorstep, you may even need to travel abroad. It is important to factor all costs associated with working at the end-client site, i.e. the cost of travel (trains, planes, automobiles), any overnight accommodation and, something which is often overlooked, appropriate levels of socialising. All of these aspects must be reflected in the contractual rate you agree with your client. I have been offered contracts on several occasions which initially looked lucrative, but when the full costs were factored in soon became unattractive.

- **Invest in yourself:** In essence, *you are the product.* You must remain relevant in terms of skills and services. Invest in yourself and qualifications that have longevity, e.g. a Certificate in Business Analysis will remain relevant long after a certificate in a specific version of Oracle Cloud Financials has become obsolete. In my case, I have consistently invested in textbooks, professional subscriptions and memberships to the equivalent value of three days of my consulting services in a year.

chapter

6

Pricing your services

We now need to get onto the part of this book that many readers will be most interested in. How much can you charge for your services, and therefore how much money will you make?

I'm going to share some strategies to determine your fees, which are summarised in Table 6.1 (see later). However, I will disappoint some readers, by saying that I cannot advise you what to charge. Even if I could, it would only be correct the moment I write these words for one service in one location. Fees fluctuate depending on all sorts of factors. The simple truth is that to determine your fees, you will have to research and experiment a little, and you will have to learn from those experiments. You also need to change what you charge from time to time.

Experienced freelance experts have a reasonably good idea of how much they can charge, although they often underestimate it. Starters in the freelancing business are usually at a loss as to what to charge.

Underlying this is a basic reality about the freelance market. The fees are opaque. There is no simple universal table you can look up which will tell you what to charge for different services. Occasionally, there are surveys and some people who research the contractor and consultant markets have data on fee rates, but rarely is this available in the public domain, and even when it is, it refers to one aspect of the market at best.

But this does not mean there is nothing to know. There are some important aspects about your fees that you should understand, which are timeless and useful. Although I am not going to tell you what your fees should be, I am going to help you to work them out.

Getting your fees right makes a huge difference. As I write this in the late spring of 2020 in the middle of the first coronavirus lockdown, I am reflecting on all the freelance experts I know and the fees they charge. There are several ways of charging – by the hour, the day, the month or a total price for a service. But if you worked them all out on an annual basis, you would find a huge range of annual revenues. If I think of the very lowest and highest, the difference between them can be vast – some freelance experts are generating revenues more than twenty times the level of others.

Right now, I am expecting that rates for services will drop after the coronavirus pandemic, as fees do fluctuate in line with the wider economy. If you are reading this in a few years' time, the economy may be booming or busting. Irrespective of this, some experts will be still charging a lot more than others, and even in hard economic times some experts will thrive. But for a moment let's ignore the differences between the services and levels of expertise. Even with experts providing broadly the same service to the same sort of customers, the amount of money they make differs significantly. Perhaps not by a factor of 20, but certainly by a factor of 2 or 3 times.

What makes this difference? The fees you will be able to charge depend on a whole host of factors, four of which are most important:

- *Your service:* is it a common service with some common price in the market or is it differentiated or unique?
- *Your clients:* what are your specific customers willing and able to pay for the service?
- *You:* what factors can you personally bring to influence the rates you charge?
- *Your units of charging:* do you charge by the hour, the day or for a service rather than time?

We will explore each of these in this chapter, and then look at the steps you can take to work out your fees.

Your service and the fee it justifies

The first factor that influences the fees you can charge is the service you choose to offer. You may choose your service based on what you enjoy doing and what you know. But if one of your personal goals is to maximise your income, it is wise to choose your services carefully as different services generate very different levels of fees.

Rightly or wrongly some services are valued more highly than others. For instance, I would typically expect someone offering strategic advice to CEOs to be charging a significantly higher rate than someone acting as a contract IT project manager.

Additionally, for some services there is a market rate or range of rates. This is often true for common services that lots of people provide. Building on my previous example of a contract IT project manager, although there are a range of rates depending on various factors, there is a reasonably well-known maximum and minimum rate for IT project managers in a particular country at any point in time. For other services though, especially where the expertise is more unusual or the service line unique, there is no market price, and it is up to you to set it.

Of course, there are limits as to what your customers will pay, which brings us onto the second factor.

How your choice of clients influences fees

The second factor in determining your fees is your clients. Some clients tend to pay higher fee rates than others. If you are advising global corporations, you are probably going to charge a higher rate than if you are charging a local business. Similarly, some sectors (e.g. financial services and pharmaceuticals) tend to pay higher fees than others (e.g. public sector and manufacturing).

This, of course, partially depends on the economic situation of your clients. Those with very limited finances and budgets are typically going to be less inclined to offer higher rates.

But within these sorts of broad generalisations, the fee rate you achieve depends on the individual client. Some clients hire a lot of different experts, and they are knowledgeable about what a typical rate is to charge for the service you are offering. Some are not. Additionally, some clients love to negotiate every penny, others are an easier touch when it comes to money.

If I think back to my personal experience, some clients have offered me significantly higher rates than others simply due to their lack of knowledge, or their unwillingness or inability to negotiate hard. But they have also paid me more money because my service was more valuable to them than others. Value is in the eye of the client. There is no absolute value of your service, and you can find clients for whom it is much more valuable than for others, who will therefore have a propensity to pay more for it.

A final thought about your clients is that in some situations there is an intermediary between you and your real client. This is common in the world of contractors where agencies often hire contractors on behalf of the clients. When it comes to negotiating a rate, you normally must negotiate with the agency. Given that their full-time job is hiring contractors, you are dealing with a very knowledgeable person who understands what the typical rates are. This is not necessarily a bad thing, but it does tend to limit quite how high your fees can go.

You and your fee rate

So far it seems that your fees depend on the service you offer, and who you offer it to. There is another critical factor in determining your fee rate – and that is you.

Not all experts are alike, even if they offer apparently equivalent services. Your level of experience, and how that experience relates directly to the specific needs of your current client has a significant influence on your fees. No two engagements are the same, and sometimes you will have done work before that relates more closely to your current client's needs than another similar expert. This will normally enable you to charge higher fees.

When a client hires an expert, there is always a risk that the expert won't be able to help them in the way they hoped. The proof of the pudding is always in the eating. There is value to the client in anything that reduces this risk. Factors which may be perceived to reduce risk in the client's eyes include experience and qualifications. The best situation from a client's perspective is to have a known expert they have worked with successfully before, which is why a deep relationship and repeat business are so valuable to a freelance expert. Although it is not quite as good, clients also value recommendations and referrals, especially if they come from people they directly know and trust. Any or all of these give you leverage when it comes to negotiating fees.

Which brings me to the next point. Fees are usually not just set, they are negotiated. Therefore, one critical factor in your fee rate is your capability to negotiate and persuade a client to pay more. This in turn depends on your communications and negotiation skills, and how you present your expertise in relation to the client's current need. Sometimes, it can be as simple as being willing to ask for more money. Never underestimate the opportunity for higher fees simply by asking.

Chapters 8 and 9 will explore these topics in more detail.

Your unit of charging

When I talk with independent contractors and consultants there is usually an assumption that when it comes to charging fees, the unit of charging is the day. However, some other experts charge by the hour, and some by other units such as the month.

Logically, it should not make any difference whether you charge by the hour, the day or the month, but psychologically it does. This depends on the specific client who may think that an hourly rate sounds fine, but when a day rate is quoted it sounds excessive, even though it is just eight times as much. But the opposite can also be true. Some day rates may sound high when quoted as a day rate, when quoted as an hourly rate they can sound astronomical even though they are in the end the same amount per unit of time. This is something you just must find out – different clients prefer different units of charging.

As an important aside, which we will explore in more detail later, your unit of charging is not just about generating revenue, it's going to affect how much work you put into selling and administration. A consultant selling by the month can only logically sell 12 units of work a year, and usually will sell fewer units, as each engagement will last for several months. That same consultant probably raises one invoice a month. In contrast, an expert selling by the hour has an awful lot of hours to fill in the year, and lots of invoices every month. Consequently, for freelance experts selling their work by the hour, marketing and administration are typically a larger part of their work than for those selling in much larger chunks of time.

A lot of freelance experts sell themselves in units of time. In fact, most of the consultants, contractors, interim managers and coaches I know do this. But there is another way, and that is to price for a service. That is to ignore the length of time a piece of work will take and price it as a unit of work. The advantage of this is that it is often possible to charge significantly higher fees, by associating the charge not to your effort, but to the value of the completed work to the client.

Successfully charging for a service depends on presentation of value for that service. By analogy, if a doctor tells you an operation is going to cost £25,000, you may think this is an excessive amount of money. If instead the doctor tells you she will save your life for £25,000 it may sound like a very reasonable price to pay.

Normally, sales of your expert services will not be as dramatic as this, but my example does help to highlight that the way you present your fees makes a significant difference to how reasonable your fees sound. Jonathan Stark's book, *Hourly Billing is Nuts* brings this home even when you only read as far as the subtitle – *Essays on the Insanity of Trading Time for Money.*

The evidence from many experienced freelance experts is that such service-based pricing, or as it is sometimes called, *value pricing*, can lead to significantly improved revenues. Your ability to do this is constrained by your customer's expectations and willingness to explore a price for the service rather than a price for time. Some customers really like the idea, as it gives them certainty even if it comes at a higher price. For other customers, it is a no-go simply because they do not work that way. But you will never know if you do not try! (See Chapter 9 for more on value pricing.)

Where do I start?

All this may seem like very fine advice, but still leaves you thinking – *'ok, but where do I start? At what rate should I pitch my fees to my clients?'*.

As I said at the start of this chapter, I cannot tell you what fee rate to charge. But there are some do's and don'ts. I'll get to the don'ts a bit later. To do's are:

- **Understand the minimum you will work for.** Hopefully, most of the time, you will be earning a lot more than the minimum, but it's helpful to know what the lowest fee rate is that you must earn to get by (see the calculation below).
- **Use the available data.** There isn't much easily accessible data on rates, but there is some. If you are an accredited profession – such as a coach, translator, copy editor and so on, the society associated with your accreditation will usually provide benchmark rates to aim for. These are guidelines, not rules. However, for many freelancers there is no such group. In this situation do a web search – you can find reports, job adverts and bulletin boards and opinion pieces that will give some guidance. If there are no data for your specific service line, look at what similar roles pay.
- **Use your network.** The main place for this will be your own network. You will be very unusual if there are no other freelance experts in your network. I now know literally hundreds, and probably thousands of contractors, coaches and consultants. You will know at least a few. Ask them what they think would be a reasonable rate for your service. Also, you probably know some people who hire experts from time to time. Ask them what sort of rates they pay. Now this advice needs to be all taken cautiously as you cannot be certain you are hearing the full truth,

but it gives you some indication and is better than plucking a number out of thin air.

- *Experiment, accepting that you won't maximise your fees in one step.* Every piece of work you price is an opportunity to experiment and learn. Sometimes a client will bite your hand off to work for them. This usually indicates they would have been willing to pay you a little more. Don't get too obsessed with thinking about the extra you could have earned, be happy with the fact that you are earning fees at a rate you are willing to work for and that you have learnt for a future sale. I include some points below on increasing your fee rate.

- *Don't be worried if a client says your fees are too high.* Do not fret about the odd client who says no to you because of your fees. If this never happens it probably means you are not trying to increase your fees enough. If your service is good and differentiated, and your fees are not ridiculous, there will be work for you even though you are too expensive for some. (See Chapter 9 for more info.)

In some markets the rates you can charge are set to some extent. For example, IT contractors and some other experts are often approached by agencies who will tell them an indicative day rate, although even here there is usually some room for negotiation. Many agencies have online bulletin boards or job listings on which they place roles with rates advertised. Even if they are not directly your service line, it will start to give you an indication of what you can charge.

If you have come from a professional services firm, such as a consultancy, and you are now setting yourself up as an independent, you will know the sorts of rates the large firms charge. In my experience, it is rare that an independent expert will be able to charge more than a fraction of these rates, but they do at least give a benchmark to target.

If you can, try service-based pricing rather than time-based charging. To do this, you must have a sense of how long the task will take else you could easily undercharge, and ideally you also have a sense of how valuable the service is to the client. If you can do this, service-based charging offers the opportunity to generate significantly higher revenues than time-based. Again, a little research into who is charging on what basis will help you to work this out.

When you have done what research you can do, and your first client asks you your rate, take a gulp and then quote them a rate. You will quickly learn whether you can push higher or lower. (See below for more info.)

The minimum fees

There is a minimum you should charge. My rough rule of thumb works it out in the following steps:

1. Determine your equivalent *minimum* annual salary if you were in a full-time job. That is the minimum you need to survive. Let's call this X.
2. Decide how much time you are going to work to earn this (e.g. how many months, weeks, days or hours per annum you will work). Let's call this Y.
3. Calculate the unit of charge per unit of time based on this – i.e. X/Y.
4. Take account of the costs to being a freelancer and a high likelihood that you will not be 100% busy by doubling this – e.g. your minimum charge should be $2 \times X/Y$.

For instance, if your minimum equivalent salary is £40,000 per annum, and you plan to work 10 months a year, I'd suggest as a minimum you should be charging fees of £8000 per month ($2 \times 40,000/10$).

I stress this is a very rough and ready calculation. If you follow this guidance, you may end up earning a lot more than £40,000 per annum. Also, you may be more or less risk adverse than me and so use a different factor in step 4 of my calculation, but be careful you don't start dreaming.

The 'so what?' comes down to this. If you do not think you can earn £8000 per month, then you risk having to work more months in the year or reduce your salary expectations. Assuming neither of those is acceptable, then you need to find a different way of earning an income if you cannot earn this minimum.

Increasing your fees

You now know the minimum fee rate you need. This is a level you must not go below. The next question is usually 'how can I earn more than this?'.

There are several ways which we will explore at different times in this book. They all build from three concepts you should always have in your head.

1. *Your maximum fees depend on how much the service is worth to a client.* What is the value to them? Think back to the reasons I shared in Table 3.1. You can get more when your skill set is rare, and a client needs help urgently. Sometimes, even what seems simple to you, is hugely valuable to your client. But you will tend to earn less when your service is very common, and the client is less desperate for help.

2 ***You don't need every client.*** Some clients will never pay what you want. Don't work for them, and say no, nicely, to their requests for help. Find the clients who value your service. I always ask clients very early in a conversation what level of money they are willing to pay. I don't want to waste their or my time if there is no way they will pay my rate.

3 ***You can persuade the clients to pay more.*** In Chapter 9 we are going to look at selling, and a big part of selling is agreeing a price. But at its simplest, negotiating a higher rate is about asking for more and explaining to the client why it is worth them paying more. This is a conversation you should prepare yourself for. I know some people hate doing this, but you need to get used to it if you want to increase your fees. If you are uncomfortable negotiating, remember most clients don't mind some negotiation, and many really are happy to pay more!

You won't get to your maximum fees in one step. Don't worry if you are not earning as much as you want initially, if it is more than your minimum.

After every piece of work, try to increase your fees by a small amount. After all, you are now more experienced, and your service should be of higher value. If you do this, it won't be long before you are earning significantly more, even if each increment is only a few percent.

As I said at the beginning of this chapter I cannot tell you what to charge, but I can give you an approach to determine your prices. Table 6.1 summarises this with a series of questions for you to reflect on.

Table 6.1 Self-reflection questions to help working out your fees

Element of pricing	Self-reflection questions
Your service	- Is your service unique, or are there others providing a similar service?
	- What do they charge? How can you find out?
	- What do the most successful freelancers in your field charge?
	- How could you differentiate your service to make it more valuable?
Your clients	- How valuable is your service to your target clients?
	- What is their propensity and ability to pay for your service?
	- Do you understand why they typically buy (see Table 3.1), and how this influences what they are willing to pay?
	- Is there a different client with a greater willingness and ability to pay more?

Element of pricing	Self-reflection questions
You	- How can you present yourself as a credible expert in your field whose skills and style of working justify the highest fees?
- How can you increase your credibility – either in reality, or in the client perception (e.g. the way you present your expertise)?
- How do the most successful freelancers present themselves, their skills and their service?
Unit of charging	- What is the best unit of charging for your service?
- Is this the best basis for charging?
- Could you reposition your service for value-based charging?
Increasing your fees	- Do you know your minimum fee (your walk-away price)?
- How can you influence your clients to pay more for your service? (See Table 3.2)
- Have you thought about how you negotiate for higher fees? (See Table 6.2 and Chapters 9 and 13)
- Do you have a compelling pitch? (See Table 8.1)
- As you build experience and clients, how will you increment your fees upwards?

Four Don'ts

I want to end this chapter with four short, but important lessons when it comes to fees. These are all things you should not do, but which you might be tempted to do to get your first piece of work. There are always exceptional situations in the real world, but think carefully before you do any of these.

1. Don't sell cheap

The first one is to avoid selling your services cheap. At times we all must discount our fees to some extent to win work. There is an economic reality, we all have competition and clients have other options than you. We cannot just charge what we like. But if you think about those points too much, you may be tempted to discount your fees to a low rate to get business.

There is no doubt that low rates can get you work, and sometimes at the start of your career getting your first gig so you can build up experience is of paramount importance. But low rates can cause a few knock-on problems. Dare I say it, but there is a price to low rates.

The first is that it can be hard to try and increase your rates from a very low basis. In contrast, it is quite easy to discount a high rate on a temporary basis for a client. Once you have set yourself a low rate, clients tend to bracket you as a low-cost supplier and expect your future rates to be similarly low. It is not impossible to move your rates higher, but you are giving yourself a big future challenge.

Within a single client, once they know your rate, they are unlikely to accept anything other than nominal or inflationary increases above your current rate. Even if you go to another client, they may want to know what you previously charged and to understand why you think you can justify charging them more.

The second problem is that you may end up with the wrong clients. The best clients for you are not the ones looking for the lowest rate. All clients want to feel they are getting value for money, many will want to negotiate on your rates, but that is not the same thing as selling cheap. The sorts of clients who want to haggle over every penny and want you to work for the lowest rate are generally the clients to avoid. With these tight-fisted clients your life will be a non-ending series of justifications for your fees. Clients who want very low fees, in my experience, tend to be difficult to work with and for.

2. Don't work for free

Worse than undercharging for your work, there can occasionally be a temptation to do some work for free. Avoid it. Have faith in your abilities and always try to charge something. Remember you must make a living and you must pay your bills.

There are two qualifications to this.

1. *Pro-bono work for a good cause:* perhaps a local charity needs some help in an area you have expertise in, and you want to help them. That's a great thing to do, and if you are so inclined, do it. It's not only good for society, it's good for you and can feel extremely rewarding beyond what money brings.
2. *Give away some advice as part of your marketing:* e.g. blogs, podcasts, talks and so on. This can work well, and such *content marketing* may be required for you to improve your profile as an expert in your area (see Chapter 8). But I strongly advise against crossing the line between marketing and doing work for clients for free. There is no black and white line between one and the other, so you must make a judgement. I always want to produce high-quality and engaging marketing materials, which some clients will find useful without ever coming to me

for advice. That is just part of the price of being a freelance expert. But I sense when I am going beyond this and start talking to clients about individual and specific situations and issues in which I am veering towards giving free advice, and that is a step too far.

The killer question is: 'How much work for free is too much?'. If someone wants a quick chat for 10 or 15 minutes, the balance is usually in favour of sharing a bit of your knowledge for free. It creates goodwill and develops relationships. I'll chat to anyone for a short while. But as a rule of thumb, for me, anything that takes longer than an hour is too much for free. And, that hour might literally be a single hour, or it might be several 10-minute conversations.

It's about finding a balance. Most people will respect that you can only do so much for free. Of course, some will push their luck and then you must be firm and say no. On the other hand, there will always be exceptions for whom I am willing to do more for free. For example, when I'm speaking to a previous client who I know well and believe there is a high probability of getting future work from, I am usually willing to do a bit more work for free to maintain the relationship.

Whatever you decide, always remember your time is valuable. If you are essentially selling yourself, that is the most valuable commodity you have. Make sure you get paid for it most of the time!

If you find it hard to say no to doing free work, tell the person asking that you are too busy with fee-paying clients – even if you are not. Most people accept that earning money takes priority over helping out. If someone will not stop asking, you need to be blunt: 'Sorry, I charge for my time. If you would like to agree a price for this work, we can discuss that. Else, I must get onto my other client work.'

3. Don't be afraid to negotiate

Don't just accept any rate that is offered to you. Rarely will a client reject your services because you ask for more money. They may say 'no' to your request for more money, but they won't offer you more unless you ask. You can accept their rejection or reject them as a client.

But asking has little cost, and it is always worth a try. Sometimes, you will end up on a substantially higher rate. Literally, just ask.

Later in this book we will explore how you can influence clients, and you can use these skills to influence them to accept your fees. But without getting into anything complex or advanced, the best way to talk about fees is clearly and avoiding any temptation you may feel to apologise for them.

When you state your fees, do not hesitate or present yourself as having to think too long about it. This indicates to the person you are negotiating with that you do not have a set fee or are willing to be flexible. If a client thinks you are flexible, they will usually ask for a reduction. Do not give them the encouragement! Table 6.2 provides a few examples of do and don't says when negotiating.

Always hold in mind, that while a client has choices, doing the work to find a good freelance expert is an effort for them and takes them time – time which has a value to them. Sometimes, it is better for a client to accept a higher rate rather than have to go through all the hassle of finding another expert. If you don't ask, you won't get!

For more ideas and advice in this area I recommend *Never Split the Difference: Negotiating as if Your Life Depended on It*, by Chris Voss.

4. Don't confuse fees with income

There is one simple mistake many freelance experts make early on in their careers, and that is to assume that they can multiply their fees by the number of units of time, and this will determine their income. If only life was so simple.

Table 6.2 Do and don't say when negotiating

Do say ...	Don't say ...
What is this work worth to you? When this is done, how much easier will your business be?	My fees are flexible
	I'll charge in a range of £xx to £yy *(clients hear the £xx not the £yy)*
For that type of work, I charge £xxx per hour / day / month.	I'm not sure what to charge
	I've not done anything like this before
My fees depend on the details of the work. We can talk them through when I understand what it is you want exactly.	I always discount
	Let's split the difference
	I'll do anything to get this work
This is good value for the sort of work you want and reflects market rates.	I don't have any other work on at present
	I'm finding it hard to find work
My clients find my fees reasonable and realistic.	
My work adds value well in excess of my fees.	
I have no problem finding clients.	

There are three problems that get in the way of this easy calculation:

- the costs of running your business
- the reality that you are unlikely to be 100% utilised
- there are non-fee-generating tasks which will take up time.

I'm not going to go into these in huge detail, as some require specialist advice and depend for example on factors such as the tax regime of the country you are working in, but I want to explain them a little more and give you pointers as to where you may find more help.

There are costs to running any business. Some of these may be tax deductible, some not – but, anyway, they are costs. For instance, you may need equipment such as laptops and mobile phones, and you may need to pay your own adviser such as an accountant. There will also be taxes and other fees to pay, which will depend how you pay yourself, and factors like your business's legal structure (sole trader, limited company, partnership etc.). This is one area where you will need specialist advice. Certainly, for me, paying for accountancy services is essential and valuable.

Unless you are very lucky, you will not be 100% utilised. For me that has never been a problem, because when I became a freelancer, decades ago, I never wanted to be 100% utilised. I wanted to take advantage of many of the benefits of independence from being an employee. I do know other freelance experts though whose main drive is to maximise their income, and for them utilisation is important. The more they work, the more they earn.

Nevertheless, for pretty much everyone I know who works as a freelancer there have been periods when the work has dried up. I personally aim to be 60–75% utilised in a year and 80–95% is certainly achievable at times. Other freelancers want other levels of utilisation, but if you assume you will have enough work to be constantly 100% busy, you are making a mistake. Hence my factor of 'multiply by two' in my calculation of the minimum fee rate above.

There is another reason why you cannot be utilised on chargeable work 100% of the time. That is because there are other non-billable activities you must do. Back in the introduction I described the lifecycle of work – eight core tasks which all freelance experts must do. Only one of these, task 5, is billable to your clients.

Some of the eight tasks in the lifecycle of work are periodic and should not use up much of your time. For instance, I am constantly refining my service, but it's a background task rather than one which competes with my time for clients. But some of these tasks will take real time and reduce your ability to be working for clients. Running your business is one of them, but especially selling services to clients can take substantial time.

We think about the time we spend working and the money we make, but any time you must spend gaining clients has a cost as well. In the jargon of professional salespeople this is known as the *cost of sales*. We are going to talk about this more in Chapter 9, for now I just want to flag it as something you need to consider.

I'll leave you with an example to bring this home: often I have seen freelancers chasing after high-paying clients, and putting so much effort into winning the work, that the effective fee rate taking account of the time to win the business was much lower than that from a client offering a lower rate, but also an easier sale.

If you want a certain income, your total fees must be in excess of that desired income. How much in excess depends on many factors, such as the way you run your business, your local tax regime, how much of your revenue you want to convert into your personal income every year and if you employ anyone else in your independent business. There can be huge variations here, but as a rule of thumb I'd assume that *at least* 25% of your revenue will be unavailable to become your personal income, and realistically it may be as much as 50–60% of your revenue.

Bringing Chapters 2-6 together: defining your freelance business

In Part 3 of this book we are going to move on from designing and planning your business into running your business and getting paid. Before we do that, I want you to summarise everything you have thought about so far as you have read the book. There is a template to do this in Table 6.3 and two worked examples in Tables 6.4 and 6.5.

You can think of this as a summary of your freelance business vision. If you find this hard to do, it's best to think some more until you are clear. Don't be surprised if at first this is hard. It is worth getting right. Don't think you are boxing yourself in, as you can always come back and modify this. Nevertheless, this is important.

Without clarity you will struggle to find good customers, sell yourself and do value-adding work. As you work through the following chapters, you are going to use the information in Table 6.3 to help define your sales messages.

To make this a little more real for you, a couple of examples are given in Tables 6.4 and 6.5.

6 ■ Pricing your services 81

Table 6.3 Your freelance vision

I am a...	Who does...	In this way...	For...	Because...	I will charge them...
Enter the title or label you are going to use (see Table 2.1)	Briefly describe your specialist service (see Chapter 4)	What style will you use with your customers? (See Table 4.2 and Figure 4.1)	Describe your ideal client (see Chapter 5)	Describe why the customer wants this service (see Tables 3.1 and 3.2)	How much will you charge? What is your unit of charging? (See Chapter 6)

Table 6.4 An example for a coach

I am a...	Who...	In this way...	For...	Because...	I will charge them...
Coach	Helps people in business to be promoted	I build deep relationships with my customers, so I understand them individually and I advise and encourage them	Mid-level managers in large corporations who are seeking promotion to executive roles	They lack the confidence and the capability to do this on their own	£1800 over 6 months for a monthly 1-2-1 meeting, with additional short check-ins through the month

Table 6.5 An example for a contract ghost-writer

I am a...	Who...	In this way...	For...	Because...	I will charge them...
Contract business ghost-writer	Helps busy professionals to write a book	I write the book for them	Technical experts who know their specialist field well and have important insights to share	They lack the motivation, confidence and the capacity to do this on their own	A fixed fee depending on the length and nature of the book

One important final point. Sometimes when I ask people to do this, they respond that they have two freelance roles which are quite different. For example, I am a writer and I am a consultant. Although there is a relationship between the two, as much of what I write about is concerned with my consultancy work, they are different in many ways. For instance, the clients are different. As a writer, my clients are publishers and book readers. As a consultant, my clients are senior managers in large businesses.

If you are like me and you have two (or even more) freelance roles, you should think of them as separate businesses, and you should create a separate table like Table 6.3 for each freelance business.

An independent voice

Diane Wiredu, Lion Words – Localisation Expert, Translator, Content & Copywriter

It was clear at a young age that I had an insatiable appetite for words. Communication was my superpower and just speaking one language wasn't going to cut the mustard. I juggled my love affair with English, French and Spanish as a teen, later throwing Italian into the mix for good measure.

After a degree in modern languages, followed by an MA in translation, I worked in a few operational roles, then I jetted off to Spain. I methodically stepped into a professional role in the translation industry with no intentions of becoming a freelancer.

'I want to be a manager', I boldly proclaimed during an interview for a junior role at a top multinational translation company. Fast forward 4 years and I was promoted to Media Department Manager, overseeing a team of 40 and liaising with stakeholders worldwide. But despite relishing the challenges and responsibilities I'd longed for, I still wasn't fulfilled.

After some time it dawned on me. I was a cog in somebody else's machine, and while I was in the industry I loved, I couldn't feel the difference I was making. What I really wanted, was to be *the* manager.

Now I run Lion Words, which helps businesses grow, connect and expand their reach via impactful and engaging marketing content. I provide translation, writing and content marketing services to global companies, as well as brand consultation. By guiding their internationalisation efforts, my role is to ensure they communicate effectively with their English-speaking audiences, get the traction they deserve and see tangible conversions.

My transition to freelancer was a natural progression, albeit boosted by a craving for location independence. It wasn't, and isn't, always easy. I spent time building my business on the side before making the leap and I had to make some personal sacrifices to get it off the ground. There have been restless nights and a few underquoted projects along the way, but I have regained a sense of purpose and control. I get to spend my days helping clients find their voice and reach their goals using the expertise I've honed over the years. And I'm doing something I love, on my terms.

My tips for anyone considering a freelance career

1 **Work on value-based pricing.** Understand the value you provide your clients and charge accordingly from the get go. Too many freelancers struggle for years trying to climb the freelance status ladder, forgetting that you can decide to start at the top, or better still, just throw the whole ladder away. You choose where to position yourself in your market, and whether you earn 1k or 5k for that contract is often down to mindset. Be an expert instead of a freelancer 'for hire'.

2 **Create a support network.** Freelancing can be a lonely place for extroverts and introverts alike. As an outgoing writer and translator, I have found it particularly isolating at times. Joining industry associations and trade organisations is a great way to connect with others in your field as well as through social media and local networking groups. Not only will you stay up-to-date on your industry, they offer great opportunities to learn from others and have people to bounce ideas off.

3 **Market your services.** Market hard and consistently even when you are busy – in fact, especially when you are busy. Stable clients can disappear, and, as we saw during the 2020 pandemic, things can take a dramatic turn overnight. I've learnt this the hard way. Your biggest client cuts their budget and 'poof', you're skating on thin ice. In this same light, don't put all of your eggs in one basket. Diversifying your client portfolio is the best way to minimise risk.

4 **Don't always DIY.** Suddenly becoming the CEO, CMO, sales manager, accountant and content strategist all rolled into one can be overwhelming, particularly for creative freelancers. Outsource your weaknesses where you can, setting up strategic partnerships or expertise exchanges in the beginning when your start-up budget doesn't stretch that far.

If you want to get in touch with me, connect with me at:

- Web: www.lionwords.com
- Email: diane@lionwords.com
- LinkedIn: https://www.linkedin.com/in/dianewiredu/

chapter 7

Preparing yourself for freelancing

If you have done all the things discussed in this book so far, you are getting close to working with real clients. Your first engagement is close at hand. Before you do this, now is a chance to take a breath and make sure you are prepared, both practically and psychologically, for what you are about to do.

Do you remember starting a race when you were a child? Everyone would shout excitedly as the race was about to begin: 'Get ready ... Get steady ... Go'. We were all waiting to hear the word 'Go' shouted out. But as sprinters know, getting ready and being steady before a race are very important. So, before we go, I'm going to take a short pause and think about getting ready.

Setting yourself up as a freelance expert is easy. It's not one of those complicated businesses that you need to go out and hire staff, rent fancy premises or buy complex and expensive equipment. You already have most of what you need – in your brain! Most of it is right there. There are few simpler businesses to start. But simple does not mean you need absolutely nothing other than what's inside your head. There are a handful of things you should have in order before you take the leap into being a freelancer.

Preparing for independence

Some people follow their path into independence as a slow, deliberate and well-planned exercise. I have known people plotting their break into independence over a period of years and deliberately getting all the preparatory tasks done. On other occasions, it is a very quick process. The most extreme is when redundancy from an employed role makes you rethink your work and you end up deciding to go independent.

If you have time, there are a few things you will benefit from getting right before you start. The benefit of thinking ahead is you can do these things thoroughly and calmly. If you do not have the luxury of time, don't worry, as much of this can be sorted out very easily and quickly. You will have to do the best you can and perhaps do some of these tasks as you start to work as a freelancer. Fortunately, there is little here that is complex.

I think of the preparatory tasks in the following five categories:

- Develop credible expertise and experience
- Build your network and visibility
- Check the viability of your intended niche
- Get your finances in order
- Sort out the right equipment, facilities and administration.

Let's briefly look at each of these in turn.

Develop credible expertise and experience

By 'develop credible expertise and experience', I mean getting yourself to a position in which you will be accepted as an expert by your clients. The important word here is *credible*. Credible is a state defined by your clients not by you or anyone else. If beauty is in the eye of the beholder, credibility is in the eye of the client.

One advantage of having employment before you step into independence is that you can think through your future independent business niche and your target customers. Based on this, you can start to develop the skills you need, while you are still being paid a secure monthly amount.

Many freelancers drift into freelancing. It is better to go into it as a deliberate and planned activity. Think about the type of freelance career you want, and what experiences and expertise your future clients will expect you to have – and then seek opportunities to gain these as you work.

Although I have enjoyed my independent life for a long time, I was an employee for about a decade at the start of my career. It is the expertise and experiences I built up in those employed roles that were the foundation of setting up my own business.

For instance, if you plan to sell yourself as an expert project manager – what project management skills and qualifications can you acquire before you become a freelancer? If you plan to set up a coaching business, what coaching experience can you get while you work in a full-time job? There are lots of skills, experiences and qualifications that will be directly useful in demonstrating credibility to future clients, that you can gain while you are working.

Most clients do not expect you to know everything, but you must be perceived to know enough to be useful and for you to seem like a good choice when a client needs some help. Although you will be freelancing, experience gained while employed is often held in high regard by clients.

I have mentioned qualifications. In some roles you need formal qualifications and accreditations. For instance, to work as an accountant or independent financial adviser you must be qualified. In other areas, you can work without qualifications but there is a high expectation you will have them. But generally, expertise is more concerned with relevant experience than exams and certificates.

On the one hand, I know some freelancers who have an array of professional qualifications and these have helped them to get clients. On the other hand, they have been of little value to me. Never once in my freelance career have I been asked about my qualifications. Clients are only ever interested in my relevant experience.

It's great to be qualified, but before you invest in all the possible certificates your domain of expertise has, check that they are necessary or helpful. You can invest a lot of time and effort in things no one cares about.

Build your network and visibility

A lot of your success as a freelance expert will come down to having a productive network that you can find clients in and to which you can advertise your services. Much of my network was built since I have become independent, but I was also fortunate in having good contacts and possible clients before I set up my own business. For instance, my very first client was someone who had previously been part of my team, and my second client was an old boss of mine.

Anything you can do to build your network now, before you take the plunge into independence helps. If you have the chance, nurture the network you need, build that social media profile and maybe set up a website.

What is important in doing this is to remember that you are not seeking out people who are useful to your current job, or advertising what you do now, but that instead you are building the network and visibility you need for when you become independent.

Check the viability of your intended niche

You may be certain that there is a business in what you are planning to do. But why take an unknown plunge into the dark? Is anyone else doing something similar – are they thriving or struggling? What are they doing right, and what can you do better?

Ask around. Talk to trusted colleagues and friends. Find a few experienced freelance experts to chat to. Explain to them about what you intend to do and see if the response is what you would expect. A little market testing never does any harm and you may well learn some useful ideas in the process.

Get your finances in order

I know what I am about to say may be a luxury some people cannot afford. But if you can – make sure your finances are in order before you jump into freelancing. The earnings potential is high, but it is far from certain. You cannot rely on a fixed level of pay at the end of the month. In fact, to begin with, even if you win business on your first day of independent work, you may not have any money coming into your bank account for a couple of months or longer.

Starting out as a freelancer, in the time before you have been paid for a few pieces of work, can be stressful enough without having to worry about paying your immediate bills. If you can put some money aside to cover those first few weeks while you are waiting to earn good money, it will make your life much better! This is the first step in learning to be aware of your cash flow.

James Watt, the co-founder of BrewDog and the author of *Business for Punks* wrote: 'The lifeblood of your business is cash. If you can't manage a cash flow, then you can't run a business.' Working as a freelance expert may be a simple business, but it is still a business and these words hold true.

Sort out the right equipment, facilities and administration

One of the great things about a freelance business is that you need very little beyond yourself to get started. But you do need a few things, and some of these may require you to splash out a little money and take a little advice. In both cases the important word for me is 'little'.

Whatever you do, unless you have lots of cash to spare, keep your equipment and facilities simple and reliable. Do not go overboard on things like the highest spec laptop, a fancy agency-designed logo or a complex website. All those things have value, but you can sort them out when you have been in business for a little while.

This is partially about saving money. Cash is king, especially for someone running a small business. It is also because, until you have been in business for a while, you won't quite know what's best or needed for you. The world is full of over-specified laptops, boxes of never-given-out business cards and un-visited websites. You need the minimum to start with. So before splashing out, give yourself a little time and experience of working, to determine exactly what you need.

Table 7.1 lists ten things you should consider when setting up your business.

Table 7.1 Key considerations in setting up your business

	Equipment, facilities and administration	Comments
1	Legal structure / company registration and company name	When I started as an independent consultant, there was an ongoing debate as to whether it was better to work self-employed / sole trader or via your own company. Increasingly there is no choice, and you generally must have a recognised legal structure such as limited liability company (Ltd) or limited liability partnership (LLP). Seek specialist advice – it should not be expensive.
2	Online presence	There are lots of options – such as your own website and social media accounts. What's best varies, but you will need something. If you don't know what, there are lots of people who will advise you. However, don't listen to everything you hear – if the advice you get sounds like nonsense, it probably is. If it's going to cost you a fortune or lock you into paying for a high ongoing service charge, don't do it. Rarely, to begin with, do freelancers need anything beyond the most basic online presence. Don't listen to anyone who tells you that you need to be a huge influencer with millions of followers. You don't. Once you have run your business for a while you can think again.

	Equipment, facilities and administration	Comments
3	Company bank account and credit card	You should have a bank account for your business separate from your personal accounts. (If you set up as a company this will be a legal requirement.) A company credit card is not essential, but it's very helpful and a good way to deal with expenses.
4	Cash float	You will not get paid immediately and will need some money to keep the business running. When you first start it may be some months before the first client payment is made. It is easy to keep the costs of a consultancy business low, but they will not be zero and therefore a modest cash float is required.
		I separate this from a personal cash float you may also need, depending on how you will pay yourself during the initial stages of your business. Most independent advisers, who run their own business, receive a combination of relatively small salary and dividends from profit. The focus on dividends is due to the inability to forecast the company revenues accurately and hence the need to keep the cost base and salaries comparatively low.
5	Accountant and tax setup	You may not legally need an accountant – that depends on the legal structure of your business. I'd always recommend you have one. It does not need to cost much, their advice will be helpful, and you can get into all sorts of mess if you do not understand taxes. It helps to find one who understands small-business tax and specifically freelance businesses.
6	Accounting system and expenses tracking	There are many excellent and inexpensive accounting software packages like Xero and QuickBooks. Talk to your accountant. Best get something that you can use to simply track your expenses as well.
7	Professional indemnity insurance	Arguably this is not mandatory, but if your clients are large businesses, they may insist on it as part of their contract with independents. I recommend you at least consider it. You may be giving such low-risk advice it is not required, but on the other hand it does not cost a lot and if you ever did get sued it could bankrupt you.
		There are many insurers who offer PI insurance, and some specialise in certain sectors. If you belong to a professional body related to your area of expertise, they can advise and may even have recommended insurers. If not, ask other freelancers who work in your field. A question on LinkedIn or other platform usually gets good responses.
		Cover may be from a few thousand pounds to tens of millions. While this sounds scary, unless you are in a high-risk area, premiums tend to be low, as it is rare to be sued. In fact, the only reason I have it is because my clients insist on it. I've never had to call on it, and don't expect to.

Table 7.1 (continued)

	Equipment, facilities and administration	Comments
8	Somewhere to work, and associated facilities	For example: mobile, laptop, desk, stationery etc. You can start working on the corner of the kitchen table or in a coffee shop, using a battered old laptop.
		Don't go overboard – you can splash out the money when you are generating a good income. Start with the minimum you need and keep it simple and reliable.
		I recommend no one starting out renting an office or other commercial property. It has a high cost and you may well find you don't need it. Once you are generating good revenues you can think again. If you really can't work at home, at most go for some short-term flexible space in a multi-tenanted office. Avoid long-term contracts you may soon not want.
9	The business essentials every small business needs to know	There are some things that you need to know if you run any business nowadays. This book covers many of them, but is not a small-business primer. There are things you should understand and research more widely. Most of it you can learn as you go along, but it is at least worth being aware that there are things you need to learn. These are, mostly, not complex, and there are people who can help you. I am specifically thinking of:
		▪ Your legal responsibilities as a business owner.
		▪ Basics of accounting and tax. Your accountant will take care of this, but you should have some understanding of at least the categories of taxes you must pay.
		▪ Data protection laws, which even the smallest of businesses must follow. In Europe, the most important of these is GDPR, which limits what client information you can keep and how you must keep it.
		I suggest you get a book such as the *Financial Times Guide to Business Start Up* as a reference for these.
10	The specific tools of your trade	Depending on the nature of your freelance service, you may need additional equipment or facilities related to that specialisation. For example:
		▪ As I regularly present at events and run workshops, I have my own projection equipment, flip chart and a professional microphone.
		▪ As a coach, you may need access to a place to meet and talk with your clients.
		Even though these are important to your work, what I said in point 8 still counts. Don't go overboard – you can splash out the money when you are generating a good income. Start with the minimum you need and keep it simple and reliable. You may be able to pick up good-quality things second hand.

The transition from another job

Very occasionally I meet someone who has become an independent adviser straight out of school or university. But it is rare for the simple fact that to be credible to clients you must have some expertise, and to be perceived as credible in having that expertise there needs to be a few miles on your clock. I'm not someone who believes you need vast experience, but you do need enough. And this means that most people setting themselves up as a freelance expert are transitioning from another job. One useful question is what is that transition like?

The answer depends on what your past job was, and what sort of freelance expert you plan to be. Let's consider one common scenario – you have worked for a business or public sector organisation doing various tasks and acquiring expertise. Now, as an independent expert, you want to step outside of that organisation and possibly sell your expertise back to organisations like the one you worked for.

You may not, yet, think of yourself as a fully seasoned professional or the world's greatest subject matter expert, but you are on the way. You know many things that would be useful to other people in similar roles. You may have some management and leadership experiences, which gives a little more credibility to your expertise.

This brings us to the first and most obvious thing that is going to be different in your career as a freelance expert. As a freelancer you are no longer a doer of the work of that organisation – you are an adviser or helper. Of course, even being an adviser requires doing things, but they are different things from your previous career.

You won't be leading a team based on role, position or authority, but instead you must influence through ideas, insights, experiences and wisdom. You won't be directly doing your clients' work; you will be helping them to do it.

How do you feel about this? Some people make great doers, but terrible advisers. On the other hand, some people were relatively modest in their achievements as a doer – but make great advisers. For example, look at the number of great sports coaches who were not first-class sports stars before. Another way of putting this is: Do you enjoy helping others succeed rather than directly succeeding yourself?

To answer that question, you should understand what's different about providing expertise. If we unpack the rather broad concept of shifting from being a doer to being an adviser: What is going to be different in the work you do? How will it feel?

You may find it liberating. Working independently, you sit outside your client's corporate hierarchy. You have no corporate baggage, you do not have to play the politics of the organisation and you can be unbiased. This is how it may seem. You are outside the corporate bubble. When you turn up at a new client you may know no one there. But if you want to advise effectively in it, you still need to be aware of the corporate politics and inter-personal relationships. And although you can avoid many of the biases and political opinions of your clients, you will find, as a freelancer, that you will develop biases of your own.

You are likely to find the work a little strange to begin with. Your value will be completely based on the influence you have within the organisation. There will be no power associated with a job title or a position which you may have enjoyed previously. Yes, you are an expert in your field, but there are lots of experts and not everyone will respect your expertise. Your clients will be judging you as you appear to them in this instant – not for any badges or titles you hold, not for any past glories or successes you have had. You will need to start to think more deeply about relationships, influence, perceptions of you and how you advise as well as what you advise.

Your time horizons will contract. Previously, you may have thought of your career in terms of years. While you may want a 20-year career as a freelancer, any individual engagement tends to be relatively short. You must get used to the fact that you will be with the client for a short period of time and must make a positive impact in that short period of time.

I am conscious of this shortened time horizon. I always start to plan my exit from the start of an engagement – that may sound premature, but only by doing this can I be sure to achieve what I need to achieve in the time available. For instance, in a six-week engagement, I must sort out the logistics, plan the work, gather the data, come up with conclusions, create deliverables, advise the client confidently, refine my deliverables and tidy up any loose ends in those six weeks. It's not a lot of time.

Your work will typically be narrower in scope. You will be hired for your expertise in a specific area. Even if this is a broad topic like leadership or strategy, you will not have to deal with the full range of areas that an employee or line manager in a normal organisation does. Your broad specialisation will be focused onto a specific area only. You will have to keep focused and ignore the peripheral, else you will not finish your work on time or within budget.

If you are a subject matter expert, being able to focus purely on your subject matter expertise alone may be attractive. You are doing what you enjoy and nothing else. But it comes with a price: the levers with which you influence people are restricted to your direct personal influence.

The final big difference is one you will be aware of from day one, but it won't necessarily hit you until the end of your first month. There will be no nice pay coming out from your employer into your bank account on a regular interval. Frankly, I never think about this nowadays, but for my first few months as an independent it worried me.

Let's end this section with a positive thought. If I am chatting with a group of freelancers who used to have corporate careers, there is one thing that there is almost unanimous agreement about. That is the joy of never having to do a company performance review, annual objectives setting or career planning session. Just think of the pleasure of never doing one again. It's in your grasp!

An independent voice

Leonie Scholten, Purposeful Growth Coach and Consultant

I have always been interested in what makes people tick. What excites us? How do we make choices? I have worked for over 10 years in product marketing and strategic brand marketing with a global brand consultancy. In early 2010 I started to specialise in purposeful branding. In that time, the concept of purpose in a business context was seen by many as a fluffy intangible thing. Boy how that has changed. Today there is a general consensus that businesses of the future have to deliver both profit and purpose.

I have never been the typical tough and number-focused left brain consultant in a suit. I thrive on human connections, deep understanding, seeing the bigger picture, collaboration and self-exploration. Empathy is one of my biggest strengths (proven time and again through the various management style tests you'll do when working in a consultancy). At times I felt like an outsider in the hard business world, but slowly I started to realise that this was what made me great at what I loved doing: helping businesses grow through building human and meaningful connections with their internal and external audiences, coming from a place of purpose.

There was just one thing that I was missing: direct impact on people. In my early 30s I was going through a difficult time due to major surgery. This was my 'reset' moment. I worked with different coaches to clarify what I really wanted in life. Where could I find fulfilment? What was my own personal purpose?

It was mind-blowing how much similarity I discovered in what they were helping me with, versus what I had been doing for businesses all this time. The pieces of my puzzle started to fall together. I invested in a renowned coaching education, and a whole new world opened for me. This was it! I wanted to make an impact on the lives of others through coaching. Helping them to go for change, live with purpose and do what matters.

At the moment of writing this, I am only at the beginning of my new journey as an independent Purposeful Growth Coach and Consultant. If you are curious about where I am now that you are reading this and to see how my story has developed, then have a look at www.leoniescholten.com. I am always keen to make new connections and hear other people's stories!

My tips for anyone considering a freelance career

Full focus

I have thought about starting my own business for years. There were always reasons that held me back from doing it. They were related to me working in a full-time, well-paying job. I was scared to give up certainty and I was not willing to sacrifice all my spare time to get started. My desire to do my own thing got bigger and at some point I realised I needed to go all in. It was all or nothing. The 'doubt-filled in-between place' didn't get me anywhere. Not in the job I was doing and not with my plans to start. So dare to choose!

Hire a coach

And I'm not just saying this just because I am one! There are endless reasons why working with a coach is no luxury when starting out as an entrepreneur. While it's great and exciting, it's also lonely and stressful. It requires your full belief and energy. In weaker moments you will have doubts and maybe even difficulty connecting with the WHY you did it. A coach helps you to stay on track. It can also help to put things in perspective. It helps you to regain confidence in what you are doing. And it helps to provide clarity in how to move ahead. So really, invest in a good coach.

Prepare for your weaknesses

In hindsight, I should have prepared better for my weaknesses. When you start your own business, it's usually because you are super passionate about the core of your business. However, being independent means taking responsibility for every aspect of your business, and it is unavoidable that you will need to think and work hard on things you don't like. For me this is client acquisition.

Sure, in my business plan I wrote down some ideas for my sales funnel. But when I started working on the business I was focusing on the fun stuff: writing my offer and story, building my identity etc. On top of that the world was changing because of the Covid-19 outbreak, which gave me even more reasons not to focus on it. I was lying to myself! I should have started with acquisition from moment one! Instead I pushed it aside, which has set me back.

part
three

Selling and winning your first engagement

chapter

8

Marketing and finding clients

In this chapter I'm going to explore the ways in which you can find clients.

Before you can sell, your clients must know about you and your services. There may be billions of individuals in the world, but only a small proportion are potential clients for you. On top of this, there are millions of other businesses trying to sell to them. Everyone's lives are full of people trying to grab their attention and convince them to spend some of their money. It can seem an impossible task to find the individuals who might be good clients for you, and to get them to focus on you. How do you raise clients' awareness about what you do in a way that they will listen to?

We might loosely think of the topic of this chapter as marketing. Marketing goes hand-in-hand with selling, which I deal with in the next chapter. Marketing and selling together form what is often known in professional services as *business development.*

In our line of work as independent experts, there is no hard and fast boundary between marketing and sales activities. There are activities, like putting out a blog or a podcast, which are clearly marketing. There are also activities, such as agreeing a price and the terms for a new piece of work, which are purely sales. But many activities are a bit of both. For instance, you may start a conversation with a potential client simply to make them aware of what you do, and by the end of the conversation have sold some work. Does that count as marketing, sales or both? It doesn't really matter, and you will find as you read these next two chapters that I jump between marketing and sales concepts.

Nevertheless, it's useful to look at marketing and sales separately, as there are various skills and techniques associated with each of them. It is going to be important for you to acquire some knowledge of marketing and sales for you to work independently. How much you need to learn, and which skills and techniques you need, depend on you and the decisions you make about how you want to run your business. There are some common fundamentals we all need to understand, but there is no single right way to market and sell expert services. There are different ways that suit different services and situations. I will explore the options in this and the next chapter.

Filling your sales funnel with valuable conversations

The nature of expert services is such that you will virtually never sell without talking to your customers. The start of any sale is a conversation. Not just any conversation, you want to have *valuable* conversations with potential clients – valuable conversations being those that lead either directly or indirectly into sales. One way of thinking about marketing is that it opens the door to being able to talk to clients.

Let me qualify the point about all sales starting with a conversation with two small caveats. The first is that someone probably occasionally sells an expert service without ever talking to their client. The world is complex, with our billions of people and trillions of interactions, and so at some time virtually everything has happened! But I think it is rare. Rare enough to assume that all sales need some form of initial direct dialogue. The second caveat is that once you have an existing relationship with a client, they may well buy you again and again without needing much more conversation. This is one reason why relationships are so important in our business.

Sales professionals often talk about the *sales funnel* (see the diagram at the end of this chapter), the funnel being a metaphor for capturing all the times we catch the attention of clients. It is a funnel because it narrows as some clients lose interest and do not want to follow on from conversations with us. We start with a certain number of potential clients – or *leads* – being interested in our service. At each of the various stages of selling some potential clients lose interest. Typically, we need to have several client leads entering our funnels to generate one sold piece of work. Marketing is the way we fill this funnel. Sales converts what comes into this funnel into paying business.

What do you want to fill this funnel with? To answer that, let's reflect on two basic ideas.

Firstly, you don't need lots of customers. As I have repeatedly said, you need enough. I know one independent adviser who between 2007 and 2017 generated fees in excess of £5m from one client. His client was a senior executive in a global organisation, and the adviser I know was his trusted adviser for a decade. Over those 10 years, the adviser did not need to do any marketing or have a sales funnel.

This is an extreme example, as one client is too few for most of us, but it shows what is possible.

What is enough for you? Enough is more clients than you can do work for. More, because it gives you the ability to pick and choose clients. Being choosey gives you freedom, flexibility and the ability to raise your prices. But there is little point having 10 times as many potential clients as you can deal with (unless you are trying to move on from being an independent to building a firm of advisers or experts, a conversation for another day and another book, but which I briefly touch on in Chapter 14).

Given this, it is only necessary to do enough marketing to give you a sufficient number of clients. Any more is wasted effort, and will waste time – time that you could use doing more valuable things.

How many leads you need depends on how good you are at converting leads into sales, and how many sales you need. I do know a few experts who convert pretty much every sales lead into a sale. But they are rare.

If you sell work by the hour and want to be busy 40 hours a week, you may need 40 sales each and every week. To make 40 sales every week, you probably need to be marketing to hundreds of people every week. On the other hand, if you sell work in six-month chunks you need a maximum of two sales a year – you may need only half a dozen conversations to generate these two sales. If you are selling on a value-based pricing, you need to sell enough pieces of work that will generate the income you want. The arithmetic is easy. The starting point is back to what you sell, at what price and therefore how many sales you need to make.

In Chapter 6, we looked at how to calculate your minimum income. From this, you can calculate how many sales you need to make. For instance, in that example we calculated that the freelancer needs to generate £8000 per month in fees for 10 months, totalling £80,000 per annum. As a further worked example, this means:

- If you are a coach charging £250 per hour, you need to invoice 32 hours of work a month. If an average client hires you for 8 hours work, you need to sell to 4 clients a month, and 40 clients in a year.
- If you are an IT contractor charging £500 per day, you need to invoice for 16 days' work a month, or 160 days over the 10 months a year you plan to work. If an average client hires you for 50 days, then you need 3–4 clients a year.

Secondly, you don't want to market to just anyone. You want to attract the sort of clients who want your service, and who you want to work with. Marketing can be indiscriminate and attracts all sorts of people who you don't want or need as clients. You want to focus the time that you spend on marketing, gaining the attention of the right people who may, realistically, become clients.

Good marketing will deliver you with a flow of a sufficient number of clients. Better than this is when you find clients who pay you well and quickly, give you repeat business, and recommend you to other clients. Best of all is when your marketing and reputation is so good that you don't need to look, because clients proactively come a-knocking at your door, asking you to help them. This happens to some people at the top of their game. Rather than looking for clients, they are well enough known to be found by them.

Your pitch

At the heart of all your marketing and your sales activities are the things you say about yourself and how you present yourself to your clients. To sell, you need a set of words that explain to clients, ideally in a pithy and compelling way, why it is that they should buy a service from you. We can call this 'your pitch'. Without having a good pitch, there is little point marketing your services, as what will you say when you manage to generate an opportunity for a valuable conversation?

Large corporations spend huge amounts of time and money on their sales messages and there is both an art and a science to getting them right. We do not need to go through all the complexities of a big business, but having a good pitch is a key step in being able to market and sell yourself. The first

8 Marketing and finding clients   101

and most important point about such a pitch is to remember that it is not primarily about you. It will say some things about you – but it is primarily about your customers and why they should buy you and your service.

In Chapter 6, we developed a vision for your freelance business. This was about you and what you do. You need this information for your pitch, but you will translate it into something that is orientated towards your target clients. When they try to sell, many freelancers make the mistake of only talking about themselves, whereas what you really need to do is to talk about your clients.

A good, straightforward and yet powerful way to do this is using the template shown in Table 8.1.

To give you a better idea of what I mean, I've built on the examples in Tables 6.4 and 6.5 to create Tables 8.2 and 8.3.

It is worth spending the time to get this right, and to be able to give your pitch confidently and succinctly whenever it is required.

Table 8.1 Your freelance pitch

I will help you by . . .	Which will achieve for you . . .	I am best placed to do this for you because . . .
Imagine you are having a conversation with your ideal client. Start by describing what you do that will help them. This needs to be very brief – as you should be mostly talking about the client and not yourself, as is described in the next two columns in this table.	Next explain, in doing this, what it will achieve for them. Describe the value it will give them. For example, you might consider factors like: - Will it save them time or money? - Will it make their life less hassled or stressful? - Will it help them be more successful or happier? - Will it take work or a problem away which they don't like dealing with? Think of the factors in Table 3.1. The better you know your client, the better able you are to understand their problems and to pitch your service as the solution.	Finally, explain why you are the right person for them. For example, you might consider factors like: - You are conveniently located - Your fees are good value - You have the right expertise - You have knowledge about them personally which will help you provide an excellent service - You are highly recommended - You have unique insights that can help them etc. The better you know your client, the better able you are to understand what is important to them, and what to stress when selling to them.

Table 8.2 The pitch for a coach

I will help you by ...	Which will achieve for you ...	I am best placed to do this for you because ...
Supporting you through the next six months of your career as you approach the promotion round.	Access to a guide who will ensure you are prepared for the promotion and able to present yourself as a confident and engaging manager who is ready for the next step in your career. At the end of my support you will be facing your promotion calmly, confidently and well prepared.	I specialise in coaching people just like you and have a long track record in helping people gain promotions. As an ex HR director, I understand the promotion processes in large organisations and know what makes a candidate successful.

Table 8.3 The pitch for a contract ghost-writer

I will help you by ...	Which will achieve for you ...	I am best placed to do this for you because ...
Writing a professional quality book for you about your specialist area.	A high-quality book with your name on it, produced without hassle, which will improve your profile in your profession and show you as a world-class expert. My books have helped experts gain speaking events, consultancy roles, as well as increasing their earnings and gaining promotions.	I have written dozens of books for experts like you and can provide you with a long list of recommendations from other experts whose books have helped them greatly. Some of these books have sold tens of thousands of copies, won industry awards and been translated many times.

The importance of relationships and trust to selling

When we pay someone for their expertise, there is always an element of risk associated with it. There is the risk that their expertise may not be as good as we hope it is. Usually, we are not able to judge how good their expertise is. After all they are the expert, we aren't, that is why we are looking to hire them. There is also risk that they will not do the work we have hired them to do very well. When they are finished, we may or may not know whether they have done a good job, as often it needs another expert to make the judgement.

We are all conscious of this whenever we make a choice to hire an expert – whether it is choosing a garage to repair our car or a dentist to fix our teeth. I'm sure you know that feeling of discomfort and uncertainty when you choose someone to do anything that you yourself do not understand.

In this situation we seek to reduce the risk in various ways. One way is that we only choose experts who work with a recognised brand. The brand indicates a certain reputation and experience. Another way is that we hire people we already have an established relationship with – people we trust. Finally, if we don't have anyone we personally trust, we seek an expert via other people we know and trust – we look for recommendations and referrals. We seek to hire an expert that someone we trust recommends.

Now let's turn the table. Imagine the situation in which you are not hiring an expert, but instead you are selling yourself as one. This is something that a freelance expert needs to do all the time. Your clients will usually feel the same sense of uncertainty when it comes to hiring you. And they will seek to reduce the risk in the same ways that you would.

As Maister, Green and Galford wrote in their book *The Trusted Advisor*, 'How does one sell? By demonstrating (not asserting) to a client that we have something to offer and that we are someone in whom they can place their trust'.

Occasionally, clients will do this by looking for a well-known brand. As a freelance expert it is hard, but not impossible, to build a trusted brand. You can probably think of a few experts you know who have a brand which they may have developed by writing books, giving seminars and podcasts, or through their active presence on social media. Normally, in these cases the recognised brand is their own name. Some of your marketing activities may be concerned with building up your personal brand.

Often, clients will reduce their risk by hiring experts they already know, who have provided a service they found valuable and helpful in the past, and experts who they liked working with. This is one of the most important ways of selling for freelance experts – repeat business. Clients do this because the trust already exists. It is much less risky to hire someone known than to hire a completely unknown expert.

Where they do not have direct experience, clients will also regularly seek recommendations and referrals from other clients. Experienced freelance experts know one of the best routes to more business is via existing clients – and by getting referrals from their existing clients to other new clients.

Your routes to market

How you should market depends on your route to market. (I am indebted to my colleague Alastair McDermott, www.marketingforconsultants.com, for some of the ideas in this section. You can find out more about Alastair at the end of this chapter.) If you have not heard the phrase before, a *route to market* is a bit of business jargon referring to the way you connect with your particularly desired clients. For instance, if you are a supermarket chain with a range of physical shops, your route to market is those shops. In contrast, the route to market for Amazon is the Amazon website.

What are your routes to market? There are three main routes:

- Indirect – using third parties to sell your services
- Direct – finding your own customers and selling to them
- Reverse – having customers come and find you and ask you to work for them.

Depending on your preferred route to market, your marketing will have a different focus. Each of these three routes has variants, which I outline in Table 8.4.

Table 8.4 Routes to market for freelance experts

	Route to market	Explanation	Marketing implications
1	Indirect – agents	Using third-party specialists who specifically market freelancers to other organisations, normally called *agents*. This is very common in the contracting and interim management markets.	Marketing needs to focus on developing relationships with agents. Agents typically need up-to-date CVs and references from your prior clients. Agents' ideal freelancers are those who they can place at clients again and again over a long period of time, while making a profitable margin on top of the freelancer's fees.
2	Indirect – partners	Working with other freelance experts who generate more business than they can serve, and who want partners to fulfil the needs of their excess clients. This is quite common in the consultancy and interim management markets. (See Chapter 14 for more information.)	Marketing needs to focus on developing trusting relationships with partners. For such partners, their client relationships are valuable. Partners' ideal freelancers will be those who reliably do work and help to maintain or even improve the partner's relationship with their clients. They won't want to take a risk with freelancers who they feel might damage their client relationships. Hence marketing to partners should focus on building your credibility as a reliable freelancer in your chosen domain.

	Route to market	Explanation	Marketing implications
3	Direct – cold outreach (e.g. cold calling)	Identifying and proactively contacting/calling potential new clients, who you have no relationship with, to generate sales.	Marketing is focused on identifying and finding the contact details of potential clients and developing persuasive messages to quickly give to the client. Quickly, because on a cold call the client will typically only listen for a very short time. This may be as little as a few seconds and if you do not capture their attention quickly you will not sell. If the client contact is successful, you may also need to provide supporting materials or content to develop the relationship.
4	Direct – warm outreach (e.g. warm calling)	Contacting clients you have an established relationship with and who you have worked with before for follow-up work.	Marketing is focused on maintaining up-to-date information on your past clients and staying in touch with them on a regular basis. Given you have an established relationship, simply remaining in touch may be sufficient to generate some business.
5	Direct – content marketing	Creating content (e.g. posts, podcasts, articles, books etc.), related to your expertise and building a reputation as an expert based on that content.	Marketing is focused on creating compelling content and placing it in the appropriate platform for visibility to potential clients. This could be by email or on your website, but often this requires active use of social media. Content marketing requires regular creation of compelling content. It also requires making the effort to build a large enough group of followers, containing potential clients, who are interested in the content.
6	Reverse marketing	Responding to direct client requests to help them.	Marketing is focused on building a pool of clients who trust you and value your service, who proactively contact you when they need help. This often is supported by content marketing and warm calling.

Any of these routes to market can work, and there is no reason to only use one route. There are marketing activities which support several of these routes to market. For instance, the development of great content and building a reputation based on it, can support all of these channels. Additionally, the creation and maintenance of up-to-date contact information (while complying with data protection laws), is essential for several of them.

In general terms, the only route to market I do not recommend is cold calling. It can work, but it is a lot of effort and the success rate is low. The challenge is that, as we have all experienced when we receive a cold call from someone we do not know, we start in a position of low trust. Most people find cold calls at least irritating, and sometimes deeply annoying. This is a hard place to move on from to develop a sufficient relationship and trust to sell expert services from.

The one I suggest everyone does is number 4. Not keeping in touch with clients you have already developed a good relationship with is as close as you can get to throwing business away! Never assume that clients will just remember you. They won't. Some degree of regular reminders of yourself and your services keeps you in your clients' minds. Content marketing is often a good way to support this. When they have a problem, if you are in their mind, they are more likely to reach out to you for help.

The one we all want to try and achieve is number 6. Once you are at the point where you can minimise your time working hard on marketing (or sales) because you are regularly called by clients with offers of work, you are in a great position to grow a strong freelance business.

A final consideration is that some of your marketing activities can be outsourced. For instance, there are plenty of businesses, including other freelance experts, who will help you with content marketing. And, while I personally don't recommend cold calling, I know experts who have paid a specialist outbound sales agency to generate leads for them via cold calling which have turned into paying clients.

Where to start

So many options, so much work to do! Luckily, you do not need to start your freelance business with a fully planned marketing approach. Most people's marketing develops over time with a combination of experimentation and learning. I have relied a lot on content marketing based on my books over the years. This has generated me a reasonable flow of business, including clients who have asked me to work with them simply based on reading a book of mine. But I did not start out with this plan, I learnt it as I worked. I started seeing my writing and my expert services as separate businesses. They have come together over time as I have learnt.

Experimenting and learning what is best for you takes time. To begin with, you will want some business to get the revenues flowing into your business.

My advice is always to start with people you know. Call a few of your contacts. Talk about your services. See if they, or anyone they know, is interested. If they do not need your service, ask them if they can recommend you to someone else.

Starting with those you know is a good idea because trust and a relationship are already there. And if a contact refers you to someone they know, you inherit to some extent the trust that existed between your contact and your client.

As McMakin and Fletcher wrote in *How Clients Buy* '... consulting and professional services are bought differently from products. They are bought on reputation, referral, and relationships'.

When thinking about the people you know, don't just think about potential clients. If you know other freelancers, talk to them. They will have lots of tips and advice, and they may know a client or two who you are just right for. Over the years, a lot of my work has come from other consultants and contractors, and I have often introduced freelancers to my clients.

Occasionally, I meet someone who knows half a dozen CEOs of global corporations very well. She can phone them up anytime, and has no trouble filling up their order book with work. But most of us don't have quite such a network. That is just a reality. But it is not a disaster, as lots and lots of services aren't bought by the CEO. There are plenty of other potential clients, and some of them will be people you already know.

When you win your first piece of work, there is one thing that should be on your mind before anything else – and that is to do a great job. You are constantly building your reputation as a freelance expert. Your reputation will be your best aide in marketing your services, and you need to build it from the first day you work.

If you are recommended by someone else, make sure you return that trust by doing a great job. Every time someone refers or recommends you, you are being given a valuable gift. Don't damage it by doing shoddy or half-hearted work. If you do, you will not only spoil your relationship with your new client, you will probably damage the relationship with the person who recommended you as well.

Direct experience of your services is the way you gain repeat business. It is also the way you generate those valuable recommendations and referrals that will do far more for your business than any other form of marketing.

As I have indicated, referrals are of huge value to the freelance expert. The best way to get a referral? Ask for one. But you are unlikely to get one unless you have already done a good piece of work or have a strong relationship with the person you are asking.

The importance of your network

You won't have a conversation about any sort of selling nowadays, especially selling yourself as a freelance expert, before the topic of your network comes up. My advice about networks tends to be straightforward and simple, and I think it is sufficient for most people. There are lots of complex models of networks, and if it is of interest to you, there is a lot of good advice available that a little research will give you access to.

When I think in terms of my network, I categorise it into four pieces.

1. The people I directly know who I have a strong relationship with. These are people I can call anytime to chat, ask advice, or talk about my services without introduction.
2. My wider network of people I am connected to, mostly on social media. These are people I can reach out to, but for some of them if I do this it is only marginally better than a cold call. Simply being connected on social media does not mean we have a strong relationship. Importantly though, these are people who are likely to see my posts and social media interactions and from this may develop into closer relationships.
3. My network's network. Although my network is finite, those people in turn know millions of other people. If I want to find a client who I don't know, I start by finding people I know who know this client. Plus, when my network shares or forwards my content it will be seen by some of these people. I have indirect, and somewhat unreliable access to them, but I do have access, and over time many of my network's network has become part of my network.
4. Everyone else, who currently I have no connection with. These are the people who potentially may become future members of my network, and from that point may become future clients. For now though, I don't know them, and they don't know me – and I do not have access to them.

I visualise this network in the way shown in Figure 8.1.

The easiest place for me to sell business is with group 1, and the hardest is with group 4. For groups 2 and 3, my content marketing helps to bring me into contact with them. For group 4 it is harder to connect to them. These are

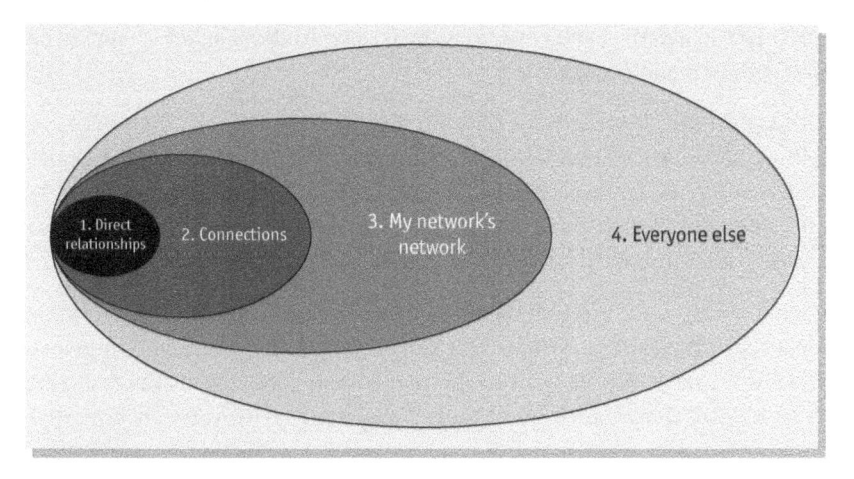

Figure 8.1 My network

the contacts that some freelancers try to access using a cold calling approach. I try to regularly expand my network to include people in group 4. I do have one advantage. Given I have published several well-known business books, I often get approached by people in this group who have read one of my books and who want to build a relationship with me.

I am constantly trying to grow my network, as experience shows that a larger network makes it more likely that I will be brought in contact with people who will want to buy my services. (It also helps me to sell books, but that is a separate point.) But I am not trying to grow it randomly. I know the sort of person who I want to sell to, and who is likely to buy my services. There are not millions of these people. My aim in growing my network is to have as many of the right people in it as possible.

A lot of people worry about the size of their network. It is no doubt useful to have a big network. The bigger the network the more likely that within it are some people who are ideally suited to be your clients. But for the freelance expert, far more important than size is the quality of your network. By quality, I mean the propensity of the network to throw up relationships which lead to you finding the sort of work that you want.

I know there is a lot of chatter on social media from those people with hundreds of thousands of followers. Well if you want to be one, then go ahead as this may well give you a lot of satisfaction. But for many freelance experts it is simply irrelevant. For instance, some successful interim managers I know have very limited social media presence and relatively small networks. If you intend to let agents do all your sales, then beyond those agents you may be fine with a small network.

This is brought home when McMakin and Fletcher write in their book on selling consultancy about *rainmakers*. Rainmakers is another piece of sales jargon and refers to those sales professionals who generate a lot of sales. As McMakin and Fletcher write: 'Rainmakers tend to *know* a lot of people, but it is not the number that matters – it is the quality of those relationships'.

If you have thought through the ideas in Chapter 5, you will know who your ideal client is. You know the sort of people you want to attract. A network of a few hundred people with a high percentage of potential clients is a lot more helpful than a network of tens of thousands with very few potential clients.

Nevertheless, building and developing a network is an important activity for most freelance experts. It takes time to build one in the first place, and it requires ongoing maintenance.

If you want to shortcut the effort of building a network, there are organisations that will give you access to their networks, for a fee. They usually claim to know a group of senior people with a direct interest in the type of work you do, whom you could get direct access to. I would tread warily before taking up these offers, especially if the fee is any significant amount of money. I've never paid for access to a network, and neither has any successful person that I know of. I'm not saying it definitely won't work for you, but I remain sceptical of it.

The role of social media

If networks are important, then one of the most important tools in building and maintaining a network is social media. Social media has an important role to play for many freelance experts. Platforms like LinkedIn provide a great set of capabilities to manage and build a network, and a forum to engage in a variety of marketing activities, especially content marketing. But social media, even if you do not choose to pay for any of the premium packages, has a cost. It takes time and effort to do it well.

At its best, social media can turbo charge your business. I know people who have used different platforms to build their reputations, create large numbers of followers and generate a lot of business. Is it for you? Probably, but not necessarily.

You can also invest a huge amount of time and generate very little business. Those who are keenest on social media are usually those whose business is selling advice on how to use social media. Not surprisingly they have a vested interest in making you think it is the be all and end all. It can be, but it does not have to be.

There are freelance experts who have no social media presence, and there are those on the other end of the scale who spend hours every day using it. I am probably on the middle of this scale. Most days I engage in my social media accounts. I comment on and engage with other people's content. I develop and place my own content, and I have successfully found business using social media. My main platform, as I write this, is LinkedIn. Whether in a few years' time it will still be LinkedIn or another platform has yet to be determined. Social media platforms evolve at quite a pace, and you must be prepared to move on.

One aspect of social media is the rise of the *influencer*. There is a business in being an influencer and it can be combined with being a freelance expert, but it is fundamentally a separate business. There can only be so many real influencers, by which I don't just mean people influencing lots of followers, but actually making a significant income from it.

A few influencers are generating truly huge incomes, and it's easy to get swept up into feeling you are missing out on something. Don't get too depressed when you see all those smiling faces with thousands of comments and likes after their posts. Most of them are not actually making that much money, if any. After all, if you are helping your clients there is not so much time left for social media.

The idea that you are a no one because you have a very limited or zero social media presence is blatant nonsense. It is a tool and can be a very useful and powerful tool if you learn to use it correctly. It can support a great business. It can make you visible to lots of clients. It can be a route to finding new clients. It can support successful content marketing. But don't forget that there are successful experts who keep their profiles low, and it does their business no harm. You need to choose if it is right for you.

If you do decide it's going to be important for your business, you can always choose to outsource the work. There are businesses who, for a cost, will maintain your social media presence with updates and the like. Some of my freelance colleagues do this successfully, tending to be those who need to generate a relatively large number of sales leads.

How much marketing do you need to do?

This is a great question and it depends hugely on your services and how you find your work. On the one hand contractors I know, for instance, do virtually no marketing, relying instead on a relationship with one or more agents to find them work. On the other hand, for some freelance experts business development activities are a significant proportion of their time.

Like many other things you need to do as an independent freelancer, you must determine what is the right balance for you. From a business perspective the more time you can focus on applying your expertise and thereby earning money, the better. However, you cannot do this without clients, and you will not be able to raise your fees unless you have more clients than you need. So marketing is going to be something that you will need to spend some time on. How much? Well, that is up to you.

If you would like to look into this area more, a really good approach to developing a marketing plan is given in *The 1-Page Marketing Plan* by Allan Dib.

To bring this point home, I am going to reference some material from my book *The Management Consultant: Mastering the Art of Consultancy*. In that book I also explore the topic of sales and marketing, but from the specific perspective of being a management consultant rather than a freelancer. But there is a lot of commonality, and I want to go back to the concept of the sales funnel that I introduced at the start of this chapter.

Figure 8.2 compares two sales funnels for two freelance experts. They both start with the same number of five sales leads, and both end with one sale. It might be thought that they are equally good then. They are not. The one on the right is better. If you are only going to make one sale from five leads, the sooner you can let go of the other four leads the better. The sooner you can focus on the one client who will give you business, the less effort you will be spending on winning that business. Also, the sooner you can stop chasing leads that will not get you work the better. Perhaps an ever better sales funnel than either would be one that only needs one lead for one client engagement.

With this thought in mind, it's time to start thinking more about sales and move onto Chapter 9.

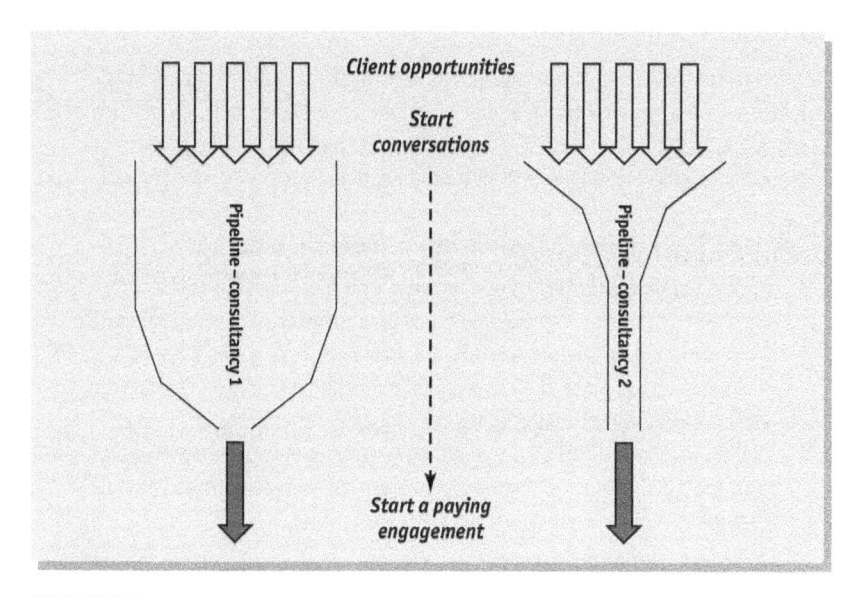

Figure 8.2 The sales funnel

An independent voice

Alastair McDermott, Marketing for Consultants

I have a business – and podcast and blog – called MarketingForConsultants.com where I work with independent consultants and boutique firms who are frustrated to be so dependent on referrals for business development. I help them position themselves as authorities and thought leaders, and leverage that to generate inbound leads who are enthusiastic ideal clients.

My background was software and web development, and for 12 years I ran a web consultancy called 'WebsiteDoctor'. This operated like a typical local digital agency: providing a whole range of website and digital marketing services to all types of businesses. 'All things to all people.'

I had been tweaking my strategy and positioning over the years, but I was still very dependent on referrals. After a lot of investigation and conversations, I realised that I needed to specialise vertically, i.e. pick a specific target market.

After going through the process of specialisation I had picked a vertical – business and management consultants – as my specialist niche and I started researching, writing and networking. It took about two years to 'turn the ship', but I'm very happy with the results. These are some of my favourite clients to work with, and marketing in the B2B professional services is a different and – in my opinion – a more challenging problem than in the consumer realm!

My tips for anyone considering a freelance career

1 **Pick a vertical market.** People say there's no silver bullet in marketing. They're wrong: vertical specialisation is the silver bullet! Pick a vertical market, i.e. one industry to specialise in. Choose an industry you're interested in, that has the ability to pay and a challenging problem that you like to solve. You want a target market that congregates – industry conferences, associations and trade journals. This allows you to be laser focused with your marketing and networking. Subscribe to the journals, join the associations and attend the events.

2 **Research and write.** Becoming an authority and thought leader is the path to higher fees and having your ideal clients coming to you. You don't become an authority without writing or producing content in some way – speaking, podcasting, videos, blogging, or writing a book like this one! Writing about a topic is a great way to develop your own thinking on a topic, and to demonstrate your expertise and knowledge to your audience.

Do some kind of independent research, perhaps survey your target market about the problems that they're encountering. This can be a fantastic source of content for you to use in your articles and talks.

For example, I surveyed over 850 management consultants about marketing and lead generation. This helped me understand my clients better, and it taught me the internal language of the industry. It also helped me grow my email list, connect with people like Richard, and it gives me talking points to help get on podcasts as a guest.

I think research is particularly important if you are an outsider and need to establish some credibility in an industry.

You can see more of my research and writing at https://MarketingForConsultants.com/thinking

chapter

9

Selling and making sure you get paid

This is the longest chapter in the book, but then it deals with two of the most important aspects that often worry freelancers most: (a) how to sell to potential clients and (b) having sold to a client, making sure that they get paid.

Some people love to sell. They like the buzz of winning work, closing deals and that psychological 'ka-ching' at the thought of money. Others dislike selling intensely. They feel it is somehow grubby or distasteful. This latter response is common among people in professional services. You rarely find lawyers or management consultants talking about selling with pleasure. With freelancers, selling is a very personal process, as you are selling yourself. You are the product and the service.

I know freelancers who are excellent salespeople, but on balance I'd say more of my freelance connections dislike selling than like it. Whatever your feelings, if you want to work as a freelance expert, sales is going to be something you will have to get used to doing. In this chapter I want to increase your confidence that you can sell. I will help you understand that, if you have followed the advice so far in this book, selling is not hard.

The need to sell

Tom Hodgkinson, among other things author of *Business for Bohemians*, wrote: 'Things do not, very sadly, sell themselves'. This is obvious, but it needs pointing out as it is too often forgotten. The world is full of people who bemoan that no one buys their wonderful products or services, but they have not really tried that hard to sell them. They will probably be bemoaning their sale-free fate until the end of time.

Unfortunately, no-one will beat a path to your door to ask for your service (at least not until you have a well-known reputation). You must actively sell. A little later, in the same book, Hodgkinson adds: 'Those of us who have ambitions to retain some autonomy over our working life and use our own creativity must, to some extent, out ourselves in the role of salesperson.'

Here is an important point. Selling yourself should not be viewed as some painful necessity like going to the dentist. It is the act which enables you to be independent. When you put it like that, it starts to become something you feel good about.

Even if you refuse to budge on your feelings and decide to resolutely hate the idea of selling, you need to develop some sales ability if you want to build a freelance business. The good news is that selling yourself as a freelance expert does not need to be difficult. In my experience, anyone can sell themselves if they think about it a little. You are not trying to sell ice to Eskimos. You are trying to sell yourself and the service you provide to clients who need help.

In this chapter I'm going to give you some things to think about, then explore some practical steps to writing proposals and dealing with Terms and Conditions, before finishing with exploring how to make sure you get paid.

The sales basics

You should have a good basis for selling if you have followed the advice in this book so far. You now have a clear niche and a vision of the clients it is suitable for. You have done your marketing, and you have started to have some valuable conversations with potential clients. You have a compelling pitch to discuss with those clients. At this point you have done most of the hard work. You just now need to answer the question: 'How do you convert your conversation into a sale?'

Firstly, when you talk to clients it must be obvious that you are selling. Even if it's a friendly chat, make clear that you are interested in selling to them. Not every conversation is going to lead to sales, but every conversation should be considered as a contribution towards selling. Don't be shy. Now is not the time for subtlety. If you are selling, people need to know you are trying to sell to them.

I originally found this difficult. Perhaps this is because I am English. I am not making a claim, I am just making a factual statement. Like any cultural background, it comes with pluses and minuses. One of the minuses is that English people can be a little indirect when it comes to selling. We hint and expect people to magically pick up on our hints. I have learnt this does not work. Your potential clients need to clearly know that you are looking for work, and that you think they could be your client.

On the other hand, you do not need to ram this down their throats like some high-pressure second-hand car salesperson. But at some point in a conversation with a potential client, you must make it clear you are looking to sell your services to them. If they don't want to buy, hopefully they will clearly tell you in return that they won't, so you can avoid wasting time trying to sell to someone who is not interested.

Secondly, remember people always need help. To update John Donne's famous line – *no person is an island*. None of us can do everything alone. All of us at some point need help – every individual, business and organisation in the world. They all need help now and again. Some of them need help all the time. Better still, many of them actively want and are seeking help and have the resources to pay for it. One way to think about selling your services, is not as selling at all, but instead as helping the client to decide what they are going to buy.

Let's not over-emphasise the challenge of trying to sell yourself as a freelance expert. Generally, you do not need to create client demand for your services, you need to find it.

The three steps to selling

When you get an opportunity to sell to a client there are three main steps.

1 Convincing the client that they need to buy the service you have
2 Convincing the client to specifically buy from you
3 Closing the sale by agreeing the terms that are mutually acceptable.

In all of these, you need to move beyond generics into the specific needs, wants, constraints and desires of an individual client. In most cases, if you are even talking to a client, it means they are some way towards a sale, and recognise they want help. Mostly you will be nudging them towards buying your service rather than starting from ground zero.

When they buy any form of expertise, the client is looking for help, but they are not looking for exactly the same help as anyone else. They are looking specifically for the help they need. Now, this is not to say that clients do not have similar problems which require similar expertise. Of course, they do! But what is important to them, and what will encourage them to decide to buy your services, varies from person to person.

This is why good salespeople generally start conversations with questions. They want their clients to answer questions which enable them to understand the motivations and desires of the person in front of them. Then they tailor their sales messages to the answers given by the person they are talking to. These can be quite general questions of the form: What are you looking for? What would make your life easier? What would be a great outcome for you? What is valuable to you? How much money do you have to spend?

The more you talk about the client and their needs, and the less you talk about yourself and your service, the more likely you are to sell.

If you want to sell, ask yourself what client needs does your service fulfil? Start by thinking through why anyone needs the help you have on offer. From this you can work out what things you are going to say about your service to encourage the client to buy it. But, as you talk with the client you will discover specific things about them as individuals, and your sales messages should be tailored to those specifics. And never forget – you are not selling to yourself. Don't think about what you might like, try to discover that this client wants.

You do not need a hundred and one sales messages. Usually half a dozen points you can talk about are enough. Selling is not about having multitudes of good reasons for your clients to buy, it is about having a few compelling reasons to buy.

Unfortunately, all your great sales talk can go to waste if you convince a client that they need to buy a service of the type you offer, but you do not convince them that you are the right person to buy it from. Sometimes, just because you are the person talking about a service means the client will carry on and buy it from you. But not always, and you should not confuse a client realising that they want to pay for some help, with them deciding they will pay for you.

Hence, you not only need to have some messages about why your service is so great and will fit with this client's needs, you need to have some messages to explain why you are best placed to help them. There is, after all, almost always someone else providing a similar service.

We summarised these in your pitch, but it's good to have a variety to be attractive to different clients. One client might be worried about price, another about how quickly you can do your work. Your sales messages about you might be about your great experience, your price, your flexibility, your availability and so on.

You need to find some reasons why you are the right person, now and in this location, for this client. That does not mean you have to make yourself sound like the best in the world. Few of us are ever looking for the best help in the world. But it does mean you should make yourself sound like the right choice for the client here and now.

The right choice may be as simple as because you are ready and talking to the client now it saves them the effort of looking for anyone else. In other situations, the right choice might be decided by other factors such as price or experience.

There are lots of reasons clients buy from a specific person, but always remember three simple things.

1. Clients are more likely to buy from people they like, so try to be likeable!
2. Enthusiasm goes a long way to convince people you are great as an expert. So, try to sound excited and enthusiastic about what you are offering and your desire to work for this client. Enthusiasm can often make up for a lack of expertise.
3. Clients want someone they can trust. So, try and come across as trustworthy. Be honest, be authentic, be open and generally do all those things that make you trust other people. Yes, some salespeople can successfully use manipulative methods to get people to buy almost anything. But most of us can't, and if you want a long-term relationship with your clients then openness and honesty go a long, long way.

Once you have got the client to the point in which they want to buy your services, you now can move onto agreeing the details.

The logic of the freelance sales conversation

Let's assume you have a potential client you are just about to talk to. What should you say to them? There are lots of things to think about in these situations, which at first may seem hard. Don't worry if to begin with you do not remember everything. Selling is like most things – practice makes perfect.

I am always a bit suspicious of the boilerplate sales technique. You and your service are unique, and you and your clients are unique. There is no universally right thing to say, or wrong thing to say. But there is a general flow of where you should be trying to lead the conversation if you are trying to sell.

I think of this flow in four logical steps.

1 *Provide insights to your client:* you want your client to buy a service from you. The first thing you want to do is to get your client interested, and to show your credibility. When your service is based on expertise, the best way to do this is to share some insights about that service. I'm thinking of statements like: '64% of people find this useful', 'the best investment strategy is . . . ', or 'typically, this will last 10 years'. They do not have to be unique or original, although it helps if they are, but they do have to show a level of understanding about your area of expertise. And insights are not about you, they are general ideas or concepts you are giving for free to show you are an expert in your field.

2 *Explain why your service matters to them:* next, explain why the service you are offering is important, helpful or useful to them. A lot of freelancers talk about themselves and lose sight of the fact that the client wants a service because they have a need. Talk about this client need, and how you can fulfil it and the way you can add value. Start with the five reasons clients hire freelancers described in Chapter 3 and, as you find out more, become more specific.

3 *Describe the benefit they will get by buying your service:* what will be the tangible benefit or value the client will get from your service. Sometimes this will be about a monetary value, but only occasionally. Value comes in many shapes and forms and is specific to the client. If you listen to what they talk about and stress, you can usually pick up what is valuable to them. It might be money, but it might be saving them time or reducing their hassle. Tell them how your service will provide this value.

4 *Talk about yourself and your track record:* I think this should be the last thing you talk about, but you do need to be prepared to talk about it. The first three points I have described should get a potential client to the point in which they are interested in buying a service. To move this on to the point they are interested in buying you, you need to show your personal credibility while you are doing this.

As you have this conversation you should be doing one other important thing – and that is building a relationship with the client. We are going to explore this a lot more in later chapters, especially Chapters 12 and 13. But in summary you want your clients to feel you are the right person for them to do business with. You can do this by listening well to them, talking to them in their sort of language rather than yours and by building trust with them. Put simply, we all prefer to do business with people we think respect us and like us. Show respect and try to be likeable.

In reality, different clients start from different positions when it comes to selling to them. Some have only vaguely thought about your service before, while others are actively seeking help. In Table 9.1 I outline four positions clients are in, and what you should do in each of these.

Table 9.1 Client position relative to your service

	The client position	What you want...	Therefore...
1	The client will never need your service	Not to waste time, but get any benefit you can	▪ Make the conversation short – else you risk wasting your time and theirs. ▪ Ask if the client knows anyone else who might need the service who they will introduce you to. It's worth a go!
2	The client does not need your service now, but may in future	The client to remember you and contact you when they need help	▪ Focus on providing insights. This shows you know what you are talking about and builds a relationship for future sales. ▪ Get the client's contact details so you can stay in touch and regularly remind them about your service, so they do not forget you.
3	The client wants help, but does not know if they need your exact service	The client to understand why they need the service and to move them to position 4 in this table	▪ Go through steps 1 to 3 of the sales conversation from the list above. If they are interested, move onto the next position of this table. ▪ If you don't succeed, get the client's contact details and ask permission to contact them again in a few weeks. Often clients take some time to realise they need a service. Don't close doors you can keep open!
4	The client already needs help of the type you provide, but is not yet convinced to buy from you personally	To agree to buy from you	▪ Focus on steps 3 and 4 from the list above. From step 3 you show you understand them, and then build on this by explaining yourself and your track record. ▪ If they decide to buy, agree a price and the other terms. ▪ If you don't succeed, get the client's contact details and ask permission to contact them again in a few days. Often clients take some time to buy or buy from someone else and find it was a mistake. Don't close doors you can keep open!

Agreeing the price

You will get lots of different advice on pricing. You can make pricing into a science. Most independents don't have the time for this, but it is still worth thinking about carefully. If you have followed the advice I gave in Chapter 6, you will know your minimum price you will sell at, and the price you would ideally like to get. Having these numbers in mind is important, but an actual sales conversation can lead you astray. Let's think about how you present your price to your potential client.

The most important point to me is to be clear what price you want for your service – whether that is time based or value based. If you are not clear about the price you want, any negotiations become hopeless. Generally, clients will want to explore and negotiate prices, especially if you are selling to other businesses.

When you are lucky, there will be no negotiation. A client will simply accept the price you offer or will immediately walk away once they realise you are talking about more than they want to spend. Don't worry if some clients walk away, that is normal. Not everyone is ready to pay what you need. That's life.

The second most important thing about pricing is to be clear about your walk-away price. This is the minimum you will accept. The reason this is important to know is that, if you don't, there is a risk that a clever client, or one with little money, will talk your fees down and down until you have agreed to do some work at a price that is not worthwhile for you. Having a walk-away price, that you are willing to walk away at, makes negotiations much easier and less stressful. Always remember the client has a choice – so do you. You may not be right for this client, and they might not be right for you.

The third important aspect of pricing is not to confuse price with value. Prices is an absolute thing. £500 is £500 to everyone in the world. Value is relative. What a specific service is worth varies hugely from client to client. A new website is worth a few hundred pounds to some people, but tens of thousands to others. Everyone values different things differently. Some clients will find your prices too high, other will think the very same prices are a bargain.

To maximise your revenue, you are aiming to understand how valuable your service is to your clients, to find those clients who value it most highly and to price accordingly.

If you have agreed a price with your client, selling is not yet over. Before you finish talking about money with your clients there are a few details to iron out. Your fees are not the only monetary aspect you must agree with your client.

There are payment terms. These essentially define how quickly you expect to be paid. If your clients are individuals, there is no reason you should not be paid quickly. Why not ask for your money up front or straight after doing the work? If your clients are businesses, they will usually have predefined payment terms. These are worth understanding before you begin. Some of these can be quite extended, but feel free to try and negotiate them. Everything is negotiable to some extent.

You may have taxes, such as VAT (sales tax), to add to your fees. Taxes vary from country to country, so ask an accountant if you do not know. You need to be clear whether your fees include or exclude VAT. Not only do taxes vary, so do client's responses to having to pay them do. For example, right now, VAT is 20% in the UK. For individuals this means the work will cost 20% more than your fees alone. A 20% increase may put some individual clients off. However, for most businesses VAT can be reclaimed, and they may not care either way whether you must charge it or not – but they do need to know.

Finally, you may want to charge back your expenses for doing the work, for example travel costs. If so, you need to let the client know, as they need to make sure they have enough money to cover them as well.

Other terms to agree and information you need

Price is not the only thing you need to agree with your client. There will normally be other conditions for a successful working relationship. Some of these are mundane administrative points, others are core to the service you are providing. They vary depending on the service you provide – but let me give you a few examples from my work so you get a sense of what I am talking about.

Some of my work takes place in my client's offices. With this in mind, the mundane details I need to agree include: Who is going to meet me when I arrive? Will I get an access pass to the building? Where can I park – or where is the nearest public transport? Will I get access to their systems or should I bring my own laptop?

There is nothing complex about any of these, but without sorting them out it's hard for me to work successfully. I suggest you write a list of all the things you need to agree before you can work with a client. In my experience, clients do not mind you producing a list of such items. In fact, it shows that you know what you are doing.

When it comes to the core conditions of the work, the sort of questions I need to know are: When is the work expected to be completed by? What does the client expect to be different or to have when I have finished? Who will help me do my work? Are there any stakeholders I need to be aware of or careful about? I can draw up a long list of such questions.

You can see such a list in my book *The Management Consultant: Mastering the Art of Consultancy*. That list is specific to being a consultant, but there will be similar things you need to know before you can start your work. I have included a tailored version of it here as an example (see Table 9.2). Use this as a starting point to create your own checklist.

Table 9.2 Core points to clarify before starting a consulting engagement

Engagement planning and resourcing checklist	Yes	No
Do you understand the constraints in terms of timescale and resources that your proposal places on your engagement plan?	☐	☐
Do you understand the deliverables or outcome required from the engagement?	☐	☐
Do you understand the process by which you will get to the desired result (including whether you will work as a process or expert consultant)?	☐	☐
Does the client understand this process and agree with it?	☐	☐
Are the organisational scope / boundaries of the engagement agreed? (Departments, divisions, processes included in scope and out of scope.)	☐	☐
Have you included your engagement management process in the plan? Does this include all actions required by your consulting firm?	☐	☐
Are you clear about what data will be available and the level of effort to extract useful information?	☐	☐
Have you considered how Quality Assurance will be performed if it is necessary?	☐	☐
Have you defined an engagement management process taking account of the need to interact with the client, the engagement team and consulting management?	☐	☐
Are the engagement management meetings scheduled in attendees' diaries?	☐	☐
Are there any significant engagement risks you need to build into the engagement plan?	☐	☐

Engagement planning and resourcing checklist	Yes	No
Do you understand the resources you require to complete the engagement?	☐	☐
Do you have access to all the resources you need (or a process to get access to them)?	☐	☐
Do the resources have the necessary skills and time available to work on the engagement?	☐	☐
Does everyone working on the engagement (client and consultant) understand their role and activities in line with the engagement plan?	☐	☐
Have you included all the activities required to close the engagement down, and to sustain any change resulting from the engagement?	☐	☐

Adapted from Table 7.1, Chapter 7, *The Management Consultant: Mastering the Art of Consultancy*
© Richard Newton, 2019

You may feel that some of these terms can be left to sort out until after you have made a sale. This can be a good approach, as bringing in too many questions before closing a sale can just get in the way of selling and make it seem as if you are nit-picking. If you choose to take this approach, it is at least worth mentioning to the client that you will have some other points you need to sort out before you can start working.

Sorting out your paperwork

The final stage before you have made a sale is to get the paperwork sorted out. Whether this really is physical paperwork or something like a trail of emails depends on the client, the size of your work and the risk associated with it.

The reason for writing things down is partially contractual. You may want some legal basis to the work. Should a client prove slippery later in paying you, then you have some grounds for a claim. But at least as important as ensuring you get paid, is that paperwork can help in confirming that your expectations about the work are the same as the clients.

It's just a feature of human beings – we can spend hours talking about something and think we are talking about the same thing, but a few days later find out we were talking about different things or misunderstanding each other. I always recommend writing down what you think the client has asked you to do, for what price and under what conditions. This does not need to be a long or complex document. For a simple piece of work a few bullet points on an email are sufficient. The client then reads this and either agrees or comes back with changes. Sometimes it takes a few iterations between you and the client to get the paperwork right. Doing this may seem like a pain, but it will save you lots of hassle later on.

It is much more likely that you have aligned understanding from the written than the spoken word. After all, in English, to show we have a mutual understanding, we do say that 'we are on the same page' for this very reason.

I have done small pieces of work for clients based purely on a verbal agreement without any formally documented contract. But I try to avoid this except with a handful of clients I have known for years and who I do regular work with. It comes down to trust and risk.

For any large piece of work, which for me can be several weeks to several months, or any work which I think has risks associated with it, I insist on a written document signed by me and the client. As I work mostly with large corporations, that document is usually based on their standard contracts, not mine. You can try to insist on your contract, but if you are negotiating with a major corporation this is generally a lost cause – they have rooms full of lawyers who need something to do!

When you choose to ask a lawyer about contracts, they are always going to advise you to have as close as possible to a watertight legal contract before starting any work. If you think you need this, then it's best to go and get legal advice from someone qualified to do it. I do not have a set of standard terms and conditions that I give to my clients, but if you want to do this it is worth getting those drafted by a lawyer.

Whatever you do, do not try and be a lawyer yourself, unless you have trained as one. Do not cobble a contract together from bits and pieces of old contracts you have seen. All those terrible contracts I have seen written in an awful half-understood legalese are not worth the paper they are written on. In the unfortunate situation that you did get into a legal dispute, any good lawyer would tear them apart in a few minutes.

If you are not going to use a lawyer, write your agreement down in simple, plain, clear, everyday language that both parties understand and get both parties to sign the document. It may not be legally watertight, but it's going to be good enough for most situations. This is all I have ever done with my dozens and dozens of clients and I have never had any problems.

Writing your sales proposal and including the small print

Most of the time, I find a relatively simple proposal letter or email is sufficient to contract with a client. You write this, and ask the client to confirm, in writing that they agree with it. The language varies depending on whether you work as a self-employed person, or you provide your services through a company.

Table 9.3 shows a template structure to give you some broad guidance.

Table 9.3 Outline proposal template

Introduction	Very briefly note why you have been driven to write this proposal. It is usually a request from the client in a meeting or a phone call. I often write something like 'as we have been discussing in the last few weeks, I'm now writing to share my proposal for . . . Please read this carefully as it will form the basis of my work.'
I am going to . . .	Describe the activities you are going to perform on behalf of the client.
Which will give you . . .	Describe what this will give the client or what the outcome of the work will be. It could be a physical thing like a document or report, or it might be something intangible such as new skills, confidence. Whatever it is, describe it here.
By this date . . .	When you expect the work to start and be completed. Say that the completion date is subject to being able to start by this start date.
For me to be able to do this, I need you to . . .	Describe what you need the client to give you to be able to fulfil your work. Typically, these are things like some of their time to attend meetings, access to information or their offices and so on. Describe why this is important. Include the essentials, but try to not make it too long or it is off-putting.
For this I will charge . . .	Define your fees, noting any additional taxes and whether there will be expenses. Is it a fixed fee, by unit of time spent or some other basis?
Which needs to be paid by . . .	Say how you need to be paid – up-front, in-arrears (within how many days of completion) or as you progress. Also include how you want to be paid, and the necessary details (e.g. bank sort code and account number).
The next steps are . . .	Describe what happens now. I usually say something like 'Can you please confirm, in writing your agreement to this proposal. Once I have that I will phone you to agree how I will start this work, and when we will first meet. If there is anything you disagree with, please call me and we can talk it through so I can produce an updated proposal.'
Please confirm your agreement to this by . . .	Unless you know and trust your client absolutely, then insist on some form of written confirmation. If your proposal is a letter, leave a space for your client to sign and return it to you confirming acceptance.
Please see my attached standard terms and conditions	If you have a set of standard T&Cs include them as a separate attachment.

Other than the proposal, there is the small print or the Terms and Conditions. There is no standard set of T&Cs that are valid for all sorts of freelance experts. It depends on the work you do, its scale, the type of clients you have, and the nature of the risks associated with it. Generally, the larger the work, the bigger the business you are dealing with and the greater the risk of liability, the more formally you will need to contract with them and the more likely it is that you should have standard T&Cs.

I have never written my own T&Cs and never suffered because of this. However, I know freelancers who have them and find them helpful.

If you do want to write some T&Cs, this is one time it is good to spend a little money and seek legal advice. There are a lot of unforeseen meanings and implications of what you do and do not include, and the precise wording used. This is the domain of lawyers. Alternatively, if you belong to a professional body associated with your area of expertise, they may provide default standard sets of T&Cs or free advice on them.

Examples of the main areas I expect to be covered in T&Cs are shown in Table 9.4.

Table 9.4 Typical topics for a terms and agreement statement

Governing law	The legal jurisdiction which your work will be subject to.
Payment terms	Details of payment information including penalties for late payments.
Variation clauses	How the contract may and may not be changed midway if the client or you wish to change it.
Client failures	What happens if the client can't fulfil their agreed part of the work – e.g. do you still get paid, and if so, how much?
Your inability to fulfil the work	What happens if you cannot do your work, e.g. through illness etc.? Generally, you are trying to avoid the situation in which there are penalties for factors outside of your control.
Any copyright, intellectual property considerations	For example, can the client share the work you do for them with other people, or must they keep it to themselves? If the client re-uses anything you produce, must they make reference to you?
User guidelines	Where appropriate rules, restrictions, requirements on the use of your service – or a reference to where these are documented.
Warranty disclaimers and limitations	Limits to your liability relating to your service, and any limitations placed on the client on the use of any outputs from you.
Termination	How to terminate the service, including notice periods and what payments will be due if this happens.
Dispute resolution approach	What happens if there is a dispute. Essentially, this part is trying to avoid costly legal action and seek simpler and quicker processes like direct conversation or arbitration.
Contact details	In case of need to discuss these terms and conditions or to flag any breach in them.

Making sure you get paid – on time!

One of the concerns that many people starting a freelance career have is how to make sure that their clients pay them. I am going to explain the key things to think about to help to ensure that you do. I also want you to be calm about this. It is relatively rare. I have never not been paid for anything I have ever done for a client across many years of work. I have occasionally been paid very slowly and that can be more of a problem.

Anyone can fail to pay a bill, but there are common patterns. I find individuals are generally good at paying their bills. Small businesses vary in terms of their performance. Some are great, but some are masters at delaying. The worst organisations for slow payment, in my experience, are large corporations. They almost always pay, but it can be late.

Sometimes this is not through any deliberate action on behalf of the corporation, but simply that they are big lumbering beasts. Paying a small invoice to an individual freelancer can get caught up in payment processes that were designed for dealing with other major corporations, which often means long payment terms.

As a freelance consultant I have only once had a problem with late payment across hundreds of invoices. As a freelance writer, it happens all the time and publishers are some of the slowest payers I know, but they always do pay. Eventually!

I am going to explore the approach to avoiding bad debt in five steps:

- Ways you can remove the risk of not being paid
- Ways you can reduce the likelihood of not getting paid
- Ways you can reduce the impact of not getting paid
- Dealing with late payment
- Handling not being paid

Removing the risk of not being paid: bill in advance

There is one sure fire way of making sure you get paid for your work, and that is not to do the work until you have been paid. Ask for your money up front. Not everyone can do this, and not every client will accept it, but if you can do it, then do it. It tends to be applicable to people selling services in relatively small chunks. For instance, I know coaches and article writers who insist on being paid up front.

Before you imagine this is impossible, remember this is becoming more common. There are services you probably pay for in advance without thinking about it. An element of most phone bills is paid in advance. My dry cleaner and my shoe mender, for instance, always insist on being paid in advance.

If you do want to bill in advance, present it as part of your standard terms and conditions when you talk with a client. Be realistic, in that clients will not part with large amounts of money up front, especially with someone they do not know. But if you are offering them a few hours work, then why not ask for your money first?

Reducing the likelihood of not being paid

If you can't be paid up front, how can you reduce the risk of not being paid? Large businesses do this by credit checking new customers. Mostly, this is a luxury a freelancer cannot afford. But there are ways you can reduce your risk.

- *Build client trust:* when a client has paid you several times before, the chances are that they will again. Of course, you want new clients, but there is always a risk with an unknown party. I have had some clients I have done work remotely for, in other countries. It would be a nightmare for me to get payment if they chose not to. In this situation, I try to do a small piece of work first. If they don't pay, I won't work for them again. If they do, I start to trust them, and I am more relaxed about doing something bigger.

- *Make sure your terms are clear and the client understands them:* including the situation with regard to VAT and expenses, and penalties for late payments if you include them. Sometimes late payment comes down to misunderstanding. This is avoidable.

- *Make sure the client has the money to pay:* ask them in advance of starting your work. You have to take their word, but it is still worth asking when you start. A simple question like 'Do you have the budget for this?' usually works. If they say no, then don't do the work, or explore how they might find the money.

- *Invoice clearly and correctly:* make sure your invoice is clear and easily understandable, both in terms of the amount and how it relates to your work. Also make sure it is correct. A simple error, by you, can delay payment by weeks. Ask your accountant to check your invoices if you are not sure how to do this.

- *Deliver what you said you would:* to be paid, you need to have done the work you agreed to do. Some issues arise if this changes as the work progresses. If what is required changes, agree this in writing, along with any impact on fees as you go along. You want to avoid arguments over whether you deserve to be paid. (See Chapter 10 for dealing with changes.)

- *Manage your clients' expectations:* give clients a friendly warning with statements like 'it's now time for me to invoice you, and you will be getting a bill from me, as agreed, in a few days' time'. This avoids many problems.
- *Hold back work:* for some sorts of freelancers, you can hold back some of the work until you have been fully paid. This needs to be done sensitively, as it could damage relationships and be seen as untrusting and aggressive if handled poorly.
- *Build client relationships:* clients are more likely to pay you if they like you and understand your situation. As you work with a client try and develop a good relationship. I know this sounds ridiculously simple, but it works.

Reducing the impact of not being paid

If you think that there is nevertheless a sizeable risk that some of your clients will not pay, you can reduce the impact of this on yourself.

- *Bill regularly:* if your work is going to take some weeks or months do not bill it all at the end. Set up to bill the clients in stages as the work progresses. This way, if you are not paid, it will only be for part of the work. This is very common, and you should never hesitate in suggesting staged payments to your customers. For long engagements, I always bill monthly, not at the end. As a variant on this, for some foreign clients who I would struggle to chase after the work is completed, I have asked for 50% of my payment in advance.
- *Have multiple clients:* ideally if one customer does default you should have other customers, so this one non-payment does not cause you serious problems. This is fine for many freelancers, but many consultants or interim managers have only one client at a time and so this will not work for everyone.
- *Have cash reserves:* as I said earlier in the book, try to build up cash reserves. One reason for this is that business will sometimes be lean. Another is so any bad debt does not cause you too much damage.

Dealing with late payment

Once in a while, a customer will be late, and lateness may be the first step in not paying at all. I suggest several steps that should be part of your normal routine:

- *Confirm the client got the bill:* bills do end up in email spam boxes and getting lost in the post. A quick call to ask 'Did you get my bill?' avoids this problem and means it can't be used as an excuse by the client either. Call soon after sending the bill.

- **Keep on top of it:** contact the client as soon as the bill is late. Keep this friendly, even saying something like 'I think you may have forgotten my invoice'. As soon as a bill is overdue, I send an email. As well as reminding, this gives me an audit trail in case it gets nasty. I always try to keep these friendly and polite.
- **Chase regularly:** don't be embarrassed, after all they owe you the money and would be chasing you if it was the other way around. Do not leave it a long time between prompts. Chase at least once a month in writing or email. If the bill is important to you, chase every week. Sometimes clients are short of cash and deciding who to pay. If you keep chasing it is more likely to be you.

When the client won't pay

If none of this works then we start to get into the areas that are, frankly, best avoided. They are time consuming, can be expensive and almost always give you a headache. But best avoided is not the same as never to be done. Don't get paranoid, as I stress most people pay, and needing to do these steps is rare, but in case someone resolutely refuses to pay, there are options.

- **Confirm with the client:** check why they haven't paid. This checks they have no good reasons for withholding, improves your understanding – especially if it is a lost cause like bankruptcy – and sometimes simply keeping in dialogue encourages payment.
- **Legal redress:** is the most obvious, but it can be expensive and complex. In the UK and some other countries there are efficient Small Claims Courts who can be effective, cheap and easy to use for small invoices. Often a solicitor's letter is enough to get the payment coming to you without actually going to court.
- **Debt collection:** you can sell your debt or use a specialist debt collecting agency. This is only worthwhile with a sizeable debt and you will not get 100% of the money.
- **Embarrass the client:** sometimes it can be tempting to try to embarrass someone into paying. With social media this is quite easy. My advice is to think very carefully before doing this. I never do this. I can't deny people who have struggled getting payment, suddenly receiving it after posting about it on social media. But you need to think how the non-paying client may respond, which may be unpleasant on you. Additionally, if your other clients see this, what it will make them think of you? Some will sympathise, but others will think of you in negative ways, which can damage your business.

There is another option and that is to do nothing. Take a breath and forget the debt. If it is a small debt, I suggest waiving it. I know this feels wrong, but you can spend lots of time, stress and energy chasing debts. Time you would be better off doing work for better clients. This is often the best solution. Of course, if this happens, never work for the non-paying client again!

An independent voice

Mike Lander, Piscari Limited

My name is Mike Lander, I've been working as a business advisor and management consultant for over 25 years. I have been fortunate enough to be trained by, and work for, some of the best consultancy brands in the world, e.g. KPMG, PwC, McKinsey and 4C Associates.

I've been a solo, expert advisor since 2016 working with small- and medium-sized enterprises in the £1m–£30m turnover range specifically in the Marketing Services, Recruitment and Consultancy sectors. I help my clients solve one of three specific problems:

- How do they improve the quality and consistency of their commercial negotiations, ultimately leading to higher growth and improved profitability?
- How do they scale their business towards £1m EBITDA (Earnings Before Interest, Taxes, Depreciation and Amortization), giving them the potential option to sell their business for >£6m?
- How do they improve their sales conversion rate and value when they meet professional procurement buyers in large companies?

I believe the advisory market is at the early stages of a fundamental transformation regarding how individuals and companies access expert advice. Advisors need to provide a blended access and pricing model including (but not limited to):

- Online courses
- Workshops and webinars
- Digital products
- One-to-one
- Masterclasses
- VIP retreats.

You can see my examples of this approach here

- https://piscari.com/
- https://piscari.podia.com/
- https://medium.com and and see my article 'Everything you need to know about selling to Procurement professionals – A sellers' guide to winning more deals'

- https://medium.com and see my article 'Why turning your knowledge into an asset as opposed to time-based billing is critical – or you will face extinction ultimately!'

My tips for anyone considering a freelance career

Whether this is the first time you've ventured into the world of being an expert advisor, or you are a seasoned veteran, these are my top tips to growing a sustainable 'practice of one':

- Clients only buy niche, deep expertise from expert advisors. Therefore, define your niche tightly and become the renowned 'go-to' expert.
- You now have to be your greatest sales asset. There is no-one else who is going to be out selling for you. You have no sales admin support, you have no lead generators working for you and you have no-one writing great marketing collateral. It's just you!
- As you define your niche, check the following:
  - Are people willing to pay for expertise in that niche – find precedents?
  - Will people pay enough to make it worth your while?
  - Is your niche big enough to give you a viable long-term business?
  - Is your niche a long-term problem, it can't be a fad (unless you can make a lot of money quickly).
- It's critical to understand the buying-cycle frequency. You want to avoid 'distressed purchasing' type problems as they are extremely difficult to market.
- Always remember, trust is a critical success factor whenever any client is buying some kind of expertise. Therefore, unless you already know the client, you need to build your credibility 6-18 months in advance of any purchase.
- You will need to build and maintain a sales funnel. Use one of the SaaS tools like https://www.pipedrive.com/
- As a solo expert, pricing is an art as much as it is a science. For an expert's advice on this, look at https://www.winwithoutpitching.com. I particularly recommend the section on pricing creativity.
- Assuming you are selling B2B services, LinkedIn is likely to be a golden source of leads for you. The reality is, if you are starting out as an expert advisor, >80% of your current LinkedIn contacts are likely NOT to be in your target, niche market. You need to define your niche audience and start connecting with them using tools like LinkedIn Sales Navigator. As a benchmark, you need to be growing your LinkedIn connections at the rate of 200 new connections per month to support your sales campaigns.

For more insights/ advice, you can email me at mike@piscari.com

chapter

10

Running your first engagement

For a long time, I have been an avid runner and a walker. A day without either a run or a walk always feels to me like an unsatisfactory sort of day. Part of the reason I like these activities is that all I need to do is put on my trainers, go outside and start. They are hassle free and easy, and as long as I am somewhere I can, come rain or shine, I will go outside for a run or a walk every day.

To a large extent freelancing is like this. Unlike being employed or setting up a more complex business with other employees, assets and systems, freelancing is simple. You just decide on your service and you do it. Well, perhaps it is not quite that simple as there are a few things for you to decide as we have covered in the previous chapters of this book, but it is hard to think of a simpler business than selling yourself to provide some service to another client.

If you have been following the advice in the book up until now, you are ready to put it all into action and start your first engagement. In this chapter I want to get you quickly into the mindset for your very first piece of work, as sometimes this can seem daunting. It should not be. This chapter's short length reflects that this should not be something that you see as hard or challenging. A bit like shutting the front door after you put your trainers on – you now just get on and do your thing!

Your first engagement

The first engagement you do as a freelance expert can be exciting as you realise that the dream of independence is now in your grasp. You may also feel a little nervous. That's normal; after all, you have a lot hanging on this.

You probably don't quite feel at ease with the process of being an independent service provider to your clients. It's not like your old job. You may be overly conscious that you have no track record or credibility in this field and are therefore feeling a bit of a fraud.

Calm down. We all go through these feelings and the vast majority of us survive this intact and go on to thrive. The stress may be unpleasant for a short time, but that little bit of adrenalin may also help you to work hard and to learn quickly.

What should you be thinking of on this first piece of work? The most important thing is to do a great job. If you do a great job, everything else will tend to flow on from it. But it's worth having a little space in your mind to reflect on how your work is going and to learn from the experience. We get better and better by learning. I think I am a substantially better expert and consultant than I was when I started, and this is because I often reflect and seek feedback. So, try to build the relationship with your client such that you feel they will be willing to give you some feedback.

On top of this, you of course want to be paid. Normally, doing a good job will ensure that happens, but make sure your client is clear about the fees and when you expect to be paid. Finally, think ahead and plan out how you might be able to jump from this client to future clients. Will they be willing to recommend you on to their network, or even give you a direct referral?

Once you have been working for a while and helped out a few clients this will all come naturally. But as when we learn anything new, to begin with you need to be a little more deliberate and conscious with your approach. I suggest you go through the short checklist given in Table 10.1. This sort of checklist can be used on every engagement, but is particularly important to use on your first assignment simply because everything is all new. When you have been freelancing for years, much of this will be automatic.

Table 10.1 Engagement checklist

	Task	Details	Done?
1	Make sure the client is ready	Contact the client and make sure they are ready for you to start your work. Confirm they have read your proposal, understand it and agree with it.	☐
2	Prepare before you start work	Think through the engagement, what you need to have at hand or have done before. (Look at the checklist in Chapter 7.)	☐
3	Make sure you have the logistics right	When, where, who and so on. This is simple to do, will make your work slicker and more professional, and will reduce your stress.	☐

	Task	Details	Done?
4	Plan out the steps of your engagement	You will almost certainly have to change this, but having a plan gives you confidence and it helps to give the client confidence too.	☐
5	Think about cultural fit	Does your style of talking, dressing, behaving and so on align with the clients? Don't over think this, as you don't have to try to force yourself to be exactly the same, but it helps to be 'comfortably' similar with the client and in line with their expectations for your role. For instance, don't wear a formal shirt if your clients wear t-shirts (unless your expertise is from the sort of profession which is always expected to wear a suit). Don't think of this sort of thing as a rule, more a common-sense guideline.	☐
6	Think about additional value you can give the client	As you work, is there any way you can give your client a little more than they expected? Often something small is enough, perhaps sharing a good article you read on a relevant topic for instance. It does not take much to flip some clients from reliable paying clients, into regular repeat clients who recommend you far and wide.	☐

Finally, as you start and every day from now onwards, don't just do your work, but also learn. You are your own boss now and your success is in your hands. Every day is an opportunity to get a little better and establish yourself as a freelance expert a little more. Of course, what you choose to learn is completely up to you. This is another wonderful aspect of independence.

Delivering your first engagement

You have made a sale and you are starting to deliver your service on your first engagement. All your hard work in setting up your business has paid off. You will apply your expertise and knowledge as you go along. Each of us will do this in our own way, dependent on the service we are offering.

There are, however, two things that I want to prepare you for:

1. What you should do if you find the engagement is starting to go wrong
2. What you should if, when you start working, the client changes the brief.

Sometimes, even with the best planning in the world and for the most expert freelancer, the engagement can go wrong. There will always be things you don't know at the start, which only become apparent as you go along. Most clients are good people to work with, but occasionally you will find a client who is difficult. From time to time something new will arise which you have not dealt with before.

The thing about things going wrong is, for some unknown reason, they are easier to deal with if you expect things to sometimes go wrong, than if you always expect things to be perfect. Just hold in mind that no other freelancer ever has perfect engagements, and you won't either. It's not avoiding all problems that is the sign of excellent freelancing, it is calmly resolving them when they happen.

How can you deal with this? I suggest the steps outlined in Table 10.2.

Table 10.2 Dealing with problems checklist

	Step	Done
1	Don't panic. The world is not going to end. Problems are a normal part of everyone's work.	☐
2	Don't ignore the problem. Sometimes problems just go away, mostly they do not.	☐
3	Reflect on the problem. Make sure you really understand what is going wrong and aren't jumping to conclusions or making wild assumptions. Then ask yourself: how could you overcome the problem or change the situation such that it resolves itself?	☐
4	If you cannot come up with a solution, try to talk to a more experienced freelancer. Sometimes simply putting out a question on social media of the 'how do you ... ?' gets good advice. Sometimes this is not appropriate. Mostly, I find other freelancers are more than happy to help.	☐
5	Talk to the client and keep them informed. Let the client know that there is an issue and talk it through with them as to how you might jointly overcome it. If you can't do your work, it's a problem for them as well, so they have an interest in sorting it out.	☐
6	Change your approach, applying the solution you have decided upon. Don't be afraid to experiment a little, trying to find quick ways to know if your solution is working or not.	☐
7	Keep the client informed and updated on your progress. This is not just about what you say, but how you say it. If you talk calmly and confidently about the issue, the client is more likely to remain calm, confident and helpful. If you start to show panic, so can the client, which won't help.	☐
8	When the problem is resolved tell the client that it's all ok now and they should not worry.	☐

The other thing that can happen on our engagements is that what we are setting out to do for the client can change. This happens for several reasons. Often, clients do not really know what they want until you start work, and through the process of working with them their minds change. Sometimes, as the engagement unfolds, your and the client's understanding improves and you both realise that you need to do something different. Finally, the world moves on, and even in a short engagement what was helpful at one point in time, may not be a short while later as the situation changes.

Change on engagements is normal, and it is something you need to learn to deal with. The risk with uncontrolled change is that you end up doing a lot more work for no more money, leaving you with unprofitable work. There is also a risk that you never satisfy the client and they damage your reputation.

To minimise this risk, I suggest the steps outlined in Table 10.3.

Table 10.3 Dealing with changes to the engagement

	Step	Done
1	Keep checking what you are doing against your original agreement with the client. It is easy to slowly drift away from the original client ask and only find out at the end of the engagement that you have not done what the client wanted.	☐
2	Don't immediately worry if the situation is changing. If there is a small variance between what you originally said you were doing, and what you are now doing, then treat this as normal.	☐
3	If the variation in what you are doing is becoming more significant – which means there is a risk the client won't be happy, it is going to take longer or cost more, or you will not fulfil what you have agreed to do in your contracted proposal – tell the client there is an issue and you need to talk. Don't present this as a problem, merely something you want to chat to them about. Change is normal.	☐
4	Plan through what the options are to deal with the change. Essentially there are three options: – Return to the original agreement. *Ask yourself: is this still helpful?* – Change to the new engagement, identifying any impact on timescale and cost. *Ask yourself: will you get paid and will the client be happy?* – Look for the best compromise, but still identifying any impact on timescale and cost.	☐
5	Discuss it with the client. Find out what they want and what they are willing to give in return if it is going to be much more work for you. Not all clients respond well to this, but most are fine. Remember, however the client responds, it will be better if you do this in a structured way. Hiding away and leaving it for a crisis at the end of the engagement is always the worst option.	☐

Table 10.3 (continued)

	Step	Done
6	Change your approach as agreed with this client.	☐
7	If the change is significant, and if it is going to change your fees, get written agreement from the client. This can be as simple as a confirmation on an email. Try not to leave it as a purely verbal agreement unless you know and trust the client well. This is as much for the client's benefit as it is for you.	☐
8	Deliver your new changed engagement	☐

Completing your first engagement

At some time, your first engagement will come to an end. Coming to the end of a client engagement is not like coming to the end of a novel, when you can just put it down and forget about it. To build great client relationships and to make sure you get paid, there are a few things you should do at the end of your engagement.

When you think you have finished your engagement, quickly go back and look at your proposal. Make sure you have done what you said you would do, or if it has changed as you go along, that your client is happy with the revised outcome.

Next simply tell your client that you are finished. This may be obvious, as for instance when an hour's coaching session comes to an end. But sometimes there are things you need to pass over to the client if your work results in some physical deliverable such as something written or created for the client. Check the client is happy with the output you have produced and sort out any small niggles that the client raises. You may also have borrowed things from the client which you now need to give back.

Then I always like to check the client is happy and agree the next steps. In most cases, if you have completed all the work that was agreed, the next step is simply to say you will contact the client again soon. This may sound trivial, but it is very important.

For successful businesses most of their clients are individuals and businesses who have been their clients before. You want to agree with the client that you will give them a call or drop them an email shortly after you finish. You can suggest this is to check that everything is going well, but for you it is all about building a relationship and making sure that the next time the client wants some work they come back to you. Put some reminders in your diary to contact the client now and again to keep in touch.

Table 10.4 Engagement closedown steps

	Have I . . .	Yes?
1	Checked I have done everything that was agreed and documented that I would do?	☐
2	Asked the client if they are happy with the outcome and sorted out any niggles?	☐
3	Returned anything the client gave me to do the work?	☐
4	Agreed the next steps, including a time to follow up with them?	☐
5	Sent in my final invoice?	☐
6	Reflected and learnt from the engagement?	☐
7	Stored away any useful materials?	☐

After this, you should send in your final bill. Make sure it is correct and is clear about what it relates to and contains numbers the client will recognise as the ones they agreed to pay you for the work you have done. Then you can wait to be paid. If you don't receive your money soon, you can follow the steps in Chapter 9.

That might seem like everything is done, but there are a couple more steps I suggest. Firstly, after this engagement and every future one, take some time to reflect on how it went, and learn how you can improve for future ones. Asking yourself these simple questions provides a good framework for learning: What went well that I should continue? What went badly that I should not do again? What didn't I do that I will do next time? Finally, make sure you have filed away any useful materials or contact details for the future. However, in doing this make sure you are only keeping materials the client is happy for you to keep, including their contact details.

Table 10.4 gives a short checklist of things to check after you have completed an engagement.

From your first engagement to brilliant engagements

So far in this chapter I have outlined the main areas to get right in running your first engagement. What I have described will help, but no doubt your first engagement will at times feel awkward and there will be moments when you think 'If only I had . . . '. These are the sorts of lessons that build experience. Even now, after hundreds of engagements, I find situations which, on reflection, I think I could have handled better.

In Chapter 11, I am going to go into running engagements in more detail. You may want to read that as well before you run your first engagement. But in my experience, it is only once you have done a few engagements that you will be ready to perfect the way you run yours and become brilliant at it. If you over-prepare you will probably be worrying too much about everything you need to get right, and you will come across as stilted, stressed and unnatural to your clients.

Relax a little. Do a few engagements. They won't be perfect, but they will be good enough. If you make a mistake, tell your client and fix it. Most clients are reasonable about this. The ones who are not are the sort you do not want as clients in the longer run.

When you have done this a few times start to take on board the lessons in the next part of this book. With experience you will become calmer and find you have the capacity to take on more of the ideas and approaches I suggest. You will also appreciate better why you should do these things, and that will make them easier to learn and put into practice.

An independent voice

Ciprian Rusen, Digital Citizen

My name is Ciprian Adrian Rusen, and I run a small publishing business under the Digital Citizen brand. I manage two publications with the same name: www.digitalcitizen.life and www.digitalcitizen.ro. Both have the same content in different languages: English and Romanian. We publish How-To content, product reviews, blog posts, and opinion articles about consumer-oriented technology products.

For example, we teach people how to use Windows, Microsoft Office, their Android phones and tablets, their iPhones, and so on. We also have a lot of niche content about specialized subjects, like Wi-Fi networks, routers, and other Wi-Fi equipment. If you want to buy a new router or improve the Wi-Fi coverage in your home, you should google *Digital Citizen* and read our articles from the *Smarthome* section. I am also a book author, having published many titles about software products like Windows 10, Windows 8, Microsoft Office, and more, with prestigious publishers like Wiley, Microsoft Press, Sybex, and others. If you are curious, you can find my books on Amazon.

To summarize, my business is about creating technical content that can be used by different audiences: people who use technology regularly but are not experts in the field, companies creating consumer-oriented hardware and software products, advertising agencies that want to distribute and sell online ads, and book publishers.

People read our content online to learn how to be productive and secure in their use of technology, while tech companies are interested in Digital Citizen because they can promote their latest products and educate audiences through the content that we create. On the other hand, advertising agencies are looking for popular sites like Digital Citizen to publish well-paid ads and generate revenue from the readers that click on them. Finally, book publishers are interested in contracting authors that are well-established and popular in their niche, who can produce great books and promote them to large audiences through their publishing platforms.

My tips for anyone considering a freelance career

My tips are based on the two things that made my Digital Citizen publications successful.

1 **Networking.** You might assume that this being an online publishing business, it is enough to create great content, and companies will come flocking, paying you generous fees for access to your audience. That is also what I thought when I started working in this business many years ago, and I couldn't be further from the truth. The reality was that, even though my websites had significant traffic and content, many companies would ignore Digital Citizen and keep working with others. To change that, I had to create a habit of going to public events and engage with marketers and companies relevant to my audience. I learned that tech companies did not choose to work with us because they did not know the people behind Digital Citizen. And because of that, they wouldn't trust and contact us. Things were problematic until I managed to start a small-budget collaboration with a famous brand and do successful projects together. After that, their competitors noticed, and they got curious to get to know us and work with us. Several years later, most of the major tech companies with branches in our country know our publications, as well as who we are, and are willing to work with us on different projects.

2 **Optimizing for Google and other platforms.** When you search online on building a successful blog, you find many experts (including Google) telling you that it is all about great content. Write the best articles you can, create the most engaging videos, and Google is going to discover them and rank them well, people are going to share them on social media, and so on. Unfortunately, great content is never enough. At least not enough to get noticed and grow a sustainable business. To be successful online, you must stay up-to-date with the latest demands from Google's indexing bot, with Facebook's algorithms, Twitter's technical constraints, and so on. The internet never sleeps, and Google, Facebook, and all the other big players change their rules and algorithms every month. You must optimize your content, blog, and YouTube channel and keep your platform relevant from an optimization perspective. Your content must be liked not only by people, but also by the bots that crawl the internet indexing websites. And that can sometimes lead you to an unexpected approach on how you create your content.

part

four

Developing your business and your expertise

chapter

Improving your engagements

In this final part of the book I am going to present some ways you can excel in your career and develop the business you dream of – earning the income you want with the levels of independence and freedom that you desire. It's always important to remember that when you work for yourself there is only one person who is going to worry about your personal and business development and that is you. This part will help you to grow your business and develop your skills.

The first topic in this part is going to look at how you can improve the way you run engagements, and eventually run excellent engagements. On reflection, you might think you should have done this before you ran your first engagement, but in my experience you need to do a few engagements first and then improve the way you do them. It's only when you have worked as a freelancer for a while, that the advice in this chapter will ring true.

There is a challenge in writing advice on improving your engagements. There are many types of freelance expert, and the ways we work with clients vary enormously. For some of us, a client engagement may be a one-hour meeting or even a short phone call with a single person, for others it could be running workshops for a few days with a group of people and for some it might be months involved in a major project situated on a client's business premises working with dozens of the client's team members.

Even given this variety, there are some common aspects to all client engagements. In this chapter I want to look at some of the key elements of running an engagement. I will look at these from two angles.

1 *The mechanics of an engagement:* that is the set of activities that you need to do on every engagement – the sort of tasks you can write on a checklist, and this chapter contains an example of such a checklist.
2 *Your behaviour on an engagement:* how you interact with your customers and build the lasting relationships that are the lifeblood of successful independent consultants, coaches and contractors.

The mechanics of client engagements

Client engagements are very varied. For some clients I have been paid for an hour's advice and we have never spoken again, while for others I have worked with them and their teams for years. Nevertheless, all of my engagements, and I think all of your engagements, go through five main stages.

- *Preparation:* what you need to do before you start working with the client
- *Initiation:* how you kick-off the engagement so you have the foundations for success
- *Delivery:* doing the work you do as an expert in a way that clients enjoy
- *Closedown:* how you bring your engagement neatly to a close
- *Epilogue:* activities you should do once the engagement is finished, both related to completing your work and maintaining your relationship.

Of course, the amount of time you can spend on each of these stages, and therefore how much detail you can go into, is going to be radically different between a one-hour client meeting and a six-month client project. Irrespective of this, there are some things you need to do in every situation.

Most of the time, new freelancers will work out how to run engagements, more or less well, on their own as they do their work. But once you have done a few engagements, it's easy to create a checklist to make sure you do it well, as there are risks of omitting or forgetting important tasks which could cause easily avoidable problems for you. Reflecting on these essential tasks, I note:

- For those very short engagements, an hour or less, there is a risk that you won't have the time to do everything. You need to decide what is most important. I recommend you at least think about doing the things I am going to suggest. For those who engage in very short pieces of client work, I want to help you to develop the habit of quickly checking that you have done all the things you should do.

- On the other hand, there is also a risk of omission for long engagements as well. Although you should have the time to do all the things I am going to suggest, it is easy to become complacent, over-confident or simply forgetful and leave things out.

The aim always for these tasks is to give your clients such a wonderful experience that they will be happy to pay your bills and suggest your services to people they know. On top of this, these tasks also should help you avoid getting into an administrative mess and reduce your risk of client problems.

I always think the best way of showing the mechanics of a client engagement is with a checklist. For me, such checklists are best considered as guidelines, not rigid sets of instructions. Our lives and our client's needs are too variable to have a fixed way of working. I don't follow them inflexibly, as situations vary and require different responses. Instead I think of checklists as helpful aide-mémoires. It is far too easy to forget important activities when concentrating on working with a client. Judging what to modify on a checklist is where experience really helps.

A little later in this chapter I provide the outline of a checklist you can use. I'm not suggesting this will exactly be the checklist you use, but I am recommending that you have one of your own and you can use this one as a good starting point. Copy it out, and then amend it to be specific for you.

But before I do this, let's look at each of the five stages of an engagement in turn.

1. Preparation

In the preparation stage, your aim is to make sure you and your client are ready for the work. There are lots of small things that need to be done before you can deliver that ideal experience to your clients.

For instance, one of these is as simple as checking the client is still intending to meet with you. That may sound trivial, but on several occasions I have turned up to meet a client, for a meeting arranged weeks before, and they had forgotten. I know I am far from unique in having this experience.

2. Initiation

You might be looking your client in the eye over steaming cups of coffee, on either ends of a phone call, or facing a device having an online meeting using Teams, Zoom, or Hangouts. Whichever it is, your engagement with a client normally starts with some kind of direct interaction. It might be a rather formal meeting, or a relaxed chat.

However your first meeting goes, the old adage 'first impressions count' should be remembered every time. The way you initiate your engagement matters hugely to how the client perceives you, how they build trust in you, and the ease with which they will work with you.

What makes a good first meeting? Ideally that you 'click' with the client and you have an open discussion. To help this be prepared. Think about the key questions you are going to ask, and the client will ask you. Try to look appropriate. I'm not trying to constrain your individuality or personality, but it makes it easier for someone to relate to someone else who looks as they expect.

From time to time we all mess up our first meeting with a new client. I certainly have done. You can recover from this, but it makes life hard. Harder than it needs to be. By starting well and setting the right impressions with your client you are going to make the whole experience more enjoyable, and usually more successful.

3. Delivery

Now is the time to get on with the work your client is interested in, and which you are hopefully excited by and enjoy doing. This stage is about meeting, or even better exceeding, your client's expectations. It is when you can really show your ability to help them, and that you are a worthy expert to have hired.

What you precisely do here depends on your service. In my book *The Management Consultant: Mastering the Art of Consultancy*, I describe Delivery in more detail as a five-step process with the steps Commence, Collect, Consider, Create and Counsel & Consult. This is more detailed than many freelance experts require, but if you want more detail – especially if you are a consultant – that process may be a useful reference for you.

4. Closedown

All work comes to an end, and you want your client engagement to come to a smooth and professional ending. First impressions may count, but so do last impressions. The way you slickly bring your engagement to an end continues to build client confidence, trust and respect. Most people quickly forget wonderful historic experiences of working with you if the last experience was poor. Unfortunately, the bad experiences stick in the mind. One of my respected peers, Dave Jepson, Chairman of Partners in Change, often says, 'you are only as good as your last impression'.

11 • Improving your engagements

The good news is that creating good last impressions, in most cases, is easy. You just need to be organised and thoughtful.

There is also a practical side to closing an engagement down – getting away from the client in time so the work is profitable! You do not want to spend more time working for a client than you need to. We have all had those conversations we just want to end, but somehow, we cannot get out of them, and time drags on, time we would rather spend doing other things. Being clear about what you need to do to bring the engagement to a close helps tremendously to avoid this.

5. Epilogue

The phone call may have ended. You may have driven away from the client's offices. The engagement is over, but usually that does not mean the work has quite ended yet. Normally, there are a range of small tasks you need to do. This might be as simple as updating your records, or it may be that tedious but critical task of ensuring your client has received a bill.

Let's bring that all together in Table 11.1, which builds on Tables 10.1 and 10.2 from the previous chapter. I stress again, this is a starting point for you. For some of you this will be 100% of what you need, for most freelancers it will be at least 80% of what you need, but you should add your own actions and flavour to it. In building your own checklist, I suggest you pay particular attention to the Delivery stage, and in particular task 3.1, as this is where your own specialisation and service line is applied.

Table 11.1 Engagement checklist

Task	Done?
Preparation	
1.1 Confirm time and place of first meeting with client	☐
1.2 Complete any pre-work required to start the engagement	☐
1.3 Think through the initiation of the engagement: What will you discuss and ask you client? What will they ask you that you should be prepared to answer?	☐
1.4 Have materials prepared and at hand for initial client meeting if any are required	☐
1.5 Check logistics for travel (e.g. route, parking, building access) or for remote meeting (e.g. platform to use, contact details/ID)	☐

Table 11.1 (continued)

Task	Done?
Initiation	
2.1 Greet client appropriately	☐
2.2 Reconfirm purpose and expectations. Confirm length of first discussion	☐
2.3 Reconfirm length of engagement and how it will work	☐
2.4 Check that nothing has changed for the client and they are ok to proceed	☐
2.5 If anything has changed for you, advise client	☐
2.6 If you think necessary, confirm fees	☐
(I never do this as it was covered in my written proposal, but I know some experts who feel this is required as clients have claimed to be surprised at the fees at the end. It's best to avoid such problems, and in most cases very easy to do so with a quick confirmation at the start of the engagement.)	
2.7 Confirm the client is happy to commence, and agree next time you will talk	☐
Delivery	
3.1 Provide your client service	☐
3.2 Maintain levels of energy, enthusiasm and engagement	☐
3.3 Progress your work in line with the time you have available	☐
3.4 If an unexpected problem occurs, react calmly and resolve it with the client (see Table 10.2 for the steps to do this)	☐
3.5 If, as the work progresses, the situation changes, the client decides they want something different or you have mis-planned, discuss with your client and agree how to handle (see Table 10.3 for the steps to do this)	☐
3.6 Manage your client's expectation as you progress, and regularly and explicitly flag how it is going to them *(e.g. we are now half-done and I just need to . . . , or we are going a little slower so I want to speed up now etc.)*	☐
3.7 As appropriate, check back against original agreement for the work and ensure you are aligned with it	☐
Closedown	
4.1 Indicate to the client clearly that the engagement is coming to an end, and that they will soon receive the final invoice	☐
4.2 Confirm that you have what you need to provide and complete your service	☐
4.3 Check if the client has any outstanding questions, and answer them	☐
4.4 Agree next steps (if any)	☐
4.5 Confirm contact details	☐
4.6 Thank the client and advise you will contact them again (even if the work does not require it!)	☐
Epilogue	
5.1 Send out / follow up with any feedback or other materials as agreed	☐
5.2 Ask for feedback	☐

	Task	Done?
5.3	If the feedback is positive, ask for recommendations or referrals, perhaps even a quote for social media or your website	☐
5.4	Invoice the client and check payment has been made	☐
5.5	Update your records and administration as required	☐
5.6	Mark diary to periodically contact the client again – remember the best business is repeat business	☐
5.7	As you find new situations in which the client could do with your help, go back into sales mode and win some more work. If it is a repeat client, this should get easier each time	☐

Your behaviour on client engagements

One side of successful client engagements is what you do. The other side is how you do it. It can be surprising, but often how you interact with the client is more important than what you do. Of course, clients want you to have the expertise you claim to have, but at least as important is how they find the experience of working with you.

Is it a pleasure? Do you develop trust? Do they have confidence in what you say? Do they look forward to working with you again? None of these depends solely on what you say or act – but often more on how you say it and behave.

You can find a million and one sets of advice about how you should interact with your clients. In my career I have come across all sorts of theories and tools for having better interactions with clients, including NLP (Neuro-Linguistic Programming), Emotional Intelligence, Process Consulting and Transactional Analysis. I know some freelancers who invest a lot of time and effort learning the tools, techniques and theories associated with these and other bodies of knowledge.

If you do intend to learn some of these techniques, my advice is to learn them sufficiently. The world is full of people who have done 2 minutes reading on NLP or read a 10-minute article on coaching and who think they can apply the techniques. Often the shallowness of the understanding is quickly apparent and a little embarrassing. You don't need to be a world-class expert, but you do need to be competent.

Clients are intelligent and will see through your attempts to use a technique you do not understand. If you decide a technique is for you, try to gain a level of mastery of it, not just acquire a few buzz words! Focusing on a few buzz words is the behaviour that has given consultants and other experts a bad name for many people. A shallow understanding of a technique may get you through one situation, but it does not build relationships or trust.

What is definite is that it is important to develop an awareness of how your behaviour and your communication style effects your clients. If you think you are saying the right things, but somehow are not gaining clients or not convincing them of the value of your advice, it is probably down to how you are presenting this information, or how you have gone about developing relationships.

My interpersonal skills as a consultant have developed from several sources. Firstly, direct personal experience and learning from situations that have gone well and gone badly with clients. Some of the worst experiences have, ironically, been the most valuable in the longer term as I learnt a lot from them. When it does all go wrong, you can at least reflect that you will learn something!

I have also learnt a lot by observing and listening to the advice of others who are successful coaches and consultants. These are people who seem to naturally know how to put clients at ease, who develop relationships well and are trusted by lots of clients. For most of them, what seems like a natural talent is in fact a learnt skill – and if they have learnt it, so can you.

One particular skill they have is being able to raise difficult or controversial topics as elements of a conversation in a way that seems natural and non-threatening. Rather than becoming the start of an argument, having challenging conversations about difficult or sensitive topics becomes something the client values about working with them.

I recommend that everyone starting out as a freelance expert finds some people who will mentor them and help explore their style of work. I have found freelancers generally very generous with their time to those starting out.

As an author, I also read a lot. Partially this is to help my own writing, but of course I have learnt from it for my consulting work. I have listed about 40 books in the Further reading and other resources section at the end of the book, and I'll mention a few of them now. They are arranged thematically – you don't need to read them all, just choose the ones for the areas you feel you need most help.

As an expert adviser, my behaviour, interpersonal and communications style has been influenced by books including *The Trusted Advisor; Crucial Conversations, Tools for Talking When Stakes are High; Influence, The Psychology of Persuasion; Humble Inquiry, The Gentle Art of Asking Instead of Telling* and *The Pyramid Principle*. I could list dozens more. I am constantly looking for great new books, but many of the ones I have learnt most from are relatively old books. Well, people are still people no matter how much technology and society has changed.

When it comes to sharing my views on behaviour with clients with other experts, my advice tends to be uncomplicated and straightforward.

We are all individuals with strengths and weaknesses of our own, and styles of interacting and behaving which are natural to us. Whenever anyone asks me to advise them on how to behave with clients, I share a simple list of things to do. There is a danger that such a list of simple things reads like motherhood and apple pie. They are not. Getting these things right takes lots of practice – and those people who think they are naturally gifted at all of them tend to be fooling themselves.

My advice to you is simple:

- Be aware that behaviour is as important to your success as an expert as your expertise. Often more so.
- Generally, behave in a way that is natural to you. But occasionally stick your neck out and try something new. When it works, learn from it and repeat it. When it doesn't – learn from it too!
- Seek feedback about how others find your ways of behaving and communicating. It's not always easy asking for or listening to feedback. Getting feedback is one of the most valuable things you can do. On a personal note, it has been fundamental to my growth as a consultant and a writer.
- Take action based on that feedback. This requires that you trust the person giving you the feedback. This works best of all when you have strong enough relationships with your clients to ask them for personal feedback.
- Always try to be honest and open. Sometimes you will get away with not being completely honest and open, but more often clients detect when we are not being honest and open – and they don't like it.
- Treat your clients as people who are worthy of your respect and trust. Your track record of doing this will play out over time. In truth, will every client be worthy of this? No. But this is the attitude with which you should always approach clients.
- Be aware of cultural variations and try to be sensitive to the ways different people expect others to behave in different contexts. This is especially important if you work regularly internationally and in other cultures than your own.
- Be constantly trying to develop and improve the way you interact with clients.

We will explore important aspects of these topics more in Chapters 12 and 13.

An independent voice

Ian Williamson, Transformation Consultant

Hi, my name is Ian Williamson, I work as a Transformation Consultant and have specialist knowledge in back-office functions, systems and processes.

My career started out working for a large bank as an accountant, but I quickly realised I wanted to broaden my business knowledge beyond 'just numbers' in a spreadsheet. I like to engage with people and understand how all the different components of organisations come together - or not - as is often the case! Having this view gave early adoption to a skill I didn't even realise I had, until it was told to me 'you're a very good problem solver'!

Much of my work today is centred on solving corporate problems and inefficiencies. This can be everyday transactional type issues to more complex programmes, such as implementing tech and business change in global conglomerates.

I have been fortunate to work across a broad range of industries and sectors. While the front-line products of the legal sector differ vastly to the utilities sector, the back-office departments keeping these businesses functioning remain largely the same. This makes my skill set transferable and with this I bring diverse and alternative thinking into the design, operation, and information that informs companies.

My tips for anyone considering a freelance career

One of the most challenging factors of my role is working in differing cultures; this affects people's propensity to change, speed of decision making, and balance of change advocates and antagonists. Building early rapport with colleagues is essential to succeed. This not only helps in getting the job done, it's a recipe for a brighter day, and often removes the dividing line that is often put in place between permanent employees and contractors. With the labour market being more mobile than ever, these relationships over time build broader and stronger networks, which is key to the success of anyone working in the gig economy. The business transformation community is small, and I have found myself being hired based on recommendations from former colleagues.

Building these networks of course takes time, meaning early on in our consulting career, we rely heavily on the batteries of recruitment consultants. Love them or hate them, this diverse group of professionals and unprofessionals needs approaching with care. Some will waste your time, let you down, and ignore your calls, others you have never heard of will call you up and get you an interview the same day. There is no logic to how they operate, but it is essential to maintain a healthy relationship because you never know when they have something you need, and vice versa. I maintain relationships with around half a dozen who I can rely on to find me the right candidates when I need them, and they will work hard across their network when my own contract is due to expire.

While contracting can be financially rewarding and bring interesting role diversity, I have found taking some time out to think and reflect is a critical success factor. Managing and working on programmes can be a real energy drain, especially when cultures are complex and pernicious. I cannot emphasise more, the importance of self-care. If possible, take regular holidays, take a lunch break, travel first class, give yourself a reward, and avoid contractor fever!

If you want to know more about me, you can see my LinkedIn profile at: https://uk.linkedin.com/in/williamsoni

chapter

12

Building relationships to drive your freelance success

We are now entering a pair of chapters which explore some of the fundamental skills and abilities that all freelance experts need. These skills and abilities do not refer to your core expertise that you sell. Instead they relate to how you present and apply that expertise, and how by doing this you can be most effective both in sharing your expertise and in building the long-term relationships our businesses thrive on.

In this chapter, I want to deal with the first set of these skills and abilities. This set concerns building trust, effective listening and understanding the conditions to be able to help our clients. These are three broad interrelated areas, and are essential for you to develop a great reputation as a freelance expert. For each of the three areas covered in this chapter there is a short checklist to summarise the contents and help you apply it.

The value of trust

We all instinctively like to be trusted. It feels good when others trust us, and we have a sense of hurt when people do not trust us. For a freelance expert, trust goes beyond being a nice-to-have emotion that makes our work more pleasant. Trust is of significant practical value. In fact, being able to develop trust with your clients may well be the most important factor in the success of your career.

The nature of giving advice, if that advice is to be listened to, is that the person receiving the advice needs to trust the adviser. Yet trust is a reciprocal relationship. When a client puts themselves in your hands, they are trusting your expertise. But you also need to trust your clients. In the short term, you need to trust them to do simple things like tell you the truth and pay your bills. In the longer run, your success as a freelance expert is dependent on your clients, their responses to your service and tendency to hire you again.

One way of presenting the basic bargain a freelance expert makes with a client is: my success is your success. Personal success for you as an expert comes about by making your clients successful. Whenever your success depends on someone else, you need to be able to trust them.

The value of trust starts with your interactions with each individual client. When a client trusts you, they are much more likely to open up and tell you everything you want to know, even if it is personally sensitive information. They will also listen to your advice. In return, when you are trusted and sense that you are trusted, you are more likely to be calm and confident in sharing your expertise – and this makes you come across as more credible.

Trust then compounds its value when it comes to repeat business. Once a client has developed trust in you, they are much more likely to hire you again, and to recommend you to other clients. These are practical reasons for wanting to be trusted, and will be reflected in your business's turnover.

But the value of trust does not stop here. One of the pains that most freelance experts bemoan is the administrative hassle that often accompanies acquiring a new client, especially if that new client is a large business. There are all sorts of procedures and forms that must be completed. This can be time consuming and can delay starting fee-earning work. Freelance experts who are trusted will often find that their clients are more willing to short circuit some of the more onerous parts of this administration, and this can be a significant benefit.

Finally, trust links to the type of work you are likely to be offered and its degree of variability. Once you are trusted, a client is far more likely to ask you to do things which may not quite fit within your core expertise. Of course, you may not want to do this work. Responding to a client offer of work with a statement that you will not do that type of work because it is not your core expertise, will tend to increase your client's feeling of trust in you further. But should you wish to put your hand to different things, areas where you have less expertise – a client who trusts you is much more likely to make this possible.

For all these reasons, trust is fundamental to our work as freelance experts. It is as close as anything comes to the magic sauce that brings success!

Setting out to gain trust

Trust is earned. It is not given out for free. Even for those of us who are by nature more trusting than others, there will be certain things we will only share with and seek help about from people we have developed deep trust in. This takes time.

Earning trust starts with our first interactions with our clients. As soon as we meet someone for the first time, our mind is working away making all sorts of judgements about who we can trust. There has been plenty of research that shows that we are not always logical about the judgements we make – our subconscious minds have been conditioned by all sorts of influences.

As someone running a business based on sharing your expertise with others, you do not want to let developing trust to be left up solely to the vagaries of chance. You want to take deliberate actions that will help you develop trust. I am not suggesting you try and manipulate people into trusting you. In my experience, this only works in the short run at best, and with any client I always assume when I meet them for the first time that I am setting out to build a long-term relationship. Nevertheless, we can do simple, honest, things that help the development of trust.

Start by being conscious of the impression you are setting when you meet a client for the first time. We probably should pay less attention to first impressions than we do, but human beings seem to be hard wired to judge based on first impressions. Having formed a first impression, it is hard to break it. In the same way, your clients will judge you based on the first impressions. It can take a lot of effort to gain an initial conversation with a client – effort that can be wasted by creating the wrong first impressions.

Human beings like best to work with, and find it easiest to develop trust with, people they like. And put simply we tend to like people who are like us. I don't mean that I will only like people who look or sound like me. Fortunately, most of us are not quite that shallow. But we do tend to like people who have a degree of commonality with us. And this can be as simple as the way we dress, speak or the sort of things we talk about. It is normal in first conversations to try and find common topics to discuss: interests, family, work, people known in common and so on. This is all part of that finding of common ground, and then developing trust.

For these reasons when meeting someone for the first time it is worth thinking about the clothes you wear and what sort of things you might talk about, especially in those first few minutes of chit-chat before work starts. But also think about giving your clients a chance to ask you a few questions, and open up a bit to them.

There is a formal name for opening up – it is called *self-disclosure*. We are going to further discuss its importance later in this chapter. For now, it's important to know that you should open up first, before your client does. This is all part of making your clients feel comfortable and starting to do the groundwork to build a strong relationship. Sharing something personal signals that you want to develop an intimate relationship, which is essential to trust.

But in trying to fit in with your clients, don't go too far. Don't try to be something you are not, just to be liked by them. While we tend to like people like us, we also are attracted to people who are authentic. That is, people who we believe are speaking and acting honestly in line with their true selves. We all have great antennae for detecting people we think are being inauthentic and we do not like it. Your clients will not like it if they detect this in you.

Woven into all your conversations with your clients is your position as an expert. If someone is going to pay money for you to do some work for them, to help them or to advise them, they want to trust that you have the right expertise. To encourage this perception, you should be trying to show your expertise, but do not try and position yourself as someone who knows everything. We are easily bored by the know-it-all – bored, irritated and unimpressed. What we like is to work with people who know something and know it well. Resist the temptation to stray into areas you have no expertise in.

I know there is a trend for 'fake it until you make it'. If you don't know this expression, it simply means pretend you have the skills you need until you have the chance to develop them. I have mixed feelings about this. On the one hand, we all must learn and develop our skills and sometimes that means stretching ourselves. But there's a limit to how far we should go. The 'fake it until you make it' approach is essentially starting out on a client relationship based on a lie. It builds on an ethics that your success is more important than your clients, and its ok for them to pay you for work thinking you are an expert, when you are not.

Personally, I am uncomfortable with that. Most clients will forgive you if you are not quite as good or experienced as they expected. But if your clients realise you are faking skills you do not have, they will probably never work with you again.

The trust equation

In the year 2000, the trio of authors David Maister, Charles Green and Robert Galford first published what was to become one of the classic texts for those in professional services called *The Trusted Advisor*. This is a book concerned with how professionals can build and utilise trust. At its heart is their trust equation, which I have always liked as it breaks down the concept of trust into smaller, easier to understand components:

$$T = (C + R + I) / S$$

Let's look at each of the components, starting with 'T', which represents trust. They claim the degree clients will trust you in turn depends on four other factors – C, R, I and S.

'C' is credibility. The authors define credibility as deriving from your content expertise, in other words how good your expertise is, and what they call your presence. That is, your ability to successfully communicate that expertise to your clients. It's no good just having expertise, unless you can communicate it convincingly to your clients.

'R' is reliability, which is your client's view on whether you can be relied on as a dependable adviser.

So far this sounds as to be expected. To gain trust as an expert we need to have expertise which we can convincingly communicate, and we need our clients to think we are reliable. The next two elements are where I think this equation becomes more interesting and enlightening.

'I' represents intimacy. This is a little harder to grasp, but essentially it relates to our emotional bond with our clients. The authors claim that this bond is developed by our willingness to be open with clients and to talk about difficult topics. One aspect of this, which is well researched in psychology and communications theories, is our degree of self-disclosure. That is, our willingness to share personal details about ourselves.

When we enter into chit-chat with our clients about our love of model railways, our worries about our children, or our favourite holiday we may think of it as just part of the social dance or even just necessary time wasting. It's not, it is a critical part of relationship building. Such self-disclosure is an essential step towards developing a relationship of any depth. People struggle to trust others who disclose little about themselves. In contrast, the greater our willingness to self-disclose to others, the more they will tend to trust us – as long as what we share is socially acceptable.

One word of caution that I give regarding intimacy. Of all the aspects of this trust equation, this is the one with the greatest degrees of cultural variation. What is the norm in one culture for self-disclosure, is not in another. If you are working in a new cultural environment, tread carefully when it comes to self-disclosure. It is easy to do or say something which may be regarded as harmless chit-chat at home, but which is socially unacceptable in another culture.

The final letter 'S' represents our levels of self-orientation. Self-orientation is our tendency to focus on ourselves ahead of our clients. Looking at how the equation works, we can see we want this to be as small as possible. As far as possible, we want to be seen to be putting our client's interests in front of our own.

In all cases, it is not the absolute level of credibility, reliability, intimacy and self-orientation that matters, but our client's perceptions of it. For our clients, perception is reality. They need to perceive us as credible, reliable intimate and having low self-orientation.

Is this little equation solid science? I don't know, but I have found it to be a useful tool over the years.

Occasionally, I will meet an expert who struggles to develop trust because they are not perceived to have sufficient credibility or reliability. This can often be a problem for people setting themselves out as experts when they have very limited experience at the start of their career. One answer to this problem is to try and focus on a small niche that is consistent with less broad experience.

But far more often, I find with freelance experts who struggle to develop trust, the problem stems from their lack of intimacy or that they are perceived to have too high a self-orientation. The client does not believe that they are fundamentally putting the client's interests first. If you find you are not developing trusting relationships – ask yourself how would clients rate your self-orientation and levels of intimacy?

Table 12.1 provides a few questions to help you reflect on your ability to develop trust, based on the trust equation.

Table 12.1 Self-reflection questions for exploring your ability to develop trust

Element of trust	Self-reflection questions
Credibility	▪ How credible as an expert in your field do you think you are?
	▪ Have you ever asked anyone for feedback on how credible you are? Did you learn from and act on the feedback?
	▪ What do you do, specifically, to build your credibility?
	▪ Do you think your clients, when they talk about you, talk about you as a highly credible expert?
	▪ How could you do more or improve the perception of you as credible?
Reliability	▪ Do you feel that you come across as authentic?
	▪ How well can you explain your area of expertise to clients?
	▪ When someone has a question relating to your domain, do they tend to come to you with questions?
	▪ How could you improve the perception of you as a reliable adviser?
Intimacy	▪ How much time do you spend discussing non-work or personal topics when talking to clients?
	▪ How sensitive are you in judging what is appropriate to discuss with your clients? Are you aware of cultural variations?
	▪ Do your clients ever talk to you about their personal life?
	▪ How often do you go first in self-disclosure?
	▪ How often are you thinking about your relationship as you talk with clients rather than purely the facts about the work you are doing?
	▪ How often do you think you are on friendly terms with your clients or building lasting friendships with them?
Self-orientation	▪ Can you think of occasions in which you have been seen to put the client first ahead of your personal interests?
	▪ What opportunities are there for you to display a low self-orientation? When they arise, do you tend to take them or not?
	▪ Do you think your clients think of you as selfish or generous?
	▪ How could you be perceived as having a lower self-orientation?

Listening

If trust is the magic sauce of great relationships, your listening is the oil that makes the machinery of helping clients work at its best.

There is a purely functional side to listening. Our most important interactions with our clients tend to be when we are talking to each other. As experts, we gather much of the information we need to provide our expert service to the customer. At its most basic this is as simple as understanding what your client wants from you and their current situation.

This functional side to listening presents it as an activity, the physical process of hearing what is said. But listening is more than this. It is also a mental process in which we analyse what is being said to us, and we determine appropriate responses – such as asking exploratory questions. We also create memories we can recall later – or better still, if it is important information, we take notes.

There are many aspects to effective listening. Some of these are practical, such as simply being in an environment in which you can hear properly. But for me there is one thing that stands above all others, and that is the attitude with which we approach listening to our clients. The most important aspect of this is starting from a perspective of truly wanting to hear what your client is saying.

Too often I see experts listening not to learn what the client thinks, but to confirm what they already knew. If you start listening with a preconceived idea of what the client is going to say, it is surprisingly easy to find yourself hearing it, even if the client never meant that. Try to have an open mind and hear what the client says, not what you want to hear.

A similar problem happens when experts get so excited about what they have to say, or want to show how great their expertise is, that they stop listening to hear the client's words. Instead, they are just listening for the opportunity to speak. It's like that child in the classroom raising their hand up and saying 'me, me, me – listen to me'. We may believe we have grown out of such behaviour, but the equivalent, albeit dressed in the refined speech of the expert, is surprisingly common. If you find yourself doing this, try to relax a bit more. Don't worry about showing your expertise so much, most of the time you will get your turn to talk, if you take care to listen first.

Even if you do not get as much time to talk as you want, you will often find the client valued the conversation. You may be surprised how much your client appreciates you if you speak less and listen more. If you are a great listener, clients will like you. Often, clients will not really understand why they like working with you so much. But that's not really important, as long as they keep on working with you.

When I talk about listening, you may automatically think about words and sounds. But good listeners are not simply hearing and analysing words. Good listeners are observing the way in which the words are said and the body language of the speaker. We have all made mistakes when, for example, we have simply heard the words someone said but not really thought about how they were said, or not observed the body language which accompanied them. We all know many stories of husbands and wives misunderstanding each other because of a focus purely on the words they each said, not how they were said.

This much is straightforward, but one thing that is sometimes forgotten is that listening is also a performance. By this I mean not only do we have to listen for the practical reason of gathering information, we listen for the interpersonal reason of being seen to listen. If you have the opportunity, carefully watch the most successful advisers and coaches at work. You will observe people who spend a lot of the time listening. And they aren't just listening – it is obvious that they are listening. They make the appropriate eye contacts, and all the little noises and gestures that people listening do.

By being perceived to be carefully listening to someone else, we show respect and we show interest. It is one of the most basic human desires – to be listened to. It is fundamental to building strong relationships with your clients. If you go back to the trust equation I described earlier on in this chapter, key to being perceived as having a low self-interest, is being willing to put your clients first. In a conversation, putting your clients first means listening to them. Let them speak first, and show you are interested by being seen to listen to them.

It is self-evident that to provide advice, counsel or coaching we do at times have to guide our clients. In other words, we must be the speaker. My point about listening is not that you should not speak. You will spend a lot of time speaking as an expert adviser of any sort. But you must get the balance between speaking and listening right. If the only thing you are doing is talking – and you are not listening at all or not properly listening – then this balance is wrong.

I think of listening as one of the core skills of great experts. It is great to go out and develop your communication skills, to learn presentation and writing skills. There are thousands of people providing excellent training in these areas, and great presentation and writing skills are a real asset. But before you worry about developing these, start with something apparently simpler. Think about how well you listen and how well you are perceived by those around you to listen. If you do not know, ask a few people you interact with regularly, and listen to and learn from their answers. Table 12.2 provides a few questions to help you reflect on your listening skills.

Table 12.2 Listening checklist

	Listening checklist	Yes?
1	Are you conscious that sometimes it is best to listen rather than speak – and that as an adviser you do not always have to fill the silence?	☐
2	Are you in the right frame of mind to listen – able to concentrate and avoid distractions?	☐
3	Are you more interested in hearing what the client has to say, or in confirming what you already believed?	☐
4	As you listen, are you tending to focus on forming answers, responses or rebuttals to the client, or are you staying focused on listening?	☐
5	Do you sometimes let go of what you came prepared to say as you listen to the client?	☐
6	Do you let the client finish speaking before you jump in with what you want to say?	☐
7	When you are listening is it obvious that you are listening? (Eye contact, head nods, verbal prompts – e.g. 'uh-huh' 'oh yes' etc.)	☐
8	When you are listening do you stay concentrated on your client and avoid interruptions (e.g. phone pings)?	☐
9	Do you ever leave your client satisfied, even though you do not think you have said very much?	☐
10	Do you have someone you trust, who you can ask how well they think you listen – and what makes them think this?	☐

Helping and advising

At the core of your service are two related acts – offering advice and helping your clients. What advice and help you give will depend on the specifics of the service you offer. The ability to help and advise depends both on the degree of trust your client has for you, and your listening skills.

Success is not only about giving your clients the right help and the right advice. Equally, and often more importantly, is how you give that help and advice. Irrespective of the specifics of your specialist expertise, there are four general points that all freelance experts would do well to get right concerning helping clients.

The first point concerns permission to offer help. Before we offer up any advice or help, we should make sure that it is the appropriate time to be giving help, and that we have permission to help. This is best explained by an example.

I regularly meet up with other consultants, coaches and contractors. There might be a range of reasons which usually starts when we find something in common. Perhaps we live nearby to each other, we share a client or some connections, we think there is a business opportunity in combining our services, or we have read each other's books. I find these meetings often valuable and interesting.

On one occasion, I had agreed to meet over a coffee with a specialised coach. We were sitting there quite happily drinking our coffee and to begin with it was a good conversation. But after a while I started to get increasingly uncomfortable with that conversation. It was not going how I expected it to go. It was less a two-way dialogue and more a series of questions from the coach, to which I was responding and opening up and sharing some of my thoughts.

The problem was this: the person I had met had started to coach me. I suspect he was a good coach for some people, but I had not asked him to coach me. I had come for a friendly chat of the sort you normally have when you meet someone for the first time. Rather than finding his attempts to coach me useful, I found it rather irritating. He had made a basic mistake: he had tried to help me before he had permission to help me.

We cannot just throw help out there expecting other people to thank us for it. We can only really help people when they want our help and ideally have given us permission to help. Even doing something as simple as saying 'I am going to offer some advice now, is that ok?' can make this situation better. However permission is given – whether it is explicit or implicit – you need it, and if you are unsure if you have it, ask.

The second point concerns the relevance of the help we are offering. Is it the sort of help our client is expecting? Again, this is best shown by an example, which may be familiar to anyone in a long-term relationship.

Imagine your partner is talking to you and complaining about some problem they have that is making them angry. Let's imagine the problem has a rather obvious solution. You, trying to be helpful, offer this solution up to them. You are then surprised when the solution suggested is not responded to with thanks, but seems to increase the distress and anger your partner has. Worse still, increasingly the anger is now directed at you.

Now let's change that from a personal to a business situation. A client starts discussing a problem, and you offer a solution. Perhaps they seem tetchy with you, or maybe their response to your proposed solution, which you are sure is correct, is completely neutral. They carry on as if they have not even heard what you are suggesting.

Have you experienced something like this? What is going on here? I would hazard a guess, that what is happening is that the person you were talking to never actually wanted you to solve the problem. The obvious solution was just that, obvious. It was obvious to them as well. They never wanted help to find the solution. The help they were looking for was sympathy or emotional support. Your focus on providing a solution, and not providing the support they really wanted, is a further irritation.

Before offering your partner help, think about what sort of help they really want. It is the same with helping clients. Yes, sometimes they do want you to solve their problems directly, but not always. Perhaps they really need some coaching, perhaps they want someone to listen – or maybe they too just want some sympathy. The sign of a truly expert adviser is the ability to offer up the sort of help that the client wants at a point in time.

My third point is that for any help to be of value to your clients, it needs to be usable by them. There are lots of ways we can offer our clients perfectly sound, but in all other respects, useless help. Before I help, I like to think about the right language to communicate it in, as well as my client's resources and capabilities.

We might make the mistake of using some jargon that is related to our expertise, but which is meaningless to our clients. Always use language that is understandable, correctly, by your clients.

We can offer up solutions to problems that require far more resources than the client has. Any solution needs to be scaled to the client's resources. Offering a solution that costs millions of pounds when the client only has thousands is as good as useless. If your expertise is always going to result in large bills that the client cannot afford, it would have been better to tell the client in advance that you cannot help them.

We can suggest options that are beyond the client's capabilities. After all, we are the experts, not our clients; that is why they hired us. It is easy to think of many things I know how to do quite simply, but my clients do not know how to do. My value as an expert is not only to share my expertise, but to share it in a way they can use with their current capabilities and knowledge.

My final point is that a little while after offering our help or advice to our clients we should check it is working for them. No matter how good your

Table 12.3 Helping checklist

	Helping checklist	Yes?
1	*Before you start:* do you have permission to help? Is your relationship with the client such that they will accept the help from you? Is now the right time and situation to start helping?	☐
2	Are you offering the right sort of help? Do you understand what sort of help is most appropriate for this client, in this their context, at this time?	☐
3	Is the help you are offering, or advice you are giving, understandable and usable by your client with their current resources and capabilities? Have you avoided too much jargon?	☐
4	*After you have helped:* did the help work? Have you checked back with the client, sorting out any issues or niggles with what you recommended?	☐

expertise is, there will be occasions where the advice was not quite right. Perhaps the client did not explain everything well enough, maybe the situation has changed after you gave the advice, or possibly it was one of those situations in which you were not listening quite well enough!

There are other benefits to checking back with a client. Contacting your client after an appropriate gap of time just to check all is well, and if necessary, to modify your advice, adds to an excellent service that clients will remember. It helps to improve trust. Following up with clients also makes good business sense, as any opportunity for a further conversation is an opportunity to win more work.

Table 12.3 presents these four simple points to advice giving and helping in a short checklist.

An independent voice

Charles Cowan, ICC Wealth Management Limited

My name is Charles Cowan. I am a Chartered Financial Planner and the Managing Director of ICC Wealth Management, a Partner Practice of St. James's Place Wealth Management.

Our focus as a Practice is to work with a small, select group of clients who are generally senior business people (both employed and self-employed), company directors or those who have already retired.

We provide pro-active, financial advice to our clients, formulating bespoke financial plans which are tailored to individual needs, circumstances and objectives. The advice is holistic, and is ultimately designed to help clients achieve their financial goals. It generally covers the following areas:

- Investment strategy
- Retirement planning
- Protection needs
- Inheritance tax planning
- Tax efficiency.

Our ideal clients are those who want one trusted point of contact to help them manage all of their financial affairs, while they concentrate on their career and family life. Our clients take their financial planning seriously and appreciate the value of robust and timely financial advice. They view us as trusted partners in their life plans and value the personal, face-to-face service that we offer – it is not a transactional relationship but rather one that will be built over the years, based on mutual respect, trust and professionalism.

My tips for anyone considering a freelance career

I am a firm believer in the adage 'people buy from people'. This may be disputed in the era of online shopping and price wars, but when your offer is a business relationship to look after someone's wealth and to help them achieve their life goals, the type of person you are is extremely important. In my line of work, I believe the two most important traits someone must have and foster, are Trust and Credibility. If you lack either of these, you will struggle to build any meaningful relationships with clients.

Being credible is probably the 'easiest' one to achieve; do lots of reading, go on courses, become a subject matter expert and get a professional qualification. My role requires a level 4 industry qualification, but I have exceeded this and become Chartered (level 6) to further enhance my profile and credibility.

My role requires a very high level of technical knowledge, and all of the points above will help you achieve this, but understanding complex Trust rules, tax positions and product features is only one part. You have to be able to relay all of this to clients in a way that they understand. By proving that you are an expert in your field, helping your clients understand the reasons for your advice, and by providing simple and precise explanations, your credibility will be established.

This leads nicely onto the second point of Trust. By establishing your credibility, you will have already gained an element of trust from your client – they know they can trust what you are telling them in relation to your field. Developing this trust can then be done in a number of ways. These may seem simple, but it's surprising how many advisers / consultants get them wrong:

- Do what you say you will do
  - By committing to an action and following through, the client will know they can depend on you
- Turn up on time – for meetings or agreed calls. Don't be early, don't be late
  - This shows respect for your client and shows you are organised
- Never deflect or avoid their questions – if you don't know an answer, tell them you will find out
  - If clients feel you are fobbing them off or answering like a politician, their trust will be lost
- Always be honest with your clients – whether that is admitting to a mistake or telling them you disagree with something they say

The last point above is particularly interesting. By always giving an honest appraisal, you will provide your client with options so they can make an informed decision. Some of my strongest client relationships have developed from me telling clients not to invest money with me. Which has, in turn, led to more business.

chapter

13

Developing your credibility and influence with clients

In your independent career there will be many situations in which your voice is ignored or drowned out among all the other sources of expertise. There are, after all, many places to find advice, know-how and access to skills.

Do a quick search on YouTube and you will discover millions of videos telling you how to do virtually everything – for free. Look at a blog site like Medium and you will locate huge numbers of intelligent and insightful articles. Search on LinkedIn and you will quickly be presented with the names of tens of millions of consultants, coaches, contractors and other experts, many of them offering services in direct competition with you.

Given this, how do you make your voice stand out? Partially that is achieved by doing the sorts of things we have already discussed in this book: differentiating yourself by having a clear and valuable service; targeting the right customers appropriately and effectively; doing great work and building a solid reputation based on trust; learning how to get referrals and repeat business.

But even if you do this, you will find people who stand out more than you. They achieve this because they have *influence*. In our line of work, influence can be defined as the ability to shape how people think, and to stand out as an expert voice that is listened to and respected.

But being listened to is not always enough. If you want to become successful in your expert career you don't only want to be listened to, you want to have impact. You must be able to convince people that your approach or your advice is the right one to follow.

Sometimes as an expert you will want to sell your services to someone who does not immediately appreciate why they need them. Having sold a service to them, your expertise may point to them needing to do something that is not naturally appealing to them. After all, if the outcome of your advice is always to tell people what they wanted to hear, you are probably not adding huge value.

Whether it is selling an unappreciated service or convincing a client to follow some great advice that they do not like, your impact is determined by how *persuasive* you are.

Credibility and your ability to present yourself

I want to start by exploring what I think of as the *rational side* of influence. That is, those aspects of our work, which – if we think purely logically, ignoring emotions and the more complex side of human motivations – we might assume were the source of our influence.

If you have followed the advice given so far, you will be on your way towards gaining influence. Later in this chapter we are going to explore two models of gaining influence which take us beyond pure rationality. But before you consider these, as an expert you already have a basis for influence – and that is your expertise. More accurately it is your clients' perception of your expertise, which I call your *credibility*.

We already touched on credibility in the previous chapter in the model on developing trust. A lot of client perceptions of freelance experts are intertwined. Your clients' degrees of trust, credibility, sense of reliability, dependability and confidence in you are interrelated. Improving in one aspect tends to improve other aspects of your clients' perception of you.

As an expert, your influence builds from your credibility. Credibility is vital. Although sometimes credibility alone is not enough to influence clients, it always plays an essential role. If you have no credibility, a client will not listen to your advice or seek out your help – full stop.

What gives you credibility? Typically, credibility builds from the following sorts of sources:

- ***Track record and experience:*** of successfully providing a similar service before.
- ***Profile and public chatter:*** what public reputation or social media profile you have. Is it consistent with being an expert in the field you are discussing with this client?

- **Recommendations and referrals:** from individuals your clients trust, which is often people in similar job roles or life situations to them – especially others they know well and respect.
- **Recognised qualifications and accreditations:** in some fields these are essential. For instance, they can be university degrees, professional qualifications or society membership.
- **Relevant content you have created:** have you created books, posts, blogs, podcasts or articles on topics that show your relevant expertise?
- **Coherent presentation of yourself:** do you look and sound like an expert?

Given that new clients will always want to confirm your credibility, it is worth the effort to develop these sources. This is best done by having easily accessible materials that demonstrate these sources of credibility. You do not necessarily need all of these sources of credibility, and which sources of credibility are more important does vary between different types of experts. Nevertheless, being able to point customers to examples of prior experience, CVs, references, certificates, content you have created and relevant social media profiles all help.

I spend time every week updating and building materials that support my credibility. I have an ongoing and ever-updated plan for developing my sources of credibility including my social media profile, sales materials and writing articles and books. For some successful freelance experts, developing their sources of credibility is a daily activity.

Credibility is also improved by your ability to present and communicate your expertise. For instance, when working with a client on an engagement it is common to suggest the client changes something in the way they work or behave. Most people do not immediately like changing anything, and so your ability to present a compelling case to make the change is essential. Having a good communication style that the customer listens to is important. Having expertise, but no ability to communicate it, will bring any freelance career quickly to an end.

I do not mean you need to be a great orator or have TED quality presentation skills. Those are wonderful and valuable skills if you have them, but don't worry if you do not. Most important is the ability to explain and put forward well-structured, rational arguments that have clarity and are easily understood by your clients.

A final aspect of credibility is the need for consistency. When we get advice or help from anyone, we like to see consistency in their advice, and consistent approaches to doing their work. Little undermines our faith in someone more than them telling us one thing one day and giving conflicting advice the next day. Once we detect a lack of consistency in anyone's advice, the credibility of them as an expert is undermined. After all, if there is a lack of consistency, how do we know which part of the advice to believe? How do we know that tomorrow they won't tell us something different again?

There is another, more subtle, side to consistency, and that is the focus of your expertise. If you claim specialist knowledge, and all your past work and other sources of credibility are all in this domain, there is a consistency in your claim – and this consistency enhances your credibility. However, if all the sources of your credibility point to you doing lots of different unrelated things, clients are less likely to consider you as a true expert.

I am not saying you must only do one thing. No one cares if you are an expert in procurement, and also a keen amateur footballer. In fact, a small range of additional interests makes you seem human and more appealing as a person. But there is an assumption that to be a real expert requires a lot of focus. If, for example, your social media profile indicates you do twenty different things professionally, it seems inconsistent with that focus required to develop a real depth of expertise.

If you do many things, one approach is to keep some of them as private activities, so they do not compete with your expert persona in public. There are lots of things I do that I do not talk about on my most public social media profiles. I also have separate social media profiles for close friends who are interested in those other sides of my life.

Alternatively, if you feel you need to publicise everything you do, try to find a common theme that makes them sound like a consistent or inter-related set of activities. For instance, I consult, I teach, I write and I mentor other experts, but a lot of my work in these areas is related so I can present it as being consistent with my status as an expert.

The brilliance and limitations of rationality

I like to think I am a pretty rational person. I have degrees in mechanical engineering, philosophy and economics. Mechanical engineering is a subject based purely on rationality. Philosophy is a subject that explores the structures of rational thinking. When I was a student decades ago, economics was awash with rationality and based around the mythical rational economic man. Economists saw the world based on an ongoing set of choices and decisions that could be modelled assuming everyone was perfectly rational.

But there has been another train of thinking in economics, which came to prominence around the turn of the 21st century – behavioural economics. Behavioural economists' theories are based on a more realistic view of human behaviour than one built on the assumption that everyone is perfectly rational. Nowadays, students of economics are likely to be taught a lot of behavioural economics, which very quickly dispenses with the idea that our decision making is purely rational.

I want to explore this because rationality is generally important for experts. Expertise is often based on rational thinking and rational ideas. The people who are attracted to becoming an expert are often people who think, or at least think they think, purely rationally. Experts tend to see the world in rational terms, and like old school economists, assume the world is full of other rational people.

When it comes to the time to influence anyone, and to persuade them that our way of thinking is right, we experts therefore usually first seek to put forward the best argument. We feel we are right because we understand our subject well, and we see clearly and logically through the issues. We believe we are to be trusted because we can justify our advice by the best logical chain of arguments, and the best fact base.

If only the world really were always so logical. There is a huge amount of research showing that people are far from being the rational animals that we usually think we are. Books like Daniel Kahneman's *Thinking, Fast and Slow*; Steven Levitt and Stephen Dubner's *Freakonomics*; or Dan Ariely's *Predictably Irrational* are just a few of the many that will soon show you how little pure rationality plays in our thinking. And the deeper you research this topic, the odder we human beings seem to be. As a result, an expert relying purely on rational argument will not achieve consistently reliable and successful results, when it comes to persuading and influencing clients.

To be the most successful of freelance experts, you need to have more tools available to you than pure rational argument. Being the most persuasive and influential we can be, requires us, at times, to go beyond the purely rational.

Having said all this, I do not want to reject the value of good arguments. For all the research into the irrational nature of human beings, often a well-described and logical set of reasons for why a client should hire us or, having hired us, why they should follow our advice over anyone else's, will work. Clarity of thought, logical structure of our reasoning and based on this the production of compelling cases for trusting our advice, often work. There are many situations in which our ability to influence and persuade clients depends purely on cold rational thought.

If you know a subject well, as you should do if you are positioning yourself as an expert, you should be able to describe it clearly. Clarity of thinking, and the ability to describe the complex in simpler easier to understand parts, are often the sign of a true expert. An inability to communicate clearly and simply is often taken as a sign, rightly or wrongly, that your true level of expertise is not high.

Before I present anything contentious or complex to my clients, I always make sure that my chain of argument is based on facts, is logically sound and is easy to understand. This is both so I give the right advice, but it is also so I sound as if I know what I am talking about. This habit has paid dividends through my career.

But there are limits to how well relying purely on rationality will work. As a simple example, we are all aware that emotions play a large part in our decision making. There are good and bad days to tell our clients difficult things. Most of us instinctively know this. Building on this, I want to make you conscious that there is more to the expertise of being an expert than facts and logical argument. It's not that using rationality is wrong, it isn't – it's just that sometimes it is not enough.

I am not going to make you an expert in the irrational nature of human beings in one chapter. But I do want to at least make you aware of it.

Influence and persuasion

One of my favourite professional books is Robert Cialdini's *Influence: The Psychology of Persuasion*. It's a book I often recommend. You might expect a book with such a title to have been written by one of the most influential and persuasive people in the world, such as a brilliant politician or salesperson. What I like about Cialdini's book is that it starts from exactly the opposite position. As Cialdini says on the first page of his book: 'All my life I've been a patsy. For as long as I can recall, I've been an easy market for the pitches and peddlers, fund raisers, and operators of one sort or another.'

Cialdini is not seeking to explain persuasion and influence from the perspective of someone who is brilliant at it. Instead he takes the perspective of a research scientist who is well aware of how easily he has been persuaded in the past, and who wants to know how this has come about.

Cialdini breaks persuasion into six components, or as he calls them the 'six weapons of influence'. These are:

- **Reciprocation:** the tendency for us to strongly feel we should return any favours given to us.
- **Commitment and consistency:** our tendency to remain consistent with decisions we have already made or actions we have already done.
- **Social proof:** our tendencies to see actions as more appropriate if other people are doing them.
- **Liking:** our tendency to be more likely to say 'yes' to someone we like than someone we do not like or know.
- **Authority:** our tendency to follow the advice or instructions of someone we believe to be in a position of authority.
- **Scarcity:** our tendencies to value opportunities more when their availability is limited.

Now to be clear, these are behavioural tendencies and not perfect rules. But Cialdini makes a very convincing case that these are reliable tendencies, and when we resist any of these tendencies, we feel very uncomfortable.

I have presented these as Cialdini does, as weapons of influence, factors which influence us. But of course, these not only influence us – they influence everyone else. And so, these are not only factors that influence our behaviour, they are tools we can use to try and influence the behaviours of our clients.

Think about these for a moment. Let's consider simple examples. Imagine two experts are helping a client. All other things being equal, the client is more likely to be persuaded by the expert they like more (liking), buy from the expert they owe a favour to (reciprocation), accept advice that is consistent with decisions they have already made (commitment and consistency), or be more influenced by the expert advising them to do something everyone else is doing (social proof).

Most of us, if we spend a few seconds thinking about this, would consider these outcomes a little less than perfectly rational; that is, unless we were talking to an evolutionary biologist, who might explain why there are very good reasons we have developed these tendencies. But in the modern world, these tendencies have lost their original value and now seem irrational. Irrational they may be, but they are also persuasive!

Influence without authority

Often the reason we are influenced by people is because they are in a position of authority. They may have formal power over us, such as our boss at work, or it may be more informally tied to a recognised position in society – such as a doctor, a politician, the head of a trade union or a religious leader.

One of the specific challenges of being a freelance expert is that usually we have no authority or power that comes from our position. We are just a knowledgeable individual, with relevant experiences who has opinions and skills that can be helpful. For a freelancer this is even more apparent than it is for a consultant or adviser from a large professional services firm.

Professional services firms may not have direct power, but they can rely on the prestige and reputation of the brand their professional services firm has. The brand gives them authority. Also, such firms often are masters at playing power politics in large organisations. While they do not have power formally, they have plenty of authority and power via relationships with senior leaders in the firm. The independent adviser can rarely rely on such things as brand and networks of relationships, and instead must rely on personal influence.

Two commentators who have specifically picked on this point are Allan Cohen and David Bradford, in their book *Influence Without Authority*. This book describes a way for influencing a wide variety of stakeholders and how to build relationships with them. They present a model for doing this, based on the power of reciprocity, which is one of Cialdini's six weapons of influence. Personally, I think Cialdini's book gives a more rounded view of influence, but what is particularly helpful about Cohen and Bradford's approach is that it provides a set of practical steps for leveraging reciprocity.

At the heart of Cohen and Bradford's book is the influence model which describes a six-step process to gain influence over other people:

- *Assume all are potential allies:* start from the assumption that everyone you want to influence could be influenced by you.
- *Clarify your goals and priorities:* be clear what it is you want from the other party and be clear what the relative priorities are if you have more than one want.
- *Diagnose the world of the other person:* put yourself in the other person's shoes and understand what drives them to behave as they do. When you find someone difficult, avoid assuming they are deliberately antagonistic or an idiot – assume they are working to different motivations, and if you can clarify these motivations you may be able to reciprocate and mutually benefit.

- *Identify relevant currencies, theirs, yours:* what is of value to the other party that you might trade with them for what you want in return? Do not underestimate what you have to give, even if you initially think you have limited value to reciprocate with. People have broad and very varied views of value and there may well be things you have that someone else values. Sometimes these may be things you personally value very little and are happy to give to the other person.
- *Deal with relationships:* develop a relationship with the other party, to give the basis for reciprocation. Deeper relationships are better, but with careful handling most relationships – even initially poor relationships – can enable reciprocation if handled wisely.
- *Influence through give and take:* influence the other party by effectively making a trade of something they want for something you want.

The authors go into significantly more depth about each of these steps, and if you are interested in influencing by reciprocity, or what we might more colloquially call 'give and take', it is worth reading their book.

What can the freelance expert learn from these models?

There is a lot we can learn from these, and other models, that explain the reality of how people develop relationships, build confidence and what makes it most likely that they will trust you. However, before using these I always advise that your position as an expert is built on strong foundations of: facts, logical argument, as well as clear and easy-to-understand communications. Additionally, you should always be seeking to deserve the trust the client places in you. As a freelance expert, your primary concern should be the benefit of your client, and therefore while you may need to influence, you should avoid manipulating them.

But sometimes this is not enough. With the models we have explored in mind, what can we learn?

The first point we should learn should be obvious. Try to be likeable! Everyone is more easily persuaded by people they like than people they do not like. I know a very experienced expert in procurement who knows how to structure the largest and most complex of deals in ways that reduce risk and maximise benefits. Unfortunately, he is also an awkward person who is difficult to warm to. While he has sufficient work, I always think he would have been far more successful if he just tried to be a little warmer to his clients.

Next, work out what things you can do for your clients that they might value, and which, having been done, can build up the sense that they owe you something and will be more willing to help you in return. Once help has been accepted from you, clients will tend to want to help in return. I am not talking about anything difficult or complex. There are many small ways we can help our clients beyond the confines of what they are paying us for, which they value, and which are often not difficult for us to do. Examples include sharing a good article you have read on a topic you know is of interest to them or acting as a sounding board when they need to talk something through.

If your clients are managers and leaders in business, do not underestimate the value that some of them find in getting an external perspective. Often managers find their confidence increases, if they feel the approach they are taking is similar to the approach in other organisations. If you can share a few tips on how other businesses solve the sorts of problems they face, you are both reciprocating and also giving them some social proof. Similarly, as a freelance expert you will tend to build a cross-industry network that may be far broader than many of your clients. Sometimes your clients really value being introduced to people in your network.

Cialdini describes how people are influenced by scarcity. If you want your advice or input on a clients' work to be more valued and persuasive, sometimes simply showing that you are highly in demand gives you authority and makes your advice more influential. For the same reason, I always recommend that you avoid telling clients you have 100% availability and no other client work, as it implies abundance and a lack of scarcity in your expertise. This both reduces your value and influence.

Clients are influenced by social proof, that is knowledge that confirms that what they are doing is similar to what other people are doing. This should be something that you as an independent expert are well placed to convince them of. Also, your own value as an expert is increased by social proof. We see this in the tendency for people with lots of followers on social media to gain more and more followers. People gain comfort in sensing that what they are doing is socially widespread. This is also why having written a popular book or having a popular podcast is valuable, as again it gives social proof.

These are all ways in which we can increase our influence as experts. But there is another way – that is, by understanding how influence is generated, we can predict situations in which we may have difficulty persuading our clients and we can plan actions to overcome their natural objections.

I am thinking of three specific situations.

The first is when our advice is for a client to do something that goes against the current trends or norms in society. For instance, currently there is a trend towards greater homeworking and more flexible working conditions. This trend is well known, and most organisations seem to be moving towards more flexibility. But imagine for an instant that you were advising an organisation to be less flexible to their staff in some area. This lacks social proof, and therefore on its own this advice may be unpersuasive.

The second situation is when we are going to advise a client to do something which is contrary to their past behaviour and decisions they have made – in other words is going to breach their need for commitment or consistency relative to their past. For example, imagine you are advising a client who for years has decided to buy some specialist equipment in Germany. Let's imagine this equipment is very good but is also rather expensive. Now, you want to advise the client that there is equivalent equipment that is better, and a quarter of the price, made in China. This conflicts with the client's need for consistency and the past commitment they have made to buying equipment in Germany.

The third example comes to liking. Not all clients will like you. No matter how you try, and how likeable you are, at some point in your career you will meet someone who does not like you, and who you probably don't like in return. I don't think anyone is liked by everyone. Sometimes, the chemistry is just wrong.

When a client does not like us, they tend to discount what we say. Feelings of dislike tend to become ideas that the other person is a fool or is working against us – even if there is no evidence of this. Because of this, when a client truly dislikes us, it can be especially hard to persuade them to follow our advice.

If we consider these examples, we can see that in each case we are going to have an uphill battle to convince the client to accept our advice. It will be harder to persuade them than if everyone else was doing the same, if it was consistent with what the client had done in the past or if the client liked us.

Yet, as an expert we will often find ourselves in such situations. Of course, sometimes as an expert you will confirm to clients that what they are already doing is right and that copying everyone else is appropriate, but often you will find there are better ways. This is when your expertise is most valuable, but that does not mean the client will want to listen.

When you find yourself in a situation in which you are going to have reduced influence because of human psychology, then the answer is that you are going to have to work harder to convince the client. You must make sure your information, arguments and the way you present your arguments are especially strong. You can use the trust your client has already built in you, knowing that you are reliable and consistent in your advice and something they can have faith in. In other words, you must find ways to counter the challenges these situations raise.

There is no standard way of approaching these situations that will work every time. But at least by understanding the levers of persuasion and influence you will be in a better position to predict resistance to your advice, and to prepare and plan your approach to convincing your client. Usually, with some clear thinking, you can find a way to persuade a client, even in a difficult situation. It can be personally very rewarding when you convince a client to follow advice they were initially resistant to.

However, occasionally the odds are stacked so badly against us that no matter how helpful our expertise could be to the client, and no matter how much effort we put into giving it, we are not going to persuade the client to trust us or to follow our advice. If this happens, the best counsel is to give up and move on somewhere else. Banging your head against a door that will never open is a waste of time. There is always another client who is better suited to you.

An independent voice

Uzma Aitqad, Magna People Change

My name is Uzma Aitqad. I am an Organisational Change and Culture Design Consultant with over 22 years of extensive and culturally diverse experience in both public and private sectors across the UK, MENA, Pakistan and Asia Pacific countries.

I have led and managed numerous transformational changes involving digital transformations and culture change initiatives. These involved applying people-focused management of change methodology with engagement/ resistance management strategies and capability development activities – all enabling people to embrace change willingly and business to transition smoothly.

My passion for driving business excellence through people, always made me think that a change can only be a success if people adopted it with full confidence and desire.

So to exercise and actualize my beliefs, I started my private consulting practice where I could apply a more focused and well-researched people-centric approach to change, focusing more on organizational culture to deliver a sustainable result that contributes to business success.

Somebody very rightly said that 'organizations don't change, but people do' – I try my level best to reflect this sentiment as part of consulting.

Besides my consulting practice, I also find my solace in teaching and building capabilities – the freelance nature of my consulting work allows me to fulfil this.

I have been a visiting lecturer on HR topics including international leadership and management, organization development and working across cultures at the University of Brighton Business School, and the mini MBA program at Birkbeck College, University of London. I also deliver bespoke workshops for corporate leadership.

It hasn't been an easy ride for me to come to this point in my career, especially as I work in the UK, which is not the country where I was born and raised. I am a Pakistani by origin. I migrated to this country after my marriage in my late thirties. That is the time when people usually are pretty much settled in their careers.

I had to start my career afresh and build my place alongside adjusting to a new environment, new culture and weather. I not only managed all of this, but I challenged the status quo of my routine life by doing a full-time consulting job with a part-time postgraduate in organizational change and management consultancy from Birkbeck College, University of London.

Would you like to know how I managed to cope with all these challenges in life?

When I was a child, I remember my mother inculcated in me that I can do anything in life if I wanted to. It is this CAN-DO mindset that I identify with and which reflects in every aspect of my life. It reflects in my consulting practice too, where I help businesses with this belief that they can achieve aspired results with the CAN-DO mindset.

My most important advice for you is to always stay connected to the belief that you CAN DO what you want to achieve for yourself and for the clients you're helping. It is this unshakeable belief and its manifestation in the form of hard work and perseverance, that makes a difference.

If you'd like to know more about my services or would like to chat with me to discuss any organizational or people issues, please reach out to me on the following links:

- website: www.magnapeoplechange.com
- LinkedIn: https://uk.linkedin.com/in/uzma-aitqad
- Email: uzma.aitqad@magnapeoplechange.com

chapter

4

Thriving and leveraging freelancing for other interests

We have covered a lot of ground in this book. I hope you have enjoyed the ride and learnt lots along the way. If you are just setting out, and still planning to set yourself up as an independent expert, then I hope I have helped you to get ready both practically and psychologically. If you are an old hand, I hope I have taught you a few new tricks and given you some different things to focus on.

There is now only a little further to go. The previous thirteen chapters have each taken an aspect of being a freelance expert and described how to go about setting yourself up and working independently.

In this chapter, I want to look longer term and discuss how to get the most from your career. To begin with I want to look at what it takes to have a long-term career.

Thriving as the world changes

I expect that you know the phrase *there is no constant but change*. As a freelance expert change is mostly a good thing – it is often people's need to cope with one or more of the myriad forms of change that creates the demand for our services. But change does not just affect our clients, it affects us too.

The main result of change is that the demand, and the associated fees, that our services lines will generate varies over time. Clients' needs, tastes and expectations continually modify. We all want to spot that service that everyone wants and is willing to pay the most for. But even the most in-demand of services will eventually become commoditised or even unwanted. Because of this, if you want to have a long-term career, you will need to adapt your services in line with those evolving client needs, tastes and expectations.

But it is not just the content of the expertise wanted that changes, it is also the style with which it is provided. When I started out as a consultant, when a client needed advice, the style was to tell them. More engaging styles of interaction, that focused more on the individual person being helped, were rare. But gradually the 'tell the answer' style of the traditional expert has given way to a 'help clients find their answer' style of a coach. Over time, how we interact with people, how we provide advice and the nature of our relationship with our clients has progressed. I have no doubt it will continue to evolve.

Hence it is worth regularly asking yourself two questions:

1. What types of expertise are clients interested in continuing to buy?
2. How are expectations about the style, in which that expertise is provided, evolving?

To help you to answer these questions, let me tell you a little bit about my story.

Decades ago, when I started out in consulting, I was mostly engaged by clients to run their projects. Essentially, I worked as a project manager. I was usually part of a consulting team, with each consultant bringing different skills. The projects I was engaged in took months or years, and I was expected to be on client location full time. I travelled to a lot of client offices and I spent a lot of time away from home in many different countries. Success was about achieving the goals of whatever project I was working on – which were often concerned with implementing new systems and processes in large organisations. Those goals were usually very tangible.

It was a great career at that time. I was learning and earning an increasing income. Project management was an in-demand skill, and although there had been project managers for a long time, good ones were in short supply.

But nothing stays the same. Over the next few years, more and more people came into the project management profession. The average skill levels went up and it was harder to stand out as particularly good. I realised that because so many people had become project managers, there was a risk that my fees were going to stall.

The principle that as demand increases, rates goes down, holds in the market for expertise. I decided to evolve my services by adding an extra skill onto my offer. In this way I planned to stay differentiated from other consulting project managers and hoped to keep up my ability to earn good fees.

Rather than focusing purely on project management, I started to develop expertise in the related discipline of change management. This worked. For a while being an experienced project manager with knowledge of change management differentiated me from other project managers, and I could keep earning good fees.

But client needs modified again. Change management skills started to become commoditised. I was finding I could not set my fees to what I wanted to earn, but instead I was constrained by rates in the market. I was at risk of being pigeon-holed into a low-paying skill set.

Whenever you find yourself being regularly categorised into a profession or skill set that mostly does not pay well, you need to think about differentiating yourself again. So, I sought ways to differentiate myself. Fortunately for me, at that time my writing career took off and I was able to get some excellent publishing contracts from well-known publishers such as Financial Times Books and John Wiley. Having written some well-regarded books, I was able to position myself as a true expert with my clients.

And now? I am still involved in project and change management. I stay involved in large projects mainly to keep my knowledge fresh. I find advisers who have been advising for many years but have stopped doing the work their advice relates to, tend to become outdated. But even so, much of my work is now as an adviser and mentor rather than hands on running teams delivering projects.

Although it is a logical progression from where I started, my day-to-day working life is very different. A lot of my work is done remotely, sometimes from different countries or even continents than where my clients are based. Many of my engagements are quite short – lasting a few days or weeks giving focused help to a single leader involved in change to overcome a particularly challenging situation. I am regularly engaged as an individual specialist, rather than as part of a consulting team. I usually have multiple client engagements running in parallel. My success is often intangible and can mostly be measured in the satisfaction levels of my clients.

I am telling you my story not for you to copy, but as an example. It would not be worth copying my story, as clients' needs and expectations continue to evolve. But it is worth thinking about the shape of my story, as it is one that is not unusual among independent experts. Swap project and change management for a long list of other disciplines and you will find many thousands of people have done something similar. They started out providing one service, but over the life of their career they have continually shifted to other services.

If I had not done this, I would probably still be busy working as a project manager, but I expect I would be earning a fraction of what I do now.

Part of my story has been driven by my personal desires. I have always had an interest in new ways of working and applying them to my domain. I have been driven by my desire to have the flexibility to manage my life as I want. So, I have developed the sort of services that enable this and selected clients who are happy to work with me on this basis. But part of my story has been driven by the larger forces in society and in the employment place. None of us is as in control as we think we are.

Some of these forces create challenges when old services are no longer wanted, but they also create opportunities as new services emerge. For instance, there are always new waves of technology and there are always changing social expectations. With those new waves of technology come people who need help understanding and utilising them. With those changing social expectations come people who need help adapting to them – people who could be your clients. It's worth always keeping your eyes open for new opportunities as new types of client demands emerge.

Whatever you start out doing, you are unlikely to be able to do it for the whole of your career, even if you really are the world's greatest expert. Part of your success as a freelancer will be adapting your skills and services over time, adapting them to the sort of work you want to be doing, and the types of services that are in demand among your clients.

Growing your business further

Money is an interesting topic to most people, and while I know a few individuals who really are not that bothered by how much they earn, they are unusual. A common question I am faced with is how to maximise revenues when you work selling yourself as an expert.

As a freelance expert you have only a few levers to increase how much money you make. Let's look at these one by one.

Firstly – and most obviously – you can try to bill more hours. If you want to bill more hours, then your focus should be on your sales and marketing as discussed in Chapters 4, 5, 8 and 9. I often come across freelance experts who are only working a few hours a week and would like to be working more.

In this situation, there is the potential to increase your income by selling more. But there is always a very clear limit to how far you can go. There is after all, a fixed number of hours in the week, and most of us do not want to be working more than a certain percentage of that time. So, by all means work harder if you want, but be aware it can only increase your income so much. And remember why you became independent in the first place – it was probably not to work all the hours of the day!

There is a second option. You can charge a higher rate. The differential in the fee rates between the best and worst remunerated experts is significant. To get to be able to charge the highest rates you need to develop the credibility as an expert who is worth those rates, and this can be achieved by following many of the lessons we have discussed through this book. They can be summarised as having in-demand skills for the right group of clients – and having strong trust-based relationships with those clients.

Billing more time at a higher rate can increase your income significantly, but even using both of these levers to increase your income there is always going to be a practical limit to how much you can earn. There are a few globally recognised gurus who can bill vast amounts of money for a single day's work, and who remain in high demand. But in truth, there are only ever a small number of these people. If you manage to achieve this, then I take my hat off to you, but it's a hard road and most people are not going to make it.

Don't despair though! There is a different way of increasing your revenue which I touched on in Chapter 6. This is to move away from billing for your time, to start billing for a service, or what is often called *value-based charging*.

Value-based charging starts on the premise that the amount you charge should not be determined by the effort you put into your work as measured by the time you spent on it, but instead should be determined by how valuable your work is to your clients. Sometimes, what seems like a relatively simple thing for you to do has huge value to the client.

For instance, an expert can often solve a client's problem quite quickly because they have successfully dealt with similar problems many times before. What may take the non-expert weeks or months to resolve, can in some cases take an expert a few minutes to sort out. You may think about those few minutes as the basis for your charges to your clients. Why limit yourself this way? From the client's perspective you have saved them months of hassle and it is worth the related level of fees.

One important thing to note is that if you choose to work this way you will find the value of a service is different for pretty much every customer you meet.

There are many examples where the client's perception of value is much higher than the cost you might charge for a service if you were simply charging for your time. A small app may take a coder only a few days to develop, but if it makes some work easier or more efficient in a large organisation it can be hugely valuable to them. A firm may benefit from the strategic insight of a consultant who knows their industry well. Although the insight may come in a flash, it could completely change the fortunes of a company. An individual may be struggling with a personal issue that a few hours of coaching may resolve, and to that individual the resolution of the issue could change their life.

At one level, using value-based charging is mostly about making a mindset shift for the freelancer, although given how long many freelancers have worked on an hourly or daily fee rate it can be hard to make that mindset change. Surely, many think, it cannot be that easy. Well actually it can be. Of course, there are risks and challenges with working in this way, but if you manage to overcome them your earnings potential is huge, and you get away from being limited by the number of hours in the day.

I am just touching on what is a whole specialist topic in its own right. If you are interested there are some useful references in the Further reading and other resources section that follows.

Freelancing as a platform for another business

This book has been all about freelancing. For many freelancers, that is exactly what they want to do, and only what they want to do. But freelancing can also be a basis to build other careers. The very flexibility of freelancing means that you can decide to use it as a basis to do anything else you want to do. For many people, freelancing enables them to make a whole series of lifestyle choices that would not otherwise be available. But for some freelancers, that flexibility gives them the time to build other careers and incomes that they want.

There are three specific types of working and earning an income that a freelance career easily enables which I want to explore briefly here:

1. *Building a pyramid*: building a business with other freelancers working for you.
2. *Side hustles*: doing other enjoyable and paid activities you like.
3. *Making money while you sleep*: finding a way to generate an ongoing income, painlessly.

1. Building a pyramid

There is a different way to increase your revenues, which is especially attractive to those who have large networks of clients and are good at sales. This is to shift to selling other experts as well as yourself.

Imagine for instance, that you are an IT contractor and a client offers you an engagement that requires half a dozen IT contractors. One response is to find a group of skilled colleagues, pay them to do the work, and you bill the client and keep a percentage of the money from the whole engagement. This can generate far more money than working by yourself ever would.

Eventually if you know enough clients and you can grow your business large enough, you may completely stop selling your personal expertise, but just work as a client relationship manager and salesperson, making your money by farming out teams of other freelance experts. I call this building a pyramid – with yourself figuratively as the apex of that pyramid, and the other freelancers who do the client work as the base of the pyramid.

You should not imagine this is that complex. A very good income can be generated by selling contracts for 10–20 other experts even with only 1 or 2 clients. If you sell more than this, you really can build a very lucrative business. At the core of being able to do this are your relationship management, marketing and sales skills. If those skills are strong, and they are what you most enjoy doing, then building a pyramid may well be a good option for you.

This is a different business from the one described in this book. It is a business that requires a whole series of other things to think about. It has its own challenges and risks. For example: how do you pay the other freelancers who are now working for you? They will often require payment before your client pays you, which can cause cashflow problems. How do you ensure the quality of the other freelancers' work is as good as yours and they do not damage your client relationships?

All of these challenges are resolvable, and this has been a proven route to success that many consultants, contractors and coaches have taken to build bigger firms. Many of them have become comfortably wealthy on the way. It was not what I wanted to do, but it may be for you. If this is what you want to do, there are many others who have trodden this path before who you can learn from.

But before you choose to do this, I will leave you with one story which has always stayed with me.

I remember seeing an Italian chef talking on the TV about his restaurant in Rome. It is a famous restaurant that has continued for several generations. It is well known for its excellent food and hospitality. An interviewer was asking the chef about the secrets of his success as a restauranteur.

He replied that he had always focused on providing the best food and running the best restaurant. He compared himself to other much better-known chefs. When they had become famous, they then opened another restaurant, and then another, until they were running a chain of restaurants around the world. Sure, they were wealthy. But were they good chefs anymore and was the food in their restaurants as good as it had been when they focused purely on one restaurant?

His view was that if you want to produce the best you need to be focused on every element, and that meant running one restaurant. And for him being the best chef he could be was much more important than having a chain of restaurants with his name plastered on them all over the world.

That has been my attitude as a consultant and adviser. I always wanted to be the best I could be. I do partner with lots of other people, some of whom have built successful businesses selling the time of other consultants and advisers – including mine. I respect them as businesspeople very much. But it was never what I wanted to do. One major reason is that it would bring me back into working in an organisation. Yes, it would be an organisation I was running, but I always felt this would impinge on the flexibility and pleasure pure independence brings me. It might, however, be just right for you.

2. Side hustles and other sources of income

One of the great things about being independent is that you can do other things. Unlike normal employment, you have control over where, when and how you spend your time. For some independent experts I know this means they have time to pursue their passions – sport, art, travel and so on.

But for others this means they have the opportunity to pursue another business as well as providing freelance expertise. These could be any businesses. For instance, I know one IT contractor who also has a chain of rental properties, and I know one coach who is also a photographer. These separate businesses have nothing to do with their work as a freelance expert, but they have time to pursue them.

However, there are certain businesses which align very well with being a coach, contractor or consultant because they utilise the same expertise that you use in your freelance business.

The most obvious and common examples are providing training, giving talks and webinars, and writing. For instance, I do not just work as a specialist consultant, I am a successful author with a long list of books. My books have been translated into many languages, exist as physical books and eBooks, and there is even one audio book. This has been an enjoyable and rewarding addition to my central work. It interacts well with my core business, as it reinforces my expertise and increases my network as well as making an income in its own right. On top of this, I increasingly spend my time in one-to-one mentoring based on my work experience and books.

I know other individuals who have built successful training businesses based on their expertise, and I know a few people who have developed a business as an in-demand public speaker, talking at conferences and webinars. For some of the people I know, what was once a side-hustle has become their main income, and their days of selling their services to individual clients as a freelance expert are now over. For others, it remains one part of a portfolio career.

All of these businesses, such as training, speaking or writing have their own challenges and opportunities, and if you want to get into them as well it is worth doing your homework and understanding what you are getting into before you do. But the barriers to entry are low and many have shown that it is possible.

3. Making money while you sleep

The dream of many people with these side hustles is to get away from being tied to working certain hours or days with their clients. The dream is to get away from earning while you work, to having an ongoing stream of income, or as it is often put *making money while you sleep*. Again, there is a track record of experts who have managed to do this, usually producing some kind of product protected with copyright and licenses that is sold to other people.

I am thinking of things like books, licensed methodologies and franchised training courses. For instance, I co-own a business project management business game with a specialist games developer called Totem Learning (see https://totemlearning.com). Every time this is sold, I make a small amount of money. Although I had to put work in up-front to create the game, now it is developed I don't need to do anything.

If you can make this work, it is fabulous. One word of caution though: I often find that people under-estimate how tricky these businesses can be, and over-estimate the revenues they may generate. I know quite a few disappointed experts who have tried this. Nevertheless, it can work and there are people who have built very successful businesses in this way.

Summarising the six ways to increase your freelance income

Throughout this chapter, and elsewhere in the book, I have proposed six ways you can increase your income as a freelancer. These are brought together in Table 14.1. In my view, some of these ways are preferable to others, but each of us lives in our own reality and the choice is yours.

Thriving and having fun

A lot of this chapter has been about money. Money is always going to be important. Even if you are not materialistic, you will have bills to pay and need a certain income. Money may not buy you happiness, but when used wisely it can certainly make your life a lot easier and less stressful. But there is a risk in the freelance trade of becoming a little overly focused on revenues. I have seen more than one contractor pushing themselves to the point of ill health because they are adamant that they will charge every hour they work.

Table 14.1 How you can leverage freelancing to increase your income

	Ways I can increase my income	How will I achieve this?
1	Work more hours	
2	Increase the rate I charge per unit of time	
3	Move to value pricing	
4	Build a pyramid	
5	Find a complementary side hustle	
6	Create an income while I sleep	

This can become an especially seductive trap to be caught by when you are charging by the hour. It is easy to fall into the mentality that every hour not worked is money lost. I know freelancers who calculate the cost of their holidays not only in terms of how much they must spend on tickets and hotels, but also adding on the fees they have not charged because they were on holiday. This is a bad mindset to get into and one that generally leads to misery and a view that every holiday is far too expensive.

Always remember, we don't live to work, we work to live!

If being a freelance expert becomes a cage where you think you must work every second of every day, then it's time for a rethink. Being a freelance expert can be so much more than this. It's within your capabilities to achieve more than this – freedom, independence, flexibility and fun. It is all possible if you stay focused enough on your goals and work in a deliberate way towards achieving them.

I wish you the very best of luck.

Final thoughts

We've reached the end of the book. The only thing that follows is a short section of references to additional resources – books and websites you may find useful if you want to explore anything I have discussed in any more detail.

Way back at the start of the book, in the Introduction I included a diagram to help guide you should you not wish to read the book in a linear order. Now you have read the book, I have adapted this diagram into a table (Table 14.2) with references to all the assets and information you can find, cross-referenced against the topics in the 'lifecycle of work' as originally shown in Figure 1. With this you can easily find all the different tables, diagrams and chapters you may be interested in.

Table 14.2 Quick reference to the key concepts in the book

Identify a specialised area of advising Chapters 2, 4, 5 & 14	■ Why do we need experts? – Chapter 2 ■ What is your service? – Chapter 4 ■ How do you provide it? – Table 4.2 and Figure 4.1 ■ Understanding you client niche – Chapter 5 ■ Growing your business further – Chapter 14
Work out a price for this service Chapters 6 & 14	■ What can you charge? – Chapter 6 ■ Reflection on price – Table 6.1 ■ Negotiating – Table 6.2 ■ By unit of time or by value pricing? – Chapters 6 and 14

14 ■ Thriving and leveraging freelancing for other interests

Find clients who want this advice Chapters 4, 5 & 8	▪ Understanding clients – Chapter 2 and Table 2.1 ▪ The right clients – Table 4.1 ▪ Client personas – Chapter 5 ▪ Determining your clients – Figure 5.1 ▪ Your service summary – Tables 6.3, 6.4 and 6.5
Get those clients to buy this service and pay for it Chapters 8 & 9	▪ Routes to market – Table 8.1 ▪ Networks – Figure 8.1 ▪ Your sales funnel – Figure 8.2 ▪ Social media – Chapter 8 ▪ Your pitch – Tables 8.2, 8.3 and 8.4 ▪ Your proposal – Tables 9.3 and 9.4 ▪ How to sell expert services – Chapter 9
Understand how to deliver the service Chapters 2, 7 & 11 to 13	▪ The foundation stones – Introduction ▪ Skills and behaviours – Chapter 2 ▪ Prepare for freelancing – Chapter 7 ▪ Handling your first engagement – Tables 10.1 and 10.2 ▪ Running excellent engagements – Tables 9.1 and 11.1
Please clients Chapters 1 & 10 to 13	▪ The skills and behaviours – Chapter 1 ▪ Handling your first engagement – Table 10.1 ▪ Running excellent engagements – Tables 10.1, 10.2 and 11.1 ▪ Developing trust, listening skills, helping and advice giving – Chapter 12, Tables 12.1, 12.2 and 12.3 ▪ Increasing credibility, persuasion and influence – Chapter 13
Run a business and protect your interests Chapters 9 to 11	▪ What you need – Table 7.1 ▪ Writing a proposal – Tables 9.1 and 9.3 ▪ T&Cs – Table 9.4 ▪ Preparing yourself – Tables 10.1 and 10.4 ▪ Managing the risk of bad debt – Chapter 10 ▪ Running engagements – Tables 10.2 and 10.3, Chapter 11 and Table 11.1
Thriving and leveraging freelancing Chapter 14	▪ Keeping your service relevant and in-demand – Chapter 14 ▪ Thinking about refreshing the way you provide your service – Chapter 14 ▪ Leveraging freelancing for another business – Chapter 14 ▪ Maximising your income – Table 14.1 ▪ Further reading and other resources section

Staying in touch

If you want to find out more about me, follow what I am interested in, or contact me you can find me on:

- Twitter at @RJNtalk
- LinkedIn at https://www.linkedin.com/in/richardjenewton/
- Goodreads at https://www.goodreads.com and look for my author profile

Feel free to contact, connect or follow me on any of these platforms.

My business website is www.enixus.co.uk where there is also a form to ping me and get in touch.

Further reading and other resources

I have referred to many other books throughout this book. If you are interested and want to find out more about any of them, they are all listed here, plus a few others that I think you might just find helpful too. I have organised them thematically by the chapters in the book they best support. A few of the resources are relevant to more than one chapter, and in this case, I have repeated them for each chapter they are relevant to.

Chapter		Additional resources
1	Why be a freelancer?	Heller, Cathy. (2019). *Don't Keep Your Day Job: How to Turn Your Passion Into Your Career.* St Martin's Press.
		Schwartz, Barry. (2015). *Why We Work.* Simon & Schuster.
		https://www.freelancer.com
		https://www.freelancesolutions.co.uk
		https://www.homeworkingclub.com
2	Different types of freelancers and what they offer	Grade, Alison. (2020). *The Freelance Bible: Everything You Need to Go Solo in Any Industry.* Portfolio Penguin.
3	Understanding why clients hire freelancers	Lewis, Martyn R. (2018). *How Customers Buy . . . & Why They Don't: Mapping and Managing the Buying Journey DNA.* Radius Book Group.
		Sartre, Jean-Paul. (2007). *Existentialism is a Humanism.* Yale University Press.
		https://copywriters.com/blog/post/why-customers-buy-two-reasons
		https://due.com/blog/5-reasons-make-customers-buy/
4	Defining your specialisation	Altucher, James. (2013). *Choose Yourself: Be Happy, Make Millions, Live the Dream.* CreateSpace Independent Publishing Platform.
		McMakin, Tom and Fletcher, Doug. (2018). *How Clients Buy.* Wiley.
		Newton, Richard. (2019). *The Management Consultant: Mastering the Art of Consultancy.* Financial Times Prentice Hall.

(continued)

Chapter		Additional resources
5	Profiling your clients	Maister, David, Green, Charles and Galford, Robert. (2002). *The Trusted Advisor*. Simon & Schuster.
		Osterwalder, Alexander and Pigneur, Yves. (2010). *Business Model Generation*. Wiley.
		https://www.strategyzer.com/canvas/business-model-canvas
6	Pricing your services	Hill, Peter. (2013). *Pricing for Profit: How to Develop a Powerful Pricing Strategy for Your Business*. Kogan Page.
		Husemann-Kopetzky, Dr Markus. (2018). *Handbook on the P$ychology of Pricing: 100+ Effects on Persuasion and Influence Every Entrepreneur, Marketer and Pricing Manager Needs to Know*. Pricing School Press.
		Stark, Jonathan. (2016). *Hourly Billing is Nuts: Essays on the Insanity of Trading Time for Money*. (Self-published, see www.jonathanstark.com)
		Voss, Chris. (2017). *Never Split the Difference: Negotiating as if Your Life Depended on It*. Random House Business.
		https://jonathanstark.com
7	Preparing yourself for freelancing	Newton, Richard and Rusen, Ciprian Adrian. (2013). *Dream It, Do It, Live It: 9 Easy Steps to Making Things Happen for You*. Capstone.
		Watt, James. (2015). *Business for Punks*. Penguin.
		Williams, Sara. (2019). *The FT Guide to Business Start Up*. FT Publishing International.
		Yocum, Jeanne. (2018). *The Self-Employment Survival Guide: Proven Strategies to Succeed as Your Own Boss*. Rowman & Littlefield.

Further reading and other resources

Chapter		Additional resources
8	Marketing and finding clients	Dib, Allan. (2018). *The 1-Page Marketing Plan: Get New Customers, Make More Money, And Stand out From The Crowd.* Page Two.
		Ducker, Chris. (2018). *Rise of the Youpreneur: The Definitive Guide to Becoming the Go-To Leader in Your Industry and Building a Future-Proof Business.* 4C Press.
		Kane, Brendan. (2018). *One Million Followers: How I Built a Massive Social Following in 30 Days: Growth Hacks for Your Business, Your Message, and Your Brand from the World's Greatest Minds.* BenBella Books.
		Maister, David, Green, Charles and Galford, Robert. (2002). *The Trusted Advisor.* Simon & Schuster.
		McMakin, Tom and Fletcher, Doug. (2018). *How Clients Buy.* Wiley.
		Port, Michael. (2017). *Book Yourself Solid: The Fastest, Easiest, and Most Reliable System for Getting More Clients Than You Can Handle Even if You Hate Marketing and Selling.* Wiley.
		https://www.amyporterfield.com/amy-porterfield-podcast/
		https://kaidavis.com/articles/
		https://rochellemoulton.com/podcast/
		https://www.marketingforconsultants.com
9	Selling and making sure you get paid	Enns, Blair. (2018). *The Win Without Pitching Manifesto.* Gegen Press.
		Hodgkinson, Tom. (2017). *Business for Bohemians.* Penguin.
		McMakin, Tom and Fletcher, Doug. (2018). *How Clients Buy.* Wiley.
		Voss, Chris. (2017). *Never Split the Difference: Negotiating as if Your Life Depended on It.* Random House Business.
		Watt, James. (2015). *Business for Punks.* Penguin.
		Weiss, Alan. (2016). *Million Dollar Consulting: The Professional's Guide to Growing a Practice* (5th edition). McGraw-Hill Education.
		https://www.salesman.org/604-what-is-consulting-explained-by-a-world-leading-consultant-with-richard-newton/
		https://www.winwithoutpitching.com/pricing-creativity
10	Running your first engagement	Newton, Richard. (2019). *The Management Consultant: Mastering the Art of Consultancy.* Financial Times Prentice Hall.
		O'Keeffe, Naimh. (2019). *Your First 100 Days: Make Maximum Impact in Your New Role.* Financial Times Prentice Hall.
		https://checklist.com/

(continued)

Chapter		Additional resources
11	Improving your engagements	▪ Newton, Richard. (2019). *The Management Consultant: Mastering the Art of Consultancy*. Financial Times Prentice Hall.
		▪ Townsend, Sarah. (2020). *Survival Skills for Freelancers: Tried and Tested Tips to Help You Ace Self-employment Without Burnout*. Sarah Townsend.
		▪ https://checklist.com/
12	Building relationships to drive your freelance success	▪ Hargie, Owen. (2018). *The Handbook of Communication Skills* (4th edition). Routledge.
		▪ Maister, David, Green, Charles and Galford, Robert. (2002). *The Trusted Advisor*. Simon & Schuster.
		▪ Patterson, Kerry, Grenny, Joseph, McMillan, Ron and Switzler, Al. (2011). *Crucial Conversations: Tools for Talking When Stakes Are High* (2nd edition). McGraw-Hill Education.
		▪ Schein, Edgar H. (2013). *Humble Inquiry: The Gentle Art of Asking Instead of Telling*. Berrett-Koehler.
13	Developing your credibility and influence with clients	▪ Ariely, Dan. (2009). *Predictably Irrational: The Hidden Forces That Shape Our Decisions*. Harper.
		▪ Cialdini, Robert B. (2007). *Influence: The Psychology of Persuasion* (Revised edition). Harper Business.
		▪ Cohen, Allan R. and Bradford, David L. (2017). *Influence Without Authority* (3rd edition). Wiley.
		▪ Goleman, Daniel. (2005). *Emotional Intelligence: Why It Can Matter More Than IQ*. Bantam.
		▪ Kahneman, Daniel. (2012). *Thinking, Fast and Slow*. Penguin.
		▪ Levitt, Steven D. and Dubner, Stephen J. (2020). *Freakonomics: A Rogue Economist Explores the Hidden Side of Everything* (Revised edition). William Morrow & Company.
		▪ Minto, Barbara. (2009). *The Pyramid Principle*. Financial Times Prentice Hall.

Chapter		Additional resources
14 Thriving and leveraging freelancing	▪	Guillebeau, Chris. (2019). *Side Hustle: Build a Side Business and Make Extra Money – Without Quitting Your Day Job*. Pan.
	▪	Senatore, Luca. (2019). *The Agency: Build - Grow - Repeat: How To Build a Remarkable Digital Agency Business That Wins and Keeps Clients*. Fiftyfive Books.
	▪	Stark, Jonathan. (2016). *Hourly Billing is Nuts: Essays on the Insanity of Trading Time for Money*. (Self-published, see www.jonathanstark.com)
	▪	Watt, James. (2015). *Business for Punks*. Penguin.
	▪	Weiss, Alan. (2008). *Value-Based Fees: How to Charge – and Get – What You're Worth* (2nd edition). Pfeiffer.
	▪	https://www.entrepreneur.com/article/303828
	▪	https://www.forbes.com/sites/alizalicht/2020/01/01/how-to-build-a-successful-consulting-business/
	▪	https://www.simplybusiness.co.uk/knowledge/articles/2019/06/how-to-start-a-recruitment-agency-in-the-uk/

I read a lot and I read widely. I always have at least one book on the go. Some of it is relevant to my freelance work, some is not. But if you are really interested to see what I am reading, and what I think about the books I have read, you can find reviews of every book I have read in the last few years on Goodreads at: https://www.goodreads.com/author/show/7068505.Richard_Newton

Index

access to clients 45, 59
accountants 5, 79, 89
accounting system 89
accreditations 175
administration 70, 87–90, 159
advising 49, 167–70
agents 104
Aitqad, Uzma 184–5
Altucher, James 51
attitude to your clients 34–5
authenticity 119, 161
authority 179
   influence without 180–1

Banger, Daljit R. 64–5
bank accounts 89
behaviour(s)
   on client engagements 153–5
   necessary to perform freelancer tasks 21–3
billing 129–30, 131
body language 166
brand 103, 180
building other careers 191–5
building a pyramid 192–3
businesses, as clients 57–9

capability, lack of, as client reason for hiring freelancers 27, 29, 30
capacity, lack of, as client reason for hiring freelancers 27, 29

cash flow 87
cash reserves 5, 13, 87, 89, 131
change
   adapting to 186–9
   management 188
Cialdini, Robert, *Influence: The Psychology of Persuasion* 178–9, 182
client leads 98–9
client persona 55–64
   dimensions of 61–2
client reasons for hiring freelancers 26–34
   hidden reasons 30–3
      being told to get help 32
      finger-pointing motive 32–3
      guidance 33
      needing support for their ideas 31
      someone to listen 31
   implications for pricing your service 28, 29–30, 34
   lack of
      capability 27, 29, 30
      capacity 27, 29
      confidence 27–8, 29, 30
      motivation 27, 28, 29
      remit 28, 29, 30
clients 20
   ability and propensity to pay for your services 44, 58–9, 130
   access to 45, 59

as always a person 59–60
attitude towards helping your 34–5
common challenges 62
demographics 62
enough 99
feedback 136, 155
fees and choice of 68–9, 74
finding 21, 97
   see also marketing
finding common ground with 160–1
functional domain 62
fundamental characteristics 44–5
geographic location 61
ideal 62–4
individuals or businesses? 57–9
industrial sector 61
job role 61
listening to 31, 121, 164–7
meeting 7–8
more than one person as 60–1
needs, and selling your service 118, 120
relationships with see relationships
selecting/rejecting 8
set of 5
shared interests 62
style of interaction with 187
   see also communication style; relationships
trust see trust
coaches/coaching 18, 36–7, 49
   for freelancers 46, 94
Cohen, Allan and David Bradford, *Influence Without Authority* 180–1
cold outreach (cold calling) 105, 106, 109
Coligan, Theresa 36–7
commitment 179, 183

communication style 154, 155, 175
company registration and name 88
competencies 21–3
confidence, lack of, as client reason for hiring freelancers 27–8, 29, 30
consistency 175–6, 179, 183
consultants 18
content marketing 76, 105, 106, 108, 110
contractors 18
contracts 125, 126
cost of sales 80
costs of running a business 79
Cowan, Charles 170–2
credibility 22, 47, 85–6, 120, 134, 162, 163, 164, 171
   sources of 174–5
   and trust 162, 163, 164
   and your ability to present yourself 174–6
credit cards 89
cultural differences, awareness of 12, 155, 164
cultural fit 137
customers see clients

data protection laws 90
debt collection 132
delivering the service 21, 130, 148, 150, 152
   first engagement 137–40
demographics, client 62
Dib, Allan 112
doing approach to helping clients 49

eight steps of freelancing xvii–xviii, 9–10
encouragement approach to helping clients 49

engagement(s) 20
  behaviour on 153–5
  checklists 124–5, 136–7,
       151–3, 249
  closedown stage 148, 150–1, 152
  delivery stage 148, 150, 152
  epilogue stage 148, 151, 152–3
  improving 147–55
  initiation stage 148, 149–50, 152
  preparation stage 148, 149, 151
  short 148
  see also first engagement
enthusiasm 119
equipment 88, 90
expenses 123, 130
  tracking 89
experience 47, 85–6, 174
experimentation 46, 106
expertise 174
  communicating your 162, 175
  developing 85–6
  focus of 176

facilities 88, 90
faking skills 161
Farley, Lyndall 13–14
feedback
  on behaviour and
       communication style 155
  client 136, 155
finances *see* money
first engagement 135–42
  checklists 136–7
    dealing with changes 139–40
    dealing with problems 138
  completing 140–1
  dealing with changes to brief 137,
       139–40
  delivering 137–40
  if things start to go wrong 137,
       138
first impressions 150, 160

Fletcher, Doug 43, 52, 107, 110
flexibility 12, 24, 52
following up 169–70
functional domain, client 62

GDPR (General Data Protection
       Regulation) 90
generalists 42, 43
geographic location, client 61
Google 143
Gould, Scott 53–4
guidance, providing 33
gurus 18

helping 22, 34–5, 167–70
  follow up on 169–70
  permission to help 167–8
  relevance of help offered 168–9
  useable help 35, 169
Hodgkinson, Tom 115, 116
home working 7, 8
honesty 119, 155, 161, 172

ideal client 62–4
income
  alternative 5–6, 24–5
  and fees 78–80
  minimum 73, 99–100
  ways to increase 5, 189–95
    build a pyramid 192–3
    charge a higher rate 73–4, 75,
       190
    making money while you sleep
       194–5
    side hustles 193–4
    work more hours 190
independence 4, 6–8, 14, 24–5, 52
  preparing for 84–90
individuals, as clients 57–9
industrial sector, client 61
influence 173, 178–9, 181–4
  long-term 23

rational side of 174-8
weapons of 179
without authority 180-1
influencers 18, 111
insights, providing 120
instructing approach to helping clients 49
interim managers 18
interpersonal skills 59-60, 154
intimacy 162-3, 164
investing in yourself 65
invoices 130

jack of all trades 18, 19, 43
Jepson, Dave 150
job role, client 61
job titles and labels 16-19
juggling between tasks 9-10

know-what versus know-how 47-8
knowledge 22, 46-7
  how you share this with your clients 48-50
  new 47-8

labels and job titles 16-19
Lander, Mike 133-4
last impressions 150-1
learning 46, 136, 141
legal redress for non-payment 132
legal responsibilities 90
legal structure 88
leveraging freelancing 21, 186-96
life of a freelancer 11-13
lifecycle of work xix, 20-1, 79-80, 196
likeability 119, 179, 181, 183
LinkedIn 45, 46, 110, 111, 134
listening to clients 31, 121, 164-7
location independence 14

Maister, David et al., *The Trusted Advisor* 60, 103, 162
making money while you sleep 194-5
marketing 83, 97-114
  content 76, 105, 106, 108, 110
  reverse 104, 105, 106
  routes to market 104-6
  sales funnel 98-100, 112, 113
  valuable conversation 98
  your pitch 100-2
McDermott, Alastair 104, 113-14
McMakin, Tom 43, 52, 107, 110
mentors 18
  for freelancers 46, 154
mobility 65
money 4-6, 13, 87
  see also cash flow; cash reserves; income; pricing your services
motivation, lack of, as client reason for hiring freelancers 27, 28, 29

network 143
  building your 46, 83, 86-7
  importance of your 108-10
  obtaining advice on fees from your 71-2
  quality of 109
  size of 109
new knowledge 47-8
niche
  checking the viability of your 87, 134
  need for a 42-4, 52, 134
  target clients for your 44-5
notice period 65

online presence *see* social media; websites
originality 50-1

Osterwalder, Alexander 57
outsider status 23, 92

paperwork 125-6
partnering with others 10, 83, 104
payment 129-33, 136, 141
   in advance 129-30
   dealing with late 131-2
   reducing the impact of not being paid 131
   reducing the likelihood of not being paid 130-1
   terms 123
   when the client won't pay 132-3
   see also pricing your services
persuasion/persuasiveness 22-3, 174, 178-9
Pigneur, Yves 57
pitch 100-2
preparing yourself for freelancing 84-94
pricing your services 20, 28, 29-30, 34, 66-80
   agreeing the price 122-3
   don't confuse fees with income 78-80
   don't sell cheap 75-6
   experimenting with fees 72
   free work 76-7
   increasing your fees 73-4, 75, 190
   influencing factors,
     choice of clients 68-9, 74
     you and your fee rate 69, 75
     your service and the fee it justifies 67-8, 74
     your unit of charging 70-1, 75
   minimum fees 71, 73, 122
   negotiating fees 69, 77-8
   self-reflection questions to help work out your fees 74-5
   using available data 71
   using your network 71-2

value or serviced-based pricing 70-1, 72, 83, 99, 190-1
pro-bono work 76
product approach to helping clients 49
professional development 12
professional indemnity insurance 32, 89
profiling your clients see client persona
project management 187-8
proposals, sales 127-8
protecting your interests 21
public speaking 194

qualifications 86, 175

rainmakers 110
rationality, brilliance and limitations of 176-8
reading 154
reasons for considering freelancing 3-9
   independence 4, 6-8
   money 4-6
   redundancy and lack of an alternative 8-9
reasons for hiring freelancers see client reasons for hiring freelancers
re-inventing yourself 52
reciprocity 179, 180-1, 182
redundancy 8-9, 85
referrals and recommendations 69, 103, 107-8, 136, 175
relationship approach to helping clients 49
relationships 59-60, 98
   building 33, 43, 131, 136, 140, 158-72
   importance of 102-3, 120-1
   see also trust

reliability 162, 163, 164
remit, lack of, as client reason for hiring freelancers 28, 29, 30
remote working 7, 8
reputation 107, 174
research 45, 114
reverse marketing 104, 105, 106
risk 4-5, 12-13
  reducing 5-6
roles 17, 18
routes to market 104-6
running a business 21, 24
  costs of 79
  see also administration
Rusen, Ciprian 142-3

sales funnels 98-100, 112, 113, 134
sales proposals 127-8
Sartre, Jean-Paul 36
scarcity 179, 182
Scholten, Leonie 93-4
Schwartz, Barry 11
self-disclosure 161, 162-3
self-orientation 164
selling 70, 97-8, 115-21, 134
  basics 116-17
  and client position relative to your service 121
  importance of relationships and trust in 102-3, 119, 120-1, 134
  and logic of the sales conversation 119-21
  need to sell 115-16
  three steps to 117-19
service-based or value pricing 70-1, 72, 83, 190-1
short engagements 148
short-term freelancing 8
side hustles 193-4
skills 21-3
  faking 161
  interpersonal 59-60, 154

social media 50, 51, 86, 88, 108, 109, 110-11, 143, 174, 175, 176
  see also LinkedIn
social proof 179, 182, 183
specialisation, defining your 41-52
style of interaction with clients 187
  see also communication style; relationships
Subject Matter Experts (SMEs) 18, 49

tax 5, 79, 89, 90, 123
  VAT (sales tax) 123, 130
terms and conditions (T&Cs) 127, 128
time, selling your 49
training, providing 194
transaction approach to helping clients 49
transition from another job 91-3
trust 7, 22, 33-4, 43, 59, 60, 102-3, 107, 119, 130, 134, 155, 158-64
  and administrative procedures 159
  and credibility 162, 163, 164, 171-2
  equation 162-4
  as reciprocal relationship 158-9
  and repeat business 159
  self-reflection questions for exploring ability to develop 164
  setting out to gain 160-1
  and variability of work offered 159
types of freelancers 15, 16-19

useable advice/help, providing 35, 169

valuable conversations 98
value of your service 120, 122

value-based pricing 70–1, 72, 83, 99, 190–1
VAT (sales tax) 123, 130
vertical markets 114
visibility, building your 86–7
Voss, Chris 78

warm outreach (warm calling) 105, 106

Watt, James 87
websites 86, 88
Williamson, Ian 156–7
Wiredu, Diane 82–3
work space 90
writing 114, 194

Zakers, Alison 23–5